MORAL STRANGERS,
MORAL ACQUAINTANCE,
AND MORAL FRIENDS

MORAL STRANGERS, MORAL ACQUAINTANCE, AND MORAL FRIENDS

CONNECTEDNESS AND ITS CONDITIONS

ERICH H. LOEWY

State University of New York Press

Published by
State University of New York Press, Albany

© 1997 State University of New York

All rights reserved

Printed in the United States of America

For information, address State University of New York
Press, State University Plaza, Albany, N.Y., 12246

Production by E. Moore
Marketing by Nancy Farrell

Library of Congress Cataloging-in-Publication Data

Loewy, Erich H.
    Moral strangers, moral acquaintance, and moral friends :
connectedness and its conditions / Erich H. Loewy.
        p.   cm.
    Includes bibliographical references and index.
    ISBN 0-7914-3131-2 (alk. paper). — ISBN 0-7914-3132-0 (pbk. :
alk. paper)
    1. Ethics. 2. Suffering—Moral and ethical aspects. I. Title.
BJ1031.L59 1997
170—dc20
                                                                96-2444
                                                                   CIP

10 9 8 7 6 5 4 3 2 1

This book is dedicated to my wife

Roberta Springer Loewy, M.A., Ph.D. (cand)

without whose advice, help and love
none of my work could have been
accomplished. What good there is in
my work, I owe largely to her.
The bad is a product of my own
mistakes and stubbornness.

Our only hope will lie
in the frail web of understanding
of one person
for the pain of another.

—John Dos Passos

Contents

Acknowledgments

This book was written in many places. Part of it was written at my former University: the University of Illinois College of Medicine at Peoria. The final editing was done at my current University, where I am fortunate to occupy the endowed Alumni Chair of Bioethics in the Department of Medicine of the University of California, Davis. A good portion of it was written while I served as visiting professor in Vienna, Austria. Actually a very great part of it was written during two extended stays in the French Alps, in a small village high up in the Haute Savoi, at L'Hôtel de La Roche in Beaufort sur Doron—a delightful, quiet and restful place, the perfect place to walk, think and write. Much thanks are due to the proprietor, Monsieur Bruno Busson, and his delightful wife, Madame Marie-France Busson. Much of it was written in their bar: not like an American bar, not raucous and filled with tipsy people or drunks loudly discussing or arguing with each other, but filled with quiet people who are having a cup of coffee or a glass of wine while conversing in very low voices. Special thanks go to Dr. Friedrich Heubel and his students in Marburg an der Lahn, Germany. I have been fortunate enough to spend a week or so a year teaching (but, frankly, mainly learning) at the University in Marburg. Friedrich is a Kantian and we certainly do not agree on a whole variety of basic issues, but there are few people whose intellectual rigor and devotion to intellectual honesty I value more. The highlight at Marburg is a weekend seminar where he and his students tear my work in progress apart—a process I find most helpful and most invigorating. Their criticisms, comments (and sly digs) have gone far towards helping me see errors.

As always and above all, my profoundest thanks go to my wife, Roberta Ann Springer Loewy, who is to be awarded the Ph.D. for which she has worked with amazing persistence and diligence for some years, commuting back and forth more than three-hundred miles to attend classes and teach. Her excellent training in philosophy, her insights into what I am trying to do, her intellectual and linguistic rigor, and above all her understanding and sense of humor have made this work possible.

My editor for this and for previous works, Carola Sautter, deserves more than just thanks. Not only have her suggestions always been well taken and her comments much appreciated but the whole way in which she and SUNY Press have helped me develop and finish this and the preceding books has been of the greatest possible help.

Last but not least I want to thank all my students: those at the University of Illinois, here at the University of California, Davis, as well as students, colleagues, and other persons who have attended my lectures or seminars in a variety of countries and settings. Their comments, questions, and criticisms have been invaluable, and are, aside from the impetus given by my wife and other colleagues, what has made my work possible.

Introduction

Erich Maria Remarque in several of his works of fiction describes the situation of refugees from Hitler Germany.[1] In these works not only the evil of the organized Nazi state but the callousness and often collusion of other nations, nations which publicly prided themselves on their humanity, is evident. In nonfictional form David S. Wyman has carefully documented the same thing.[2,3] What emerges is the callous indifference of nations and peoples toward the fate of others. But not always: invariably there were those who cared and who strove (often at great danger and often at formidable odds) to stop the outrages or to help the victims.

The experiences of this century have not made most people optimists. It has been a century in which repetitively recurring outrages have occurred, in which these outrages continue to occur and in which these outrages have been studiously ignored by those who could have done or could do something about them. The Turkish persecution of the Armenians, the Bolshevik massacres and persecutions, the Holocaust, Paul Pot, the continued and deplorable treatment of the Kurds and, as this is written, the horrible events in the former Yugoslav republic are only a few outstanding examples. These and many others could have been prevented, interfered with, or rapidly stopped if only the world community had taken seriously the belief (to which it generally paid lip-service) that for whomever the bell tolls, it tolls for us. When such outrages were stopped and the victims meaningfully helped, it was done only grudgingly and generally as the by-product of some other political end: generally pointing to these events and to the necessity for interference was used as a hypocritical shield behind which nationalistic and geopolitical interests could easily be detected. No one really cared about the treatment and eventual extermination of Jews or Gypsies: indeed, even when the battle with the Nazi state was at its height, even when Nazi defeat was obvious, American pilots were not allowed to bomb the access road to Auschwitz, the gas chambers, or the fences of the many other concentration camps.[4] And while pilots were forbidden to bomb the extermination camp Auschwitz, its fences, its gas chambers or its access road, Buna, a part of the camp in which militarily useful goods were made, was repeatedly bombed. Likewise, no one really cared enough to do anything about the fact that Kurds were gassed or Cambodians exterminated. Indeed, the United States as well as other western nations (not to speak of the actions of the former Soviet State) often and in many ways supported and, in a sense, created the problems they then reluctantly and much later were forced to address. This is true whether one looks at Hitler, Noriega, Sadam Hossein, or the situation in Nicaragua or Somalia.

Helping the victims was never high on the agenda of nations until such helping could serve palpable political and national ends. Jewish persons desperately trying to escape from Germany were denied access even when the laws of the nation would allow it: persons desperately seeking visas to the United States, even when they had the necessary "affidavits" which would entitle them to a visa, were often told that "the quota was full"; and yet the quota was never filled, never even nearly filled until after World War II had started. People (including the writer of this book and many of his no longer living friends) were simply and deliberately lied to. In more recent times, desperate boat people were turned back by the British in the Pacific and the U.S. Coast Guard (in what amounts to acts of piracy—one need only imagine the pious handwringing of the United States if Vietnam had acted in a similar way!) boarded Haitian vessels, returned the occupants to the country they were fleeing and finally seized and destroyed the ships. Helping Haitians was simply inconvenient (just as helping the victims of Nazism had been) and interfering with them served narrowly argued and narrowly conceived national interests. Furthermore, and not unimportantly, Haitians are Black just as a large number of the refugees from Hitler were Jewish: reason enough, it seemed, to abandon them. The notion that persons do not flee their country or their culture capriciously and that when they do so compelling circumstances force them to this drastic step, rarely finds expression. If it did, seeking to ameliorate the circumstances causing people to flee, rather than tacitly condoning such circumstances and often even having a hand in creating them, would be seen as being "in the national interest."

Underlying these actions lies a notion of minimal obligation towards each other. Minimal obligations (obligations of merely inflicting no direct harm on one another) justify my ignoring my neighbor's plight, be it the plight of my neighbor in another nation or culture or my neighbor down the street. The same world-view which tolerates the extermination of the Jews, the gassing of the Kurds or the mass murder of Cambodians in and by other nations underwrites tolerating poverty, homelessness and social injustice "at home." It is a philosophy of minimal obligations because it denies our essential connectedness as human beings (and, I shall argue, our connectedness with other species).

This book deals with the problem of connectedness: connectedness between and among individuals as well as connectedness between and among different communities. While it builds on my last work, it can, I hope and think, stand on its own feet. Although the initial chapter will essentially be a brief recapitulation of previous work, the chapter will go beyond what was previously done, will modify it and flesh it out. The chapter serves as a necessary springboard for what is to come. I hope to show that what Jonathan Moreno calls the "myth of the asocial individual"[5] is indeed a myth and that Engelhardt's notion of "moral strangers"[6] which leads to a respect for autonomy limited only enough to grant others a like autonomy is seriously flawed, untenable and is, indeed, representative of this myth. The concept of moral strangers, so eloquently argued for by Professor Engelhardt and so necessary to a libertarian conception of morality, holds that persons from disparate cultures, religions, or moral commitments lack a common meeting ground of moral discourse: their only commonly held assumption, the only thing of moral significance which can help mediate their disputes is the realization that each wants to live his/her own life in their own fashion.[7]

In this book, I will argue that far from being moral strangers, and while not being "moral friends," we are sufficiently morally acquainted to enable fruitful dialogue across even starkly different cultural groups. The argument will be a bio-psycho-social one as far as its framework goes, relying on universal human needs and common human experience (indeed, I will also argue that these common human needs and common human experiences are not limited to human animals but are merely different in degree as one "descends" to "lower" species).

While such a framework relies on universal human needs, biological facts and common human experience it cannot be reduced to it. It is not and cannot be reductionary in that sense. The framework and what we build within it can no more be reduced to these common needs, biological facts and common experience than it can be conceived without them: biological facts are the necessary conditions which produce common needs and enable common experience but in themselves are not sufficient. These biological facts underwrite common needs and common experience and with them form the necessary framework for all else. I have called these the "existential a prioris" of ethics: that is the necessary conditions from and with which our notions of what is proper behavior or ethics (or, for that matter, the basic rules of all religions) emerges.

These "a prioris" of all being and all ethics are at least: (1) an inborn and necessary drive to survive ("being"); (2) the satisfaction of biological necessities (food, drink, shelter, etc.); (3) the meeting of social needs (different though they may be, all creatures have social needs); (4) a desire to avoid suffering; (5) a common sense of basic logic (at least sufficient so that the incompatibility of "p" and "non-p" are evident); and (6) a desire to lead their own lives in their own way. These conditions are virtually lexical: that is, to satisfy one the preceding must be satisfied.

Recognizing such a prioris as basic for the development of ethics (and, I shall claim, for religions) does not reduce ethics to biological, social, or psychological factors. It merely indicates that these factors (and probably others) are, unless we believe that we can transcend our biology or our human condition, the necessary framework in which such an ethic can and ought to be developed.

Using this concept as grounding, I shall elaborate an ethic which necessitates more than merely respect for autonomy: in such an ethic beneficence on a personal and communal level have moral force. Such a viewpoint would, I shall argue, imply respect for autonomy as well as at least minimal beneficence for all beings with the capacity to profit from such an ethic. On an individual basis such an ethic leads to an imperative for taking at least some responsibility for the well-being of our fellow creatures and on a communal basis it implies an infrastructure seeking to supply the biological and social necessities of life to all in an equitable fashion. Methodologically such an ethic sees human interrelationships as homeostatic in nature: in seeking their own ends individuals recognize that to accomplish their personal ends being and community themselves must become a goal and communities, for their own development and survival, strive to provide maximal autonomous opportunity to the individuals of which they are composed. Such a relationship of individual to community is mirrored in the way that communities interrelate with each other and with the larger world community of which they necessarily are a part.

Even if we grant the existence of these existential a prioris, how and why do they serve to interconnect us so that we can, in fact, pursue a fruitful dialogue? Even if I understand these things about my neighbor, about the stranger I have never met or about members of another species, why should such knowledge serve to help us build a common basic ethical framework within which to develop and enjoy our cultural diversity? I shall argue that all of us (individuals and communities) are deeply aware of this connectedness: the attempts to rationalize or deny what we are doing when we fail to come to another's aid, our denial or rationalization of conditions down our streets is at least partial proof that we are not innocent or unknowing. Like those in Germany who closed their eyes to and rationalized what was going on, we are simply opportunists who when things are "going well" for us personally are quite willing to ignore the fate of others.

In this book, I shall also introduce the term "compassionate rationality" and differentiate it from "rational compassion." In doing this I shall inevitably have to address the relationship between emotion (sentiment) and reason as well as dealing with the role which curiosity and imagination must play in crafting an ethic and, ultimately, in acting ethically. Lastly I will sketch a way of dealing with contemporary problems which incorporates the various ideas I have suggested.

I have said that the experiences of this century have not served to make persons optimistic. And yet, I would argue, there is good historical reason for some modicum of cautious optimism: indeed, hope and the belief that humans can fashion their own fate in a morally and materially ever better way (one of the necessary conditions for optimism), grounds the works of such disparate thinkers as Ernst Bloch[8] and Hans Jonas.[9] Hans Jonas (not the world's most renowned optimist in his writings) likewise accentuates optimism and maintains that optimism as the basis of all acting is itself morally required.[10] We have good reason for optimism: while this century has seen outrages possibly unparalleled in their brutality, such outrages were only so unparalleled because science and technology enabled their more efficient execution. In other areas, this and the last century has seen advances unparalleled before: advances not largely created by science and technology (albeit often enabled by them) but human advances which have enabled mankind to dispense with prior outrages. We no longer have slavery and apartheid in the United States (where the institution of apartheid originated) or in South Africa; racial discrimination, while hardly abolished and, in fact, often flourishing de facto, has legally at least disappeared. At the beginning of this century, few single laborers lived in their own flats:

often, if not indeed usually, they merely hired a bed for eight hours. In looking at the "good old days," we tend to forget how very horrible they were for most persons. Gentility for some was bought at the price of misery for many. Some, pointing at poverty in the United States, will say that not much has changed. That, however, is not true: while poverty, hunger, homelessness, and social injustice are widespread in the United States, they have been at least ameliorated in a good part of the rest of the Western world. Even in the United States great improvements (even if improvements which still leave a large number of people disadvantaged) have occurred. Since the enlightenment suggested that the power of the human mind could, if it would, improve the lot of all (and even though it is fashionable to deny this), steady improvement has, in fact, occurred. Technology which can be used to create Auschwitz or Hiroshima can likewise be used to enrich the lives of all. Such a use, however, presupposes an awareness of mutual social obligation and such a use is endangered when connectedness is disregarded or our social nature is denied. Emphasizing the individual out of context with his/her necessarily social existence opens the door to the outrages this and past centuries have brought about; seeing the needs of the individual and the demands of community as necessarily interrelated and as inevitably in homeostatic balance, realizing that what we share may be far more than what divides us can create a solidarity within and among communities which furthers progress and justice.

     If this book does anything, I hope that it at least begins to argue for two things: first, that we share a common framework of reasoning which would allow us to establish a far richer than a merely minimalist ethic; and secondly that if we as a human species are to survive, thrive, and develop, we are compelled to adopt more than merely a minimalist ethic. The argument, therefore, will have two roots of justification: one which can be grounded in our inescapable common bio-psycho-social experience and the other which is more pragmatic. The one reinforces the other. I shall argue that the pragmatic solution (pragmatic not in a crass way but in a way which sees all "answers" as tentative and all solutions ultimately testable in experience) is only possible because our common experience enables a meaningful dialogue.

1 Suffering, Communities, and Interconnections

This chapter will not only review some previous work but will also try to clarify and further develop some of these concepts. These concepts will serve as a grounding for what I hope to develop in this book: the notion that all sentient beings are inescapably connected through a series of shared interests, that these shared interests provide grounds for discourse and that this inevitably entails at least some easily agreed upon mutual obligations. In prior works I grappled with the question of obligation: are our obligations minimalist and confined to not harming each other or are our obligations richer and include obligations we would term "beneficent": that is, obligations which concern themselves, in some sense, not only with not harming but with actively helping others. Obligations not only play themselves out in a community but are unthinkable outside of one: what, after all, can "obligations" be if there are not others to whom we owe and by whom we are owed obligations? Therefore, the structure of community and its relationship to its members, the relationship of the members to the community, and the relationship of communities to each other needs to be conceptualized and understood. Relationships, in turn, are at least in part defined by the obligations such relationships entail.[1]

But before we can grapple with the specific idea of obligation, we must be clear as to what can be owed obligations or, in other words, we need to concern ourselves with the question of "moral standing" or "moral worth" and how it is assigned and perhaps prioritized: how do we decide that an object or creature is of moral significance and that, therefore, our acting so as to affect it becomes a moral concern. What, putting it differently and ethically speaking, makes rocks, college students, and puppies different: what is it about rocks, college students, and puppies which makes hitting one morally significant and hitting the other under most circumstances of little moral concern? And beyond this, why should we assign ethical standing to houses, cars, or ideas? Perhaps most importantly: are there preconditions which, by virtue of being preconditions, themselves have moral standing? These questions, questions with whose ramifications I continue to grapple, are fundamental and in one way or another must be answered (or the answer assumed) in order to do ethics in any meaningful sense.

With Kant I seek the property which allows us to call an entity one for which we should have moral concern. Differing from Kant I suggest that the capacity to suffer (rather than the capacity to set oneself autonomous law) is at least one of the critically relevant facts. Entities which have that capacity have moral standing: how we act to affect them matters. Kant's conception that it is an entity's capacity to set its own autonomous law which is the ethically relevant fact necessitating our moral concern is, in my view, far too narrow: it leaves out a large number of beings who at the very least we feel not to be ethically irrelevant: puppies, the senile, the severely retarded and, in some respects, even the severe ideologues or fundamentalists who are incapable of setting their own rules. (Some of us would even argue, though perhaps tongue in cheek, that it might leave out persons who consider themselves to be orthodox Kantians: persons who follow all rules unquestioningly and implicitly and whose source of moral understanding is, therefore, heteronomous, precisely what Kant eschews!) In the past, I have claimed that what unites all of these beings and makes of them entities with moral standing, is their capacity to suffer.[2]

Being of primary worth is, I have said, always positive: no one is or can be dangerous or loathsome enough to forfeit it. Hitler, a serial murderer or a Bengal tiger ravaging a village still has positive primary worth: as a creature which can suffer, Hitler, a serial murderer, or a Bengal tiger about to ravage a village is deserving of consideration and respect. Under some circumstances, it might be ethically acceptable to harm or even to kill any of these so as to protect the vital interests of others; but it would not be acceptable to capture and then torture them or, for that matter, to affect them negatively in any way greater than that necessary to prevent them from doing harm. Unless it can be shown that even behind bars Hitler, a serial killer, or a Bengal tiger would continue their actions, doing more than using sufficient force to prevent them from being a danger is morally unacceptable. Revenge as a motif may have emotional appeal but revenge for the sake of revenge has little moral standing.

But what does it mean to have moral standing or to be of moral worth? Surely the capacity to suffer does not give an entity a complete right to be left alone, does not, under any and all circumstances, prevent us from acting on it against its will or, even under some circumstances, to cause it to suffer. And surely, all things which in themselves cannot suffer cannot therefore be acted upon wantonly. My automobile, Notre Dame Cathedral, a person's ideas or faith, or the community itself are not ethically trivial: and yet, automobiles, cathedrals, or ideas cannot, in themselves, suffer. These then are two questions which must be answered: the first concerns what having moral standing means; the second asks whether and how objects which cannot suffer have or acquire moral standing.

In the past I have argued that having moral standing gives an entity prima facie protection against being acted upon contrary to that entities interest or desire (in the case of primary worth) and, in the case of secondary or prior worth, against the interests of those who would be affected by acting upon such things. Such protection is, of course, prima facie: that is, it can be overridden by morally weighty considerations. Having "primary moral worth" (having the capacity to suffer) gives one one's day in court but having primary moral worth does not preordain the judgment one will receive. Primary moral worth, furthermore, while always positive (an entity which can suffer always has standing) is variable: it can be lesser or greater. Although being of primary moral worth is always positive and although being of primary moral worth can never be disregarded, all entities of primary moral worth are not coequal. Being of primary moral worth can, for sufficient moral cause, be set aside.

I want to be quite clear: using the capacity to suffer as the grounding (or at least as one of the groundings) for having moral standing does not mean that our only obligation concerns itself with suffering. The capacity to suffer is, so to speak, an index condition: one which identifies or at least helps identify persons and things with and on which we cannot act wantonly. Refraining from causing suffering, ameliorating suffering, or preventing suffering is not the only issue that concerns me here. As yet the question is not "what shall we not do to others" but rather what is it which makes these others, others which should be of moral concern. At times the argument has been made that such a grounding would allow us to kill persons as long as they had no foreknowledge and as long as death was instantaneous and did not entail suffering. Such objections evade the basic arguments: the capacity to suffer provides an entity with moral standing and once a thing has moral standing any action which affects it or its interests and, therefore, anything that we do or fail to do is ethically relevant. I want to be quite clear here: my using suffering as an index capacity for moral standing does not reduce our concern for such entities to a concern for suffering.

Other things than entities which can suffer themselves matter in an ethically relevant sense: cars, books, ideas, symbols. I have called such entities entities of "secondary moral worth": they have, as it were, moral standing by reflection. How we deal with such entities matters because how we deal with them (whether positively or negatively) affects another or others who has or who have primary moral worth. Secondary moral worth can be material (akin to, but not identical with, Kant's "Marktpreis") or symbolic (similar, but not quite the same as what Kant terms "Affektionspreis"):

> In the realm of ends everything has either a price or a dignity. Whatever has a price can be replaced by something else as its equivalent; on the other hand, whatever is above all price, and therefore admits of no equivalent, has a dignity.
> That which is related to general human inclinations and needs has a market price. That which without presupposing any need, accords with a certain taste . . . has an affective price. But that which constitutes the condition under which alone something can be an end in itself does not have mere relative worth, i.e., a price, but an intrinsic worth, i.e., a dignity.[3]

Furthermore, and most importantly, secondary worth (as distinct from primary worth which is always positive) can be positive or negative: whether it is positive or negative depends upon the valuing done by another whose moral worth is primary. For most, Notre Dame cathedral has a great deal of positive secondary worth; a grenade about to go off a great deal of negative worth. My ideas and symbols are of great value to me but, depending what they are, may be loathsome to others.

Being and community itself have a different kind of standing: they are, what I call, of "prior worth": their existence, their prosperity, and their continuity are the necessary conditions of all experiencing and valuing. Without being and without being in some sort of community having primary or secondary standing makes no sense.[4] Being (unless one wishes to flee into mysticism) is the necessary condition of experience and community, is the necessary condition of being and of valuing. Since without them our personal being is impossible and our community is impoverished, our environment, the ecology, and nature itself become critically important in such an ethic.

A brief but pertinent example may help: a person who after a severe automobile accident, is unconscious but has a chance of regaining consciousness has primary moral standing or worth. The physician's obligation is primarily to that patient and, barring a previously expressed wish to the contrary by the patient him/herself, the family's wishes, the fact that this very possibly uninsured patient is costing the hospital great expense or the fact that his organs might be of use to another is not important: he/she is of primary moral worth and, therefore and unless overriding moral reasons to the contrary can be shown, is the centerpiece of ethical concern. Once the patient is brain dead, permanently vegetative or comatose, however, matters change: primary moral worth is lost and secondary moral worth now becomes the centerpiece of consideration. He/she is now of secondary moral worth: positive material worth as a potential organ donor, negative material worth as a consumer of resources, and of symbolic worth to family and community. So that such a scenario can be played out, moreover, a community of persons who acknowledge having obligations, who set the framework of moral action and who are willing to act morally, is a necessary condition and, in that sense, being and community form the background and the context of all such considerations.

If one accepts such a theory, our treatment of nonhuman animals must be a matter of concern. If, on the other hand, we consider only creatures which can rationally set their own rules to be of moral concern to us, disregard for animals, except as acting on them affects humans, would result. Kant, not surprisingly, feels that we have obligations to animals only indirectly: if acting in certain ways against animals affects humans, acting on animals becomes of moral concern.

> But so far as animals are concerned, we have no direct duties. Animals are not self-conscious and are there merely as a means to an end. That end is man. We can ask: "Why do animals exist?" But to ask "Why does man exist?" is a meaningless question. Our duties towards animals are merely indirect duties towards humanity. Animal nature has analogies to human nature, and by doing our duties to animals in respect of manifestations which correspond to manifestations of human nature, we indirectly do our duty to humanity.[5]

As humans we have come to accept the premise that the way we deal with animals is not morally irrelevant. Our laws against cruelty to animals attest to this. But to Kant it is morally relevant only as such acting impinges on humans. That is because to Kant being morally relevant is a function of rationality, a function of having the capacity to reason and, therefore, to determine one's own moral laws. Those entities or things which do not have that capacity are morally relevant only insofar as they affect those who have that capacity. According to Kant "animals are not self-conscious" and, therefore, not rational. Kant does not argue this proposition—he states it as an acknowledged "fact": it seems unlikely that Kant ever owned a dog or a cat! In the language I have used here, Kant would consider all nonhuman animals to be merely of secondary moral worth.

Even those who wear fur, eat flesh, and have no concerns about animal experimentation would be troubled if we were to torture animals to death for our amusement. And we would be troubled by this even if it could be shown that such an act did not "brutalize" humans. The ability of nonhuman animals to suffer is implied by any notion of "cruelty to animals," a notion few of us would deny. Bentham was perhaps the first to give voice to this when he held that what was morally relevant was not a creature's capacity to reason but its capacity to suffer.[6] Except allegorically, we do not speak of cruelty to rocks, houses, or trees. This notion of suffering as at least one of the considerations grounding moral concern is one implicitly understood by all.

If one is to use "suffering" as giving moral standing and if by moral standing we mean at least "prima facie" protection from being acted upon, then ways of telling greater from lesser worth must be developed. Choices between harming one or another person or thing which has moral standing must be made. If such a way of looking at ethics is to be useful, we must be able to deal with conflicting interests among human persons, animals, the environment, and objects. Not all entities of primary worth have equal worth; not all entities of primary worth trump those of secondary worth (albeit that having prior worth as the condition for all else may generally be thought to take precedence): think of a mouse ruining an art object or of a human trying to blow up Notre Dame cathedral; think of a law which might favor a small group but which threatened to destroy the community.

What of killing animals? Do cows, chickens, fish, shrimp, or mussels have primary moral worth? And if so, since having primary moral worth only gives standing but certainly does not give absolute protection, how much protection is their due? I have argued that creatures endowed with the neurological substrate necessary to allow suffering and exhibiting behavior we generally associate with suffering do have such standing. That would include mammals, birds, and perhaps fish but, in the current state of our knowledge, leave out shrimp or mussels which lack the substrate conceded as necessary for suffering to occur.[7] Two things must be stressed: (1) suffering is a complex matter: it cannot be reduced to pain and has important psychic and social ramifications. While suffering cannot be reduced to the neurological substrate, suffering without the neurological substrate which allows it is unthinkable; after all, while function cannot be reduced to its material substrate, function without the material substrate which subtends such function cannot occur. The thing is greater than its parts and transcends them; but without the parts, the thing does not exist. (2) The discovery that an entity heretofore thought incapable of suffering can suffer (or, conversely, that one thought to suffer really does not) does not change the theory itself: such a discovery would merely increase or decrease the range of creatures covered by it. (3) Just because a creature can suffer and just because it has moral standing does not give it complete protection. Less developed creatures with a lesser capacity to have hopes, feelings, and aspirations may well have a lesser moral standing, but always still are due some, protection.

I have previously suggested that when it comes to making choices between creatures which are of primary worth the depth and capacity of their development to be subjects of their life may matter greatly. Creatures which have or which potentially have (socially deprived persons, for example, certainly have the same potential) a greater capacity for developing life plans, hopes, and expectations may perhaps take precedence over those with a lesser capacity or potential. Such a philosophy has certain undoubted dangers: it would tend to support dealing with the mentally deficient, the demented or, for that matter, with young infants in what we would generally consider to be socially and morally inadmissible ways. Depending on the extent of deficiency, the mentally deficient, the demented, or very young infants certainly would appear to have a lesser knowing stake in their life (to be the subjects of their life to a lesser extent) than do "normal" humans or, for that matter, intelligent apes or dogs. Such a view could easily lead to what civilized persons would consider to be atrocities, atrocities which—in view of history—are hardly beyond serious consideration.

The events of this century and specifically the treatment of disabled persons by the Nazis more than justifies these fears. And these are, therefore, fears which must be faced. Mentally deficient, demented, or very young infants are, however, socially members of the community in a way in which apes, elephants, or dogs are not. Although the primary worth of mentally deficient or demented persons or the primary worth of infants could arguably be considered to be less, such helpless beings are members of the human community and, therefore, have immense social importance and significant symbolic worth. They cannot be dealt with except on their own terms: above all their own interest and not merely the interest of the state are what matters. The thesis, which I shall develop in what is to follow in the next few chapters, is one which sees "rights" (or which sees what justifies claims) not as absolutes—as "out there" somewhere—but which sees rights as something which is socially constructed by and in communities along lines determined by reason and compassion. In forging such rights (or in determining the justification of claims) communities must be mindful of the lessons taught by history. When it comes to making communal choices, it may well be that human animals will be protected for that reason: that they would be what Professor Engelhardt calls "persons in a social sense."[8]

Communities, even when their members are well educated, concerned, and interactive, are certainly not an ideal way of dealing with such problems: the voice of God or some brilliant and totally rational convincing insight into how to go about this would be much superior. But God (if there is such a thing) chooses not to speak or if he or she does, does so to but a few unable to convince others and to date brilliant rational insights convincing for all or even for most are lacking. Under these conditions, democratic communal action (wrong-headed though it may at times be) continues to be the best of a bad lot. The argument that such choices can, at times, be very badly made or that allowing such a method is dangerous is unconvincing: bad laws do not speak against the necessity of making laws and dangerous ways of doing things cannot prevent our acting. Such arguments counsel caution when we act or choose but they cannot serve to prevent all acting or choosing.

Strict adherence to a strictly Kantian ethic arguably will not serve as a hedge against the sort of atrocity which would run roughshod over the interest of severely mentally deficient or severely demented persons or over the interests of very young infants. Such persons are certainly not autonomous in the sense Kant uses the term, certainly can only be protected in an extended and, therefore, tenuous sense. The Kantian condition for respect (the capacity to set one's own autonomous law), however, could here be invoked so that those with that capacity may have higher standing. A cow, a pig, a dog, or a mouse in such a tentative hierarchy would have standing: less standing than a human person but more than a fish. And the severely retarded, the badly demented, or very young infants would be protected by a properly functioning community which accepts (and even welcomes) such helpless beings as members of the human community and, therefore, acknowledges that they have immense social importance and significant symbolic worth.

In this scheme, higher animals have "primary" standing: acting on them against their will or interests must be defended and even then acting on them against their will or interests can be done only sufficiently to attain a goal deemed ethically appropriate under the circumstances. Just like torturing Hitler would not be permissible under such a scheme, killing animals for food or sport would seem to be ethically problematic: eating meat may please our palate (just as torturing Hitler may please our sense of revenge) but eating meat is not necessary to maintain our lives or to accomplish other morally legitimate functions. We may have to kill or otherwise incapacitate Hitler to protect millions but to reach the goal of making him incapable of injuring innocent others torture is not needed. We do not need meat to live and live very well and we do not (under ordinary circumstances at least) need to hunt or fish to accomplish an ethically appropriate objective. Under severe restrictions (and with great discomfort on my part at least), however, we might be able to defend certain forms of animal experimentation if these are vital for gaining information which could lead to curing disease or ameliorating suffering. The curing of disease or the amelioration of suffering has quite a different moral standing than does pleasing one's palate or enjoying the chase. But again: while this view might find animal experimentation ethically justifiable, it would not condone animal experimentation when other courses of action are available nor allow such experimentation to serve other than vital ends.

It is not possible to set canonical hierarchies: nor is it necessary. My thesis is that such hierarchies can only be crafted, enunciated, and ultimately vouchsafed by a community democratically acting together. Furthermore, such hierarchies or criteria cannot be set for all time. Not only will they differ depending upon the particulars of the situation extant at the time but, like all else including ethics, they are subject to learning and growth. As new information develops and as we as persons, communities and species grow in moral maturity they too will be adapted and changed.

But what causes us to have moral concerns in the first place? Why should humans worry about how their actions affect anyone but themselves? Indeed, as we shall see, there are those who think that our only obligations are to refrain from interfering with the freedom of action of others and that only because we ourselves would not want others to interfere with our own freedom of action. Ethics, in other words, is understood as primarily motivated by and serving our own interests: we concern ourselves with morality so as to better get on with our own lives. Such an asocial ethic has the individual not only as the centerpiece but also as the sole concern of ethical consideration. In what is to follow, I shall assume that our concern about ethics is motivated not merely by how our actions would affect us but how our actions affect not only other individuals but the community at large.

What, then, motivates our ethical concern, concerns which involve not only us but all others whom our acting or refraining from acting affects? What Rousseau has called "a primitive sense of pity" or "compassion" (Rousseau either refers to "pitié" or to "l'impulsion intérieure de la compassion" when he speaks of this sense) gives animals (not only human animals) a natural repugnance ("la répugnance naturelle") to see the suffering of others.[9] Rousseau speaks of this as a "natural" trait, one (normal) human and some nonhuman animals are born with. As a natural trait, this compassion for those who are suffering or weaker must play a natural role: if it had negative survival value, if acting on that trait would ultimately be a disservice to the individual or to the species, it would be attenuated or eliminated. This natural sense of pity (which, according to Rousseau can be overpowered by the instinct for self-preservation ["la conservation de soi-même"]) can, however, serve survival: a point which Darwin himself emphatically makes.[10] This sense of compassion, which leads individuals to help each other and in turn to come to expect such help, is a key element in social solidarity and, therefore, in fostering a species or a group's survival.

The misunderstanding, often one suspects the deliberate misunderstanding, of what Darwin has said, has, in my view, led to a bizarre and wrong-headed interpretation of "social Darwinism." I have written at greater length about social Darwinism in a prior work.[11] I have argued that, at the very least, Social Darwinists err in: (1) exalting physical strength above intellectual ability: the human species ability to survive is hardly its physical strength; physically weak and, indeed, physically disabled persons have made major contributions to society and, therefore, have helped it to survive; (2) believing that those who lose in our society (the weak, the chronically unemployed) are likely to be genetically inferior rather than that they are the product of the social structure of our society; (3) overlooking the role that a sense of compassion plays in fostering communal solidarity, cohesion and hence the ability to survive and prosper. The disabled in our midst (whether they are socially, physically, or intellectually disabled) are not only members of our community but our regard for them may well be an important asset which would ultimately allow societies to survive and prosper. The very fact that persons realize that even if they run into hard times and even if they or their children become disabled the community will continue to cherish and support them produces solidarity; realizing, on the other hand, that the community will cast off those who run into hard times or those who become disabled shatters it. Societies (one could point at the Scandinavian nations, for example) which have taken on responsibility for the poor, the disabled, and the weak, have attempted to remedy their lot or, when that fails, have supported and nurtured them have shown no signs of losing their strength. On the other hand, societies which have only grudgingly extended their hand to those in need have been saddled with ever increasing social problems and have, consequently, lost much of their strength.

Just like the trait of being able to see, the trait of being able to hear or the trait of having a sex drive, a natural trait such as the "natural sense of compassion" is ethically neutral. It can, however, serve as the necessary condition for actions which then are hardly ethically neutral. The sex drive is the necessary condition for sexual activity which, in turn, can eventuate in rape, incest, or an expression of closeness and human warmth. Lacking such a natural trait changes the range of actions a person is likely to have. A congenitally blind painter or a congenitally deaf composer (Beethoven's and Smetana's deafness were acquired, not inborn) is hard to imagine just as is a truly ethical individual entirely lacking compassion. A congenitally blind painter or a congenitally blind composer could go about their task in a mathematical sense: they could learn music or art theory but their works, even if one could imagine them, would perforce lack the emotional content we associate with art or music. Likewise, a person may, convinced by cold logic, adopt certain ethical precepts; but such a person would have a most difficult time having the necessary sensitivity to recognize or the internal motivation to deal with ethical problems.

Compassion, as Schopenhauer already pointed out, is the driving force (or "Triebfeder," i.e., the driving spring) of ethics.[12] On the other hand, the capacity to see or hear if it is to eventuate in truly great works of art, must be modified and controlled by art or music theory: it must, in other words, be disciplined by reason. The capacity to see and hear by themselves cannot (no matter how talented a person may be) suffice to produce truly great works of art: even those artists said to be "untrained" of necessity acquired such training in the course of their work. This interplay between emotion and reason (see the sections on what I have called "compassionate rationality" or and not the same thing "rational compassion") will be discussed at length in subsequent chapters in which I argue that emotion not modified by reason can lead to as many problems as can reason unleavened by emotion.

Persons have argued that this natural sense of pity is not a natural trait: they have pointed at well known individuals as well as national examples of such a lack. Individuals or nations which play their part in sending persons to their death in Auschwitz or back to starvation and persecution in Haiti do not persuade one of the power of such a trait. But, like all other things, nature can serve only as the necessary condition so that nurture can develop, attenuate or even extinguish the trait. An unjust social nexus or wrong-headed education can transform the impulse of self-preservation ("conservation de soi-même") into abject self-love (a wrong-headed form of "amour-propre") and overcome compassion.[13] Some individuals, furthermore, may well lack such an inborn trait: examples of such persons who from early childhood on seem to lack it, while not frequent, are imaginable and probably exist. But some individuals are born blind or deaf: a fact which does not argue against sight or hearing as a natural trait.

I spend some time on this sense of pity (spent a great deal in previous works and shall have cause to develop it further) because I believe it to be fundamental for understanding what is to come. I have held that this natural drive is essential to allow us to recognize and ultimately deal with ethical problems. It is not a purely individual trait, one which like sight an individual either has or lacks. Rather, much more than is sight or hearing (which also can, but to a much lesser extent, be influenced by social forces) compassion is developed, nurtured, and modified in the embrace of community and, in turn, compassion in the members of the community serves to strengthen or weaken its communal expression. Although Rousseau does not seem to connect compassion with the "general will" (which, as Rousseau sees it, causes individuals to subordinate their personal interests to that of the community and about which I shall have much more to say in later chapters), such a sense of communal compassion for its members may well be a variant of it.

The role of human collectives in all of this cannot be overrated. Humans as most animals to a greater or lesser extent are social creatures. Whether in families, tribes, nations, churches, or clubs, humans can fulfill their destinies only with and through others. Even an hermit has a relation, albeit it may be a negative one, with human association and could not exist without having had more than a merely superficial one. Humans as freestanding persons, as entities whose connection with others is not a necessary part of existence cannot be imagined—it is what Jonathan Moreno so aptly calls "the myth of the asocial individual."[14] Kant fully acknowledges this necessary connection: throughout his *Critique of Judgement* (as well as in his essay on Eternal Peace) Kant stresses the need of social communication, the need for the exchange of ideas as world citizens and as scholars.[15] We cannot, as it were, think without community.

Persons are not asocial beings. They need each other and contact with each other for a variety of activities. Fulfilling our ends or goals—even having ends and goals—implies a community of others with which we are somehow connected. Ethics without others with whom we are necessarily related and whose actions impinge on us as do ours on them would, in fact, hardly be a viable topic of discourse. Beyond this, Kant in stressing the need for a "realm" or "kingdom" of ends in which we all must—if we are to lead moral lives—participate and share acknowledges community and its ethical dimension. The myth of the "asocial individual" has other and prior ramifications. Thinking itself, ultimately is a social task. Without our being able to develop, share, and hone our thoughts in the company of others our ability to think would be sorely limited. This is not only quite obviously developmentally true (children very obviously need the company and stimulation of others to develop this skill), it is likewise true in adult life. If individuals were asocial, or if societies were asocial, they could not easily develop: as Kant has pointed out we need others if we are to think, others with whom we can share and correct our thoughts (Kant speaks of "orienting" our thoughts). Thinking, to Kant, is social and public and this is one of the reasons why the inhibition of free intercourse among all persons is essential to peace and understanding.

As Hanna Arendt put it so very well: "In the center of Kant's moral philosophy stands the individual; in the center of his philoso-

phy of history (or, rather, his philosophy of nature) stands the perpetual progress of the human race, or mankind."[16] And that perpetual
progress, that evolution, learning, and growth (so central, incidentally, to Dewey's philosophy as well as to an explication of what I
have to say) necessitates human associations. Ethics, in the view I
suggest here, is ultimately a social construct, is motivated and ini-
tiated by our sense of compassion and is developed (within a framework of bio-psycho-social conditions, interests and possibilities) by
our ability to reflect and reason. Moreover, crafting an ethic is, I
shall argue, an ongoing process and not one which can be seen as
more than tentative. Our "solutions" serve to get on with our task
today as well as serving as a springboard for learning and improvement tomorrow.

As social beings, individuals must interact not only with other
individuals but also with a variety of collectives of various sizes and of
various importance for the satisfaction of their individuals' interests.
I shall shortly sketch a schema of different models of collectives but
whatever the nature of the collectives, members must interrelate with
the collectives of which they are a part. Moreover, collectives must
interact with other collectives. Collectives can be seen as corporate
individuals and the relationship among collectives can be analogized
to the relationship among individuals. Ultimately, these collectives
together form smaller or larger societies or communities until they
ultimately must join in a world community whose prosperity underwrites the fate of all. Such relationships can give rise to a variety of
problems: on the one hand, individuals (whether persons or corporate
individuals) wish to pursue their own interests unhampered by others;
on the other hand, part of being a member of a collective can be
defined by the obligations one has towards the collective as well as by
the expectations one has of it. So as to meet their obligations towards
their members, collectives must expect certain things from their
members: a commercial company expects its employees to spend time
they would otherwise spend on other activities working for it; in
return, the company pays its employees a wage. A state expects its citizens to pay a certain amount of taxes the citizens would undoubtedly
rather spend on other things; in return the state provides certain services and benefits to its members.

Such relationships have often been painted as dialectic: the
interests of the individual (whether personal or corporate) for meeting its goals are opposed to the interests of the community, the state
or the collective to meet goals of its own. The tension between these
two conflicting interests results in a synthesis: a modus vivendi

which continues, however, to be an armed truth in which both the individual and the collective continue to try to compete and to change the balance in their favor.[17] This has been the classical way of looking at this problem: individual interests (also termed interests of autonomy, freedom or, put differently "human rights") are necessarily seen as being in conflict with the interests of the community which in trying to meet its beneficent obligations to its various members feels that it must inhibit individual freedom to a greater or lesser extent. Neither swamps the other albeit that one or the other may, at any given time, predominate. Thus certain societies may value freedom at the expense of the community's ability to exercise beneficent obligations: such communities, exemplified by predominantly capitalist states like the United States, may protect what they consider to be individual rights at the expense of basic human needs. Other nations, exemplified by the former Soviet societies, may do the opposite: individual rights are given short shrift compared to the perceived needs of the community. The ethos of a particular community is said to emerge from the tension of this dialectic. It is at best an uneasy truth in which each party continues to pursue its narrowly conceived interests. Readjustments occur but they are a manifestation of power rather than one of learning and growth.

In past works, I have suggested that such a dialectic way of viewing the matter is flawed. The demands of freedom are realizable only within the embrace of the conditions the community provides. Seeing the striving for freedom as in conflict with the beneficent obligations of community or seeing the interests of the community as somehow separate from the interests of its members does not give an accurate picture: without having basic needs for food, shelter, clothing, education, and health care met, individual freedom means little. Only those who need not worry about these basic necessities can afford to be cavalier about them. On the other hand, having merely one's basic needs satisfied without a due respect for individual freedom and the satisfaction of individual goals, remains empty. Ultimately, I shall argue, either situation leads to the same thing: a society in which large numbers of unsatisfied, unfulfilled individuals lead impoverished lives and in which such individuals are, therefore, unable to help the community prosper and progress.

The question is sometimes posed as one of ontological priority: did communities precede individuals or did freestanding individuals precede collectives which ultimately were formed by free individuals voluntarily associating? Such a question is a basic question of how such groupings came about, one of what has been called "social contract": did such collectives come about because freestanding individuals chose voluntarily to associate (were individuals ontologically prior) or was the collective itself the more natural state of being and did the individuals within it only later come into their own? Most writers who have worked with the notion of social contract have explicitly or tacitly assumed the priority of individuals. In such a view, collectives must be defined as voluntary associations of free standing individuals. Hobbes, Rousseau, Locke, or Rawls, as different as their visions of such a contract may be, all share this point of view.

In this chapter, I will only briefly sketch some theories of social contract and introduce an alternative way of looking at the genesis of communal association. I will leave considerable further discussion and elaboration of these view to later chapters.

Hobbes saw the original condition as one in which lives were necessarily "solitary, brutish, nasty and short": persons in the original condition were wont to assault one another and thus would be constantly hampered in pursuing their own lives. This inability to lead their own lives was the impetus to their associating with each other: their association was impelled by terror and their promise to each other was merely a promise of non-harm. Beneficence or helping one another was no part of this contract. Such a world-view (which Hobbes felt necessitated an absolute sovereign to enforce such a contract) is one which, of course, underwrites much of libertarian and crass individualistic capitalism today.[18]

But even Rousseau saw individuals as preceding their association. Indeed, these individuals were differently conceived: they were amoral creatures not out to do each other violence but already, as we have seen, endowed with compassion. Ethics or morality was a product of their association which came about not merely because they were in terror of each other but because they saw such association as facilitating their individual lives. The repugnance to see the suffering of others was a natural trait and one, which together with the need to facilitate their lives, became part of a social contract. Associations in which power was badly distributed were distortions and the morality of and in such associations would (since morality was a product of the way in which associations were constituted) necessarily be perverted.[19]

But in reality, it seems unlikely that associations came about in such a deliberate way or that individuals ever were or ever could be as "freestanding" and sufficient as such theories would have them be. Whether communities preceded and spawned individuals or whether freestanding individuals associated to form collectives is, in my view, a "chicken and egg" question, as unrealistic as it is irrelevant. We do, however, know that much: humans (and perhaps all higher animals) are born not only helpless but without a sense of self as distinct from their environment. The world and they are one and their sense of selfness only develops in the course of the next few months; a fact, which interestingly enough, is not only psychological but also immunological: early on, we cannot dissociate "self" from "non-self." Such beings are critically dependent upon the nurture of others, are anything but "freestanding" (indeed, since they cannot dissociate their selfness from their being one with all else, they can have no conception of what being free is) and are inevitably born into a small community whose beneficence enables their survival. Autonomy and freedom necessarily and inevitably develops in the embrace of beneficence: individuals are social and their individuality without a social nexus can neither emerge nor be maintained.

The relationship of individuals to the collectives of which they are a part (and, ultimately, the relationship of various collectives to each other) can likewise be sketched as other than one of each merely striving for their particular interests. A dialectic tension is not the only or perhaps even the most accurate and fruitful way in which such a relationship can be defined. If we start out with the presumption of stark individualism, of course, no other alternative remains. If, on the other hand, we hold a wider point of view a more cooperative and ultimately satisfying model may emerge. While collectives must, perforce, be constituted of individuals, individuals need a collective to define themselves. Individuals are not entirely freestanding, did not come about and cannot live or be defined that way. Even an hermit had his/her origin in some sort of social association and even an hermit inevitably defines him/herself in terms of a collective.

Defining the relationship between communal and individual strivings can be done by examining the concept of homeostasis. Homeostasis implies an equilibrium or balance tending towards stability. It is a concept which can equally be applied to organisms (and to organisms in both a psychological and physical sense of equilibrium), societies, and ecosystems. Homeostatic relationships consist of a balance between and among disparate forces serving the teleological goal of individual, species, or other systems.[20] Homeostasis denotes a dynamic equilibrium with continual change: as the environment impinges on the system (be it a cell, an organism, a species, a tribe, a society, or an ecosystem) adjustments are made for the common goal of survival. Such a steady state is, in truth, a complex series of adjustments between external forces and internal controls. In a homeostatic equilibrium the response is aimed at a balance or equilibrium which oscillates about a preset range of values. When such values are exceeded, corrective forces come into play so that what looks from afar as a steady state can again ensue. When changes are great (when disease develops, when natural enemies die out or move into the area, or when profound environmental changes occur) a new steady state will have to be created and the homeostatic range will have to be adjusted. If it is not, survival will not occur. All such natural systems are "open," prone to a myriad of diverse outside influences and not "closed" as they would be in a balanced aquarium or in a test tube. A homeostatic field results.[21] It is not a closed field, in the sense of being hermetically sealed from the outside world: indeed, many of the adaptive changes of homeostasis are due to these very forces.

Evolution (whether it is biological, social, or psychological) requires the maintenance of a relatively steady state over time as well as the ability to adapt to forces by resetting the limits within which homeostatic balance is maintained. Thus, homeostasis does not, as is often claimed, lead to dead uniformity. On the contrary: homeostasis, to be successful, maintains a relatively steady state in which adaptation to new forces can occur. Organisms or societies which can maintain relative stability within a framework of values, while dynamically adjusting as well as reexamining, and organisms or societies which have the capacity to experiment, learn, and adapt, are organisms and societies which are likely to endure.

While homeostasis implies a balancing of forces, it does not (in the same sense as a dialectic) imply constant struggle towards conflicting goals. These forces do not seek to vanquish each other for vanquishing in a well-balanced and dynamic system becomes a pyrrhic victory. Physiological forces or species maintain a balance rather than "vanquish" each other: they do this to meet the common goal of survival and growth. The notion of pursuing a common goal or interest which enables the pursuit of individual goals or interests rather than the notion of combat or struggle between antagonistic and opposed forces is what homeostasis is all about. Dialectic tension (the tension between opposed forces each pursuing its own interests) resolves itself into a temporary synthesis: a tenuous balance best described as an armed truth and one in which a struggle continues. Homeostatic balance is conceived as the dynamic equilibrium between various forces each of which seeks to maintain the balance and each of which can continue only within the context of the whole.

When viewed in this fashion, the old tension between the interests of individuals (or associations) to follow their own destiny and the requirements of the larger associations of which they are a part persists: but it persists not so that one can predominate over the other but so that the interests and the goals of the association which enable all other interests can be met. Individual interests or rights need a playing field which, so that they can be realized, the community must provide; communal interests, so that they can be realized, in turn require the willing and open contributions of individual talent and interests. Removing the individuals from the playing field as surely as removing the playing field from the individuals stops the game.

In past works, I have tried to differentiate various types of collectives and show their relationship to each other and to their members.[22] My thesis was (and continues to be) that in an ethically relevant sense individuals relate to each other and to their communities in a way similar to the way in which communities relate to each other and, ultimately, to the large world community of which they are a part. To sketch different collectives I have largely relied on the work of Tönnies. Since some of the prototypes have no proper English translation, I have relied on the original German word for particular collectives and have tried to sketch their meaning.[23] So as to make what is to come comprehensible, I will briefly review and at times extend what I said in past works here.

Collectives can come together to pursue a single goal, a few goals or a complex set of goals. When collectives become ever more complex and the range of goals becomes wider, some of these associations begin to formulate and evolve new goals. Simple collectives exist to serve limited ends and serve as means to these ends; the more complex the collective, the more do means and ends intertwine until the collective itself becomes an end in itself. The homeostatic balance within these collectives which tends towards stability while allowing change becomes ever more evident as more complex collectives are examined. As collectives become more and more complex and more and more dynamic and as they underwrite a more complex skein of their members goals they become goals in their own right.

Collectives which enable a single or a narrow range of interests lack more than superficial solidarity. The homeostatic balance in such a collective is not particularly dynamic nor can such collectives be expected to evolve new and more complex goals. Membership largely depends on personal interest and as personal interests change membership is easily abandoned. Solidarity within such a collective is apt to evaporate quickly. As the collective assumes a more central role in enabling ever more important aspirations of its members, as it became a goal in its own right, loyalty to and solidarity with it becomes ever more solid and firm.

Broadly speaking, one can in ascending order of complexity (not necessarily in ascending order of size) identify three types of collectives: "Verein," "Gesellschaft," and "Gemeinschaft." The first is almost untranslatable but will be described; the latter can loosely be translated as "society" and as "community."

A Verein is the most primitive of these associations. It could be exemplified by a group of persons who come together to play Mozart Quartets or to manufacture shoes. A Verein serves as a means to such ends. Individuals come and go as members of such an association depending upon a particular interest or a narrow range of interests at any particular time. While the association can be seen as essential to the pursuit of such an interest, the interest, as important as it may be for the individual, is not central to his/her existence and the existence of the Verein is, therefore, not generally an end in its own right. In general, a Verein does not evolve more complex goals. When one leaves such an organization, one may leave it with regret but without undue difficulty: other organizations inevitably and with not too much difficulty take its place.

A Gesellschaft (society will do fairly well as a translation) is a far more complex entity. It has many more goals and begins to have a dynamic existence and equilibrium of its own. Not only does it frequently evolve new and more complex goals, the existence of the Gesellschaft becomes more and more necessary for the achievement of a broad range of its member's goals. Loyalty to the Gesellschaft and solidarity with it becomes very much evident. Members may leave the Gesellschaft: they may, as it were, emigrate or join another Gesellschaft but doing so exacts a large price not only in delayed, abandoned, or changed goals and possibilities but ultimately also an increasing emotional price. Emigration, as I know full well, is far more than merely the loss of material goals and possibilities; other associations do not too easily take the place of the old.

A Gemeinschaft (translated adequately as community) is the most complex of these associations. There are two very different ways of conceiving of a Gemeinschaft or community: I shall refer to the one simply as community or Gemeinschaft and to the other as "cloistered community" or "eingeklosterte Gemeinschaft."

A Gemeinschaft or community in the former sense is itself the condition for the satisfaction of most of the most important goals and interests its members may have. That does not mean that absolutely all goals need be communal: but it does mean that the further from a "Gesellschaft" and the closer to a Gemeinschaft a collective will be, the more will most of the goals and most of the crucial goals be fulfilled in or through it. When I say "in or through it" I mean that while some of the goals may not be met by the collective itself (let us, for example, say specific religious or political goals), the collective even when it does not meet such goals supplies the soil on which such aspirations or goals can legitimately be met or worked towards. A Gemeinschaft or community readily evolves and experiments with new and more complex goals and very decidedly has an existence of its own. Individual diversity is encouraged and fostered: it is one of the driving forces of evolution and change and, therefore, has survival value. Solidarity within the Gemeinschaft is firm: to its members the Gemeinschaft itself and its existence is an essential goal without which their individual goals are hard if not impossible to realize.

One other form of community needs to be mentioned: it is not what I shall mean when I speak of Gemeinschaft; rather, it is almost a caricature of what I have in mind. For want of a better word, I have called such a community "cloistered": not because it necessarily is religious, albeit it often is; it can be any secular or religious association in which set points are narrow so that new values and ways of doing things are unlikely to emerge. Such a community as not only an important goal but as "the" one and only goal in itself tends to swamp all individual interests: there is stability but it is the dead hand of stability and not a stability aimed at growth and development. Members are subject to a party (be it religious or secular) discipline which stifles rather than favours individual interests and growth. The interests, values and goals of its members are narrowed: they are hemmed in rather than enabled by the monolithic nature of such an organization. Soon such an organization lacks the dynamic and voluntary character of a true community. Such a collective has a very narrow range of set points which are rigidly enforced and it lacks the elasticity necessary to adapt. When confronted by changed situations or new external forces it will not adapt and may not survive.

Leaving a Gemeinschaft is possible only at a staggering price. Often leaving a community of this sort means that in some sense the

Gemeinschaft is felt to have broken faith with more than just with the person or persons leaving it: faith has been broken not so much with the person him/herself but faith has been broken with what at least that person perceives to have been one of the central values or goals which have heretofore typified the community. Such a state of affairs could be seen when members disillusioned at various stages by the Communist party left the party: examples of this are the leaving of the party after the Stalinist purges, after the Hitler-Stalin pact, and after some of the terror at the end of World War II. Generally, internal or external emigration became necessary so that central personal values heretofore believed realizable by and through such a community could be preserved.[24]

Separation from an association may occur for reasons sometimes labeled as "nonideological" and trivialized as "merely" economic. People who are starving may leave their prior association because it now can or will no longer serve as the soil on which survival is enabled. Later in this work I hope to show that the possibility of freedom squarely rests on the fulfillment of prior material conditions, conditions which are necessary for survival. To claim that persons who flee a society which no longer can feed or house them and their loved ones do so lightly or, somehow, with less defensible reasons than if they do so for ideological reasons is cynicism: freedom can only be valued by those alive to value it. Emigrating under conditions of material need, however, leaves the cultural image of one's former community more or less undamaged: its present standing depends on its former. When economic conditions are the result of the way a community shaped itself politically such an emigration will be far different than it would be if famine were the result of natural disaster. But in either case, emigration whether for reasons of basic economy or for reasons of deep-seated ideological incompatibility is never "easy" or "lightly done."

When it comes to cloistered communities, one can think here of emigration from Bolshevik Russia or Nazi Germany; or one can think of leaving a monastery or tightly knit religious order. Emigration which occasionally was internal and was manifest by overt or covert rebellion, occasionally ended in outright suicide but more often ended in an emigration in which the emigrant felt (with much reason on their side) that the essential values and goals of that society or community (for the harder it was to leave the more it had, at least in the eyes of the emigrant, become for him or her a community) now could only be saved by the very act of internal or external emigration and alienation. The emigrant here feels that homeostasis has failed at home and that, if it can be preserved at all, preservation is possible only by internal or external emigration.

What had happened in the Nazi as well as in the Bolshevik state is that the community approached a cloistered form. By embracing the new movement, it abandoned some if its own cultural principles and gravely narrowed the setpoints of homeostasis. In this way it lost elasticity and, eventually, solidarity. The falling of such types of communities is merely a matter of time. Unless solidarity can be maintained, communities are doomed to perish.

The relationship among various collectives, I shall argue throughout this book, can be analogized to the relationship among individuals within a collective. In turn, the relationship of more complex collectives—themselves composed of less complex collectives—with their individual members can be analogized to the relationship communities and individuals have with each other. A collective which has developed a general common purpose through development of a general will can be seen as a corporate individual. Eventually all of these various collectives impinge upon one another: the fate of one ultimately affects all others. To speak of national interests outside the confines of world interests, as isolationists are apt to do, is to extend the view of the asocial individual to an asocial corporate individual or asocial society. Solidarity among collectives and the realization that ultimately we can only fulfill our personal or corporate individual goals within the embrace of a community of others is essential to our survival as a species.

To describe human relations, whether to describe them among individuals, professions, or communities, is necessarily to assent to a notion of obligation. In this book I shall consistently argue that a minimalist view of obligations grounded on the notion that individual liberty can exist outside a social nexus and that collectives exist merely or predominantly to assure the liberty of their individual members does not suffice on either theoretical or practical grounds. Obligations among persons (what I owe my particular neighbor or a stranger) exist within the more general notion of communal obligations: both the obligations individuals owe their communities and the obligations communities in turn owe their members. In part, all relationships are defined by their obligation: the concept "friend," "spouse," "teacher" or "member of a community" in order to be understood must at least in part be explained in terms of such "role" obligations. Some of these "roles" (such as friend or teacher) are voluntarily assumed; others (such as member of a given family or state) are accidents of birth; and still others ("sentient being" or "human") are inevitabilities of our existence. The world is not a simple system of individual and collective. Collectives (larger, smaller, more or less complex) coexist and their inevitable relations with each other are likewise in part defined by their mutual obligations.

Here I briefly want to speak about the grounding or justification of obligations. To do this we first of all must take a look at what we mean by the term "obligation" or "duty." I will use the terms interchangeably albeit that the term duty somehow seems to have a more absolutist flavor. What does it mean to have "an obligation" (or a duty)? If I have an obligation it is, under certain circumstances at least, something I (ethically or sometimes and, hardly the same thing, legally) must do. Such a "must do" is, however, something I could if I wished, refrain from doing. Thus to say that when my knee is tapped, my resulting knee-jerk is an obligation or to assert that a bullet shot at a target has an obligation to hit it is not what is meant. If I do not discharge an obligation or duty I could (morally or legally) be called to account. Nor can an obligation be something that I cannot do: duty is something which refraining from as well as doing is possible. To say that a pauper has the duty to feed his family or that I have a duty not to have an Achilles reflex is a meaningless statement.

How, when I claim that something is your obligation and you deny that it is, do I go about arguing? How, in other words, does one go about "proving" a proposition? One can, in one school of thought, reduce proof to authority by appealing either to "the word of God" or "natural law." Such a method, however, cannot be convincing to those who do not share the same point of view: either a point of view about God and God's commandments or a point of view of what, in fact, natural law is. Relying on authority for proof is circular: authority gives the rules and the giving of the rules proves authority. Propositions accepted on the grounds of authority are deduced from the rules given by authority.

Of course, one cannot entirely escape authority. Appealing to reason is, in a sense, an appeal to the authority of reason. The process as well as the result of reasoning, however, is an ongoing and public process prone to logical and empirical examination. Propositions "proven" by reason are not proven for all time: they are a step in the right direction, a working out of questions with answers which help one get on with whatever one is doing better than before. Propositions are "truer" because they are seen to work better, more successfully, and more humanely when they are applied to real situations, not "true" in the sense of "eternal" or "divine" or "natural" truth. The ability to reason along a basically similar line is one of the

unifying biological traits of all sentient beings: not merely of particular social classes, societies, or cultures. It is, as I shall later argue,
one of the shared traits which allows us to be moral acquaintances
rather than being, as some will argue, moral strangers.

Deductive reasoning does not exhaust reasoning and deductive
"proof" does not exhaust the possibilities of proof. In ethics, Kant's
Categorical Imperative comes close to being deductively evident.
But such propositions, while essential to any ethical reasoning, do
not suffice to deal with our obligations either as persons with each
other or as members of a community.

What is needed is a working inference which will allow us to
get on with the task at hand. By "getting on with the task at hand"
such a proposition will be further tested and refined in praxis. Looking for "absolute truth" or "absolute proof" will render getting on
with our task impossible and will complicate further testing. Justification, in that sense is an ongoing process of learning and growth;
ultimately it becomes a tool in our evolution and survival.[25]

There are two extremes to be avoided: the one is acting on a
proposition before all reasonable efforts to prove the proposition
have been made; the other is refusing to act until a proposition has
been absolutely proven. In the nature of things and in the view
advanced here, absolute proof is not something that we in the human
condition can ever obtain (or, at any rate, we have not accomplished
it to date and do not seem much closer to accomplishing it!). When
we act on a proposition without making all reasonable efforts to
prove it, we are apt to act wrongly and to recognize that we have
been wrong. We cannot only or merely test an ill-conceived proposition in experience. But on the other hand, not acting until we have
been given absolute proof freezes our acting and, therefore, makes
the testing of the proposition in experience impossible. In the human
condition, all of our acting is on the basis of probability: the more
important the consequences of our action, the more rigorous ought
we to be and the higher the probability we must ask for.

Logic, as Dewey has pointed out, consists of far more than
merely deduction. It is a dynamic striving towards warranted "solutions": solutions not in the sense of final answers but in the sense of
tentative hypotheses which serve to carry inquiry from a lesser to a
greater state of determinacy. Solutions are tested in experience: when
we have "found" a "solution" it is a more determinate way of dealing with a problem but it is not a final answer. Solutions are more
determinate because they work better in the context in which they
are used and "working better" denotes a better ability to deal with

real problems to everyone's benefit. It denotes that such solutions, furthermore, can be used to further inquiry, stimulate growth and promote survival. In a sense this way of looking at proof or "truth" bears some similarity to a homeostatic process in which a dynamic balance among forces strives towards the transcendental (in the sense of overarching and connecting) goal of development and survival. If one uses only deduction, the set points are narrow and solutions are meager; if one fails to attend to deduction, the set points are diffuse and the process cannot proceed.

In this work I shall not rely merely, albeit I will rely heavily, on deductive logic to deal with the question of obligations. Our obligations can be underwritten by a host of different reasons. Like our life experiences which do not stand alone like a heap of stones but which interpenetrate each other to form a mix in which the single components have interacted to produce a new whole (something Steward Hampshire aptly calls a "compost heap"[26]), our different ways of going about reasoning interact.[27]

Obligations of refraining (essentially those of not harming under which I would include the obligation not to lie or steal) are less difficult to argue for than are the more positive obligations of mutual help or beneficence. The former rely heavily on deduction even though supportive evidence for them can likewise be garnered from other parts of the compost heap. When one argues for the obligation of mutual non-harm one can, for example, use Kant's Categorical Imperative and fortify it further by an appeal to social contract. But when it comes to looking at more than the overall idea or looks further than at any one obligation taken out of context, problems soon present themselves. These separate obligations do, pace Kant!, manage to conflict one with the other. Appealing to deductive logic will not, I think, by itself solve the problem. When we employ strategies to evade this difficulty (whether it be the prima facie obligations of which W. D. Ross speaks[28] or other methods) we leave pure deductive logic and must employ other means. Kant, when he argues for obligations of beneficence, supports his argument in a variety of ways. The one argues that while such obligations cannot be strictly deduced from the categorical imperative (do not strictly conform to logic) willing a world in which such obligations would not be accepted would, since we all ultimately and at some time must rely on such obligations, "force the will to conflict with itself":

> We must be able to will that a maxim of our actions become a universal law; this is the canon of the moral estimation of our

actions generally. Some actions are of such a nature that their maxims cannot even be thought as a universal law of nature without contradiction, far from it being possible that one could will that it be such. In others this internal impossibility is not found, though it is still impossible to will that their maxim should be raised to the universality of a law of nature, because such a will would contradict itself. We easily see that the former maxim conflicts with the stricter or narrower (imprescriptible) duty, the latter with broader (meritorious) duty . . .[29]

Beyond this, Kant argues that there is a "realm of ends," that we have an obligation to make everyone else's ends also to some extent our own (for the proper quotation see chapter 2). If that is the case, then obligations of beneficence (which ultimately include our neighbor's needs among ours) naturally emerge. Such arguments, however, fail to suffice in arguing for welfare, public education, or a readily accessible healthcare system since they leave what we will and what we will not recognize as compelling obligations strictly up to us.

In this chapter I have tried to tie together some of my previous work and to sketch how I shall use it throughout this book. Specifically I have tried to interconnect the notion of suffering with that of community, have attempted to escape some of the vagueness which concepts like community often have been charged to have, and have tied these things together with a sense of how I shall attempt to argue for a rather wide range of obligations and understandings. Underlying all of this is my belief that all human activities ultimately must aim at serving survival, growth, and learning, They are, as it were, linked together, part of a harmonious whole in which homeostasis ultimately modulates their activities. The dissonances of everyday existence must not, I think, dissuade us from working towards a harmonious resolution.

2 Moral Acquaintances: A Way of Relating

In the last chapter, I briefly reviewed the concept of basing moral relevance or standing, on, among other things, the capacity to suffer, presented various forms of moral standing, and linked the idea of suffering and its moral implication to the notion of various types of associations. Relationships among persons, among persons and associations, and among various types of associations are, at least to a large extent, dependent upon the types of obligations such descriptions entail. Relationships are at least in part defined by obligations and obligations are at least in part dependent upon relationships: the two concepts are largely inseparable. Although one can conceive of generic obligations (of a "this we must—or must not do") without a specific relationship, even such a generic principle of obligation implies the existence of social relationships: even strangers, in that sense, have relationships with each other and they have obligations based on such a relationship. I tried to show that our obligations cannot be purely deductively derived but that they have a rich and complex connection with the way we conceive community. The way we conceive community, the way in which we envision our proper place in any collective, in turn preordains the way our mutual obligations are conceived.

In this chapter I will review the libertarian notion of isolated selves, of freestanding persons who lack social connectedness and are, therefore, termed "moral strangers."[1] The term "moral stranger" has been used to refer to persons of different cultures and beliefs who, therefore, lack social connectedness: except for knowing that all want to shape their individual lives in their own particular way, such moral strangers lack a common framework of dialogue or of understanding each other's problems.[2] I will show that the notion of social unconnectedness and of moral strangers rests, at least in part, on an acceptance of Hobbesian social contract based on terror. I will trace the development of the idea of social contract and link it to modern libertarian thinkers such as Nozick and Engelhardt. Some alternative notions of social connectedness or contract will be briefly reviewed and the centrality of Rousseau's notion of a "primitive sense of pity" or compassion to moral theory will be stressed. Finally, I will begin to sketch my own notions about social contract and proceed to expand them in the following chapters.

There are many ways of sketching obligations. The idea of obligation is invariably linked to our understanding of the individual not only in his/her relationship to specific others but inescapably in his/her relation to community. Those who conceive persons as basically asocial, freestanding individuals see their obligations (whether these be obligations owed to other individuals or obligations owed to the community) quite differently than do those who conceive persons as inseparable from their social nexus. Those who conceive individuals as freestanding and isolated, may concede that individuals by their own choice become part of a social nexus and even take on specific obligations as part of being members of such a nexus; but they see such a nexus as freely chosen and the relationship as basically contractual. Generic obligations which persons qua persons have to each other will, if one subscribes to such a vision, be basically minimalist: obligations beyond the minimalist are seen as entailing voluntary choice. Such organizations or collectives are the sum of their individuals. In Rousseouean terms, as we shall discuss shortly, such associations would consist of persons who, while they have a particular personal will, lack a general will. Their particular will, a will which is always primarily concerned with the individual interest of the person concerned, in the libertarian vision does not mature into a general one. Those who see persons as intrinsically social beings (and who see social association as not merely voluntarily entered) conceive of a far richer basic set of mutual obligations.

Since the idea of moral strangers and what that idea implies (the idea that we know virtually nothing about each other which would allow us to derive a content-full ethic) is central to what is to follow, I will, best as I can, sketch the idea of moral strangers. To do this I will rely on Professor Engelhardt's work realizing that the ideas he expressed are fundamental to most of what can be called libertarian belief. So as to sustain a starkly individualist notion of mutual obligations, it is necessary to assume that persons from diverse backgrounds or cultures know little about each other except that they all wish to pursue their own interests without being hindered by the interference of others. This lack of understanding of one another's interests has spawned the notion of moral strangers.

To be a moral stranger to another is not to share enough of a concrete morality to allow the common basis for the correct resolution of a moral controversy.[3]

So as to be able to negotiate with each other across various cultural and belief systems having an entirely different content, one would necessarily have to have a common denominator of assumptions:

When moral strangers meet and cooperate, the question is: what basis can exist for the cooperation, other than force and coercion? To find a basis for cooperation, moral strangers must look for some neutral framework (i.e., some secular framework) in terms of which they can discover what they share in common.[4]

Accordingly, the only common denominator we can all agree upon, the only assumption we can make about one another, is that we all wish to lead our own lives in our own way and according to our own (freely chosen) precepts and values. This gives us a formal and minimalist ethic, one in which respect for others and their liberty of action, insofar as its exercise does not hinder a like freedom of action for others, must be presupposed. Various ways of attempting to give a normative or prescriptive account of ethics have, according to those who hold a strongly libertarian view, failed and such attempts are doomed to fail in the future. Libertarians would deny that there is "a philosophically justifiable foundation . . . that can be shared by all persons."[5]

According to libertarians (specifically in this instance according to Engelhardt)

the question is whether one can secure a secular ethic. . . . in the special sense of an ethic not beholden to any particular faith or moral tradition, but grounded in the very requirements of a rational ethic or in the nature of man or reality itself.[6]

Such attempts, whether utilitarian, deontological, hypothetical choice, or contractor, as well as appeals to intuition or to the outcome of reflective equilibrium among one's moral principles and intuitions have supposedly failed. Likewise, except for specific persons in specific enclaves, religion has failed to provide moral guidance; appeals to "human nature" or "natural law" have been equally unsuccessful. According to such writers, it is, therefore, impossible to establish a content-full moral vision which would make dialogue and arbitration possible.

The only grounds for dialogue we are left with "even if God is silent and the project of discovering a content-full ethic fails"[7] is formal and minimalist.

> Insofar as one is interested in engaging in ethics, that is, in resolving controversies without foundational recourse to force, one can still participate in a common moral world with moral strangers. The necessary condition for participating in that world is mutual respect, the non-use of others without their consent. This side constraint is not grounded in a value given to autonomy, liberty or to person but is integral to the grammar of controversy resolution when God, facts and reason do not provide bases for peaceably resolving a dispute. Mutual respect is accepted because it is the one way to ground a common moral world for moral strangers without arbitrarily endorsing a particular ranking of values. Accepting this ground for secular ethics is equivalent to accepting the moral point of view which requires the fewest assumptions: an interest in having common moral authority for collaborative endeavours when God is silent and reason impotent. It is intellectually the least costly way of establishing a common moral world.[8]

Let us hear a little more of what the outcome of such a vision is:

> Because secular humanism is not a tradition but a way of reaching across traditions, it regards individuals outside their embeddedness in particular moral communities. This does not mean that they cannot belong to moral communities or that a sense of community should cease—far from it. It is just that moral strangers as such do not share in a concrete moral community. Secular humanism cannot supply a content full account of individuals that places them within a particular moral context. Thus, for secular humanists, individuals are salient and central. It is individuals who meet as moral strangers. It is individuals who exist before moral theories are articulated or common endeavours created. Since common moral endeavours are, from a secular humanist perspective, the work of actual individuals in actual contexts, the accent is on individual responsibility. It is individuals who will engage in empirical science and secular morality and thus sustain general

practices that have no a priori content beyond the sparse grammar that governs this function. It is individuals who through secular social structures create the fabric and focus of common endeavours. In all of this, individuals are not given precedence because they are valued. Within the sparse morality of moral strangers, one cannot talk about persons as being valued or having moral worth. They, and their consent, are simply necessary for a morality of moral strangers (only in a particular moral community can a person have moral value and worth). As moral strangers, individuals are respected, not because they are valuable, but because such respect is integral to a morality for moral strangers. Secular humanism does not involve a value commitment to individualism. Individuals are salient by default. Since one cannot discover a general, morally authoritative social nexus ontologically prior to individuals, individuals hold center stage when moral strangers meet.[9]

In what is called "the postmodern era" we have found it necessary to reject any of the conventional ways in which ethical problems were heretofore resolved. According to Engelhardt, the enlightenment, with its reliance on reason to solve human problems, is almost as dead as God: the only universal obligation that reason can show us, is the one and only obligation of strictly respecting each other's freedom. Such a minimalist point of view, aside from presupposing God's silence and the impotence of reason, presupposes largely asocial individuals. It is, perhaps, peculiar that while denying that reason can give a "content-full ethic," such an ethic perforce must rely on reason to establish the framework of "mutual respect and the nonuse of others without their consent." Moreover, the belief that God is silent (or dead or nonexistent or at least not accessible to us) and that consequently some form of secular humanism is all that is left to us (a statement with which I would largely agree) does not necessarily denote, as Engelhardt I think suggests, that we must accept the concept of moral strangers if we are to maintain peace. I do not argue against secular humanism, whatever secular humanism is supposed to mean. Unfortunately, secular humanism has been used to denote a large number of mutually incompatible world views based on the non-accessibility or nonexistence of God. Central to most interpretations of secular humanism, however, is the importance of human rationality, human experience and human welfare. Except for some rather flagrant examples to the contrary, few of us, whatever our general world view, would deny the importance of rationality, of experience or of fostering human welfare.

In what is to come and in future chapters I do not argue against the use of reason in grappling with these problems nor against the notion that one of the things we need for moral dialogue is mutual respect for others and for their freedom of action. Indeed, that seems obvious. What I argue against is a monolithic viewpoint which claims that reason cannot advance our search for an ethic beyond such respect and such freedom of action and that the condition of respect and freedom of action is the only (or even the most fundamental) ground of arbitration. What I argue for is a richer framework of decision making which allows other common and accepted grounds of arbitration and which is aimed at producing not merely maximal human freedom but much else that human welfare and happiness entails.

The fact that there is no complete philosophical foundation to be found and the fact that vast differences among individuals, individual beliefs, and individual cultures will inevitably persist, does not mean that there are not many more commonalties (and, therefore, many more things we know about each other) than libertarians would acknowledge. While such commonalties do not allow us and will never allow us to shape a complete or an entire content-full ethic all will subscribe to, these commonalties enable us to share a far richer framework of mutual understanding than a libertarian position would admit. And, I shall claim, these common understandings provide a ground of arbitration which can, even if it is not complete, begin to yield some significant content.

Most certainly humans from different cultural, religious, and experiential backgrounds will always have vast differences in their moral points of view. There can never be—nor do I think that it would be particular desirable if there were—absolute agreement about all, or even perhaps about most, specific ethical questions. To have a homogenized world would, I believe, stifle evolution and progress. To assume that adopting a secular ethic, which in a pluralist world is indeed necessary if we are to remain at peace, must inevitably lead to embracing the notion of moral strangers and to assume, therefore, that a secular ethic is perforce minimalist rests upon an impoverished view of what can possibly connect us. What I shall argue is that sentient beings have much more ground for common dialogue than such a minimalist ethic would suggest: that humans qua humans (and, I would argue that this is not necessarily limited to humans but is to a lesser extent true for many nonhuman animals) have sufficient knowledge of each other to allow a much richer dialogue among humans of all sorts of backgrounds and beliefs. This leads to a much richer notion of obligation and ethics. I shall base this argument on certain factors common to all and will call these factors "experiential a prioris of ethics": that is, they are grounded in human biology and experience and are prior to any ethical dialogue. These "a prioris," I will further suggest, are not only the factors which undergird our ability to reason about ethical issues with each other but likewise are the factors which underlie religion. It is simply not the case that only religious or freely chosen enclaves can supply a content-full account of individuals that places them within a particular moral context. And while undoubtedly the framework I am suggesting does not suffice to solve all, or perhaps even most, specific moral problems, it can go a good way towards suggesting solutions to at least some of them.

I want to be clear about this point: I am not committing what has been called the "naturalistic fallacy": I am neither extracting an "ought" from an "is" nor reducing obligations or ethics to experience or biology. In what follows I am arguing that human experience and biology provide the necessary conditions for all else, including ethics. While, on the one hand, we cannot escape either our biological or our experiential framework in shaping our destiny (and shaping our destiny includes making certain decisions about questions of ethics), we can, on the other hand, not reduce our acting to mere experience or biology. All sentient animals have taken their experience and biology, learned from it, adapted to it and, where possible, changed it. But even when we change these conditions, say when we build houses or cure illness, we do so within the necessary framework of experiential and biological understanding. We learn to use what we have, shape what we have and learn from what we have experienced. Saying that something ought to be because it is, is evidently wrong: but we cannot begin to think about what ought to be the case unless we are quite clear about what is the case.

Because the way we see our obligations is necessarily related to the way we conceive communal ontology and structure we must, before we get on with elucidating some of these existential a prioris, deal with the way communities are conceived. The notion of social contract is often used to analyze community and its social structure. It is a mistake to think that the notion of social contract is ever meant to be taken literally. Rather than being thought a historical fact, social contract is a way of examining and conceptualizing communal structure. Dewey in speaking about the historical method in its application to ethics made the point which, likewise, can be made for social contract theories: "the value of the earlier event in time is really one of method, one of giving us insights into the later conditions."[10]

The Hobbesian notion of social contract is, of course, basic to the libertarian notion of a minimalist ethic. Hobbes presupposed, even though he did not articulate, this notion when he held that life was "solitary, nasty, brutish and short" and when he claimed that asocial individuals driven by terror associated merely to enable them to pursue their own lives in their own way. In many respects Hobbes was an offshoot of a natural law type of philosophy which accepted "nature" as normative for ethics: not as the necessary framework in which humans and their communities seek to fashion their ethics and laws but as content-full and preordained. To Hobbes the right of nature, which many writers commonly call jus naturale, is the

> liberty each man hath, to use his own power, as he will himself, for the preservation of his own nature; that is to say his own life; and consequently of doing anything in his own judgment, and reason, he shall conceive to be the aptest means thereunto.[11]

To Hobbes a law of nature, lex naturalis, is

> a precept or general rule, found out by reason, by which a man is forbidden to do that which is destructive of his life . . . and to omit that, by which he thinketh it may be best preserved.[12]

To Hobbes, "right" consisted of "liberty to do or forebear" whereas "law" "determineth and bindeth to one of them."

Laws of nature can be examined because "laws of nature oblige in conscience always, but in effect only when there is security."[13] They are "immutable" and "eternal" and they are "easy to observe." Persons who fulfill these laws are acting justly (in that Hobbes makes justice also one of the laws of nature there is some inevitable circularity here: in a sense, justice consists, among other things at least, in being just).

Every man, according to Hobbes, has a right to everything. This Hobbes considers to be the fundamental law of nature. Since the "natural condition" was war of all against all, man had a right to possess himself of all he was able to get: even to the point of murder.

Therefore, as long as this natural right of all to have all endured, man was insecure and unable to safely go about his business. The fundamental and first law of nature, then, is to seek peace. The second law, as Hobbes sees it, is that

> men should be willing when others are so . . . to lay down his right to all things; and be content with so much liberty against other men, as he would allow other men against himself.[14]

Man can renounce or transfer some rights but not all rights are thus alienable. Ultimately Hobbes believes that persons alienate their rights so to bring about some good for themselves and therefore alienating some rights (such as that to defend oneself) is not possible: to Hobbes, such a right, since alienating one's right to self-defense could not benefit one, is inalienable. To Hobbes, contract involves the transferring of a right and covenant implies the trust that contracts will be kept. Justice—the third law of nature according to Hobbes—is simply the performing and injustice the nonperformance of covenant.[15] Since persons are apt not to perform covenants there must be "some coercive power" to compel them to do so. From this, eventually, Hobbes extracts his notion of an absolute sovereign to whom all power is given so as to ensure peace and the keeping of covenants: to assure that covenants will be kept (a necessity so that peace may reign), all logically turn over that power to an absolute sovereign. They do so in order to maximize their liberty of action: in a sense tyranny can be seen to come in on the Trojan horse of freedom. Although the sovereign derives his power from the initial (and logically necessary) consent of those governed, such power once given is permanently held. Interestingly enough there are other laws of nature Hobbes deals with: nineteen in all.

Hobbes' theory of social contract as I have very briefly sketched it in the previous chapter, depends upon these considerations much as later libertarians depend upon Hobbes' notion of social contract. Fundamental to both libertarians and Hobbes is that liberty of action and lack of constraint are what motivates persons to associate; where they differ is that Hobbes' view of justice and law is (at least initially, for with the emergence of the absolute sovereign to whom all powers are given all "bets are off") a far more generously conceived one. To Hobbes, all laws by virtue of being laws are just.[16] That, however, does not necessarily mean that they are good. To Hobbes a good law is one which "is needful, for the good of the people, and withal perspicuous."[17] Different than today's libertarians would have it, good laws also included taxes for public purposes and public charity:

> and whereas men, by accident inevitably, become unable to maintain themselves by their labour; they ought not to be left to the charity of private persons; but to be provided for, as far as the necessities of nature require, by the laws of the common-wealth. For as it is uncharitableness in any man to neglect the impotent; so it is in the sovereign of a commonwealth to expose them to the hazard of such uncertain charity.[18]

However, such "good laws" are laws which it would be well but not necessary for the absolute sovereign to make. They are, as it were, Hobbes' advice to any potential sovereign.

Albeit that libertarianism derives much of its world view from the Hobbesian notion of a social contract forged in terror, it differs markedly in the way it would conceive modern social structure. Whereas Hobbes would not only be satisfied with an all powerful sovereign (even if, since laws by their nature are just, such a sovereign made laws he did not consider to be good) but would indeed find such a position needful, modern libertarians would not agree: indeed, limiting the power of the sovereign (be it single or corporate) is one of its prime motivators. On the other hand and for that very reason, libertarians would not agree that public charity or the supplying of everyone's necessities was a proper thing for the state to do: or, at the very least, they would hold that while public charity might be desirable, taxation to make public charity possible could not be exacted. Forcing people to pay taxes (except to ensure personal freedom and enforce contracts) would be an incursion on their liberty. Persons could certainly contribute voluntarily (at times libertarians speak of a tax which, however, could not be forcibly collected: a voluntary tax, as it were!) but coercion to collect taxes, since it interfered with individual liberty, except insofar as these taxes were for the maintenance of peace within and without the state, could not be collected.

The minimalist ethic claims that liberty (or individual free-dom) is a "side-constraint": that is, it is a condition and not a value of morality.[19] Moral rules must conform to respecting personal liberty except when the exercise of personal liberty would directly constrain the personal liberty of another. Government is constituted for that purpose, a purpose which necessarily includes enforcing freely entered contracts and defense against external attack. Levying taxes to accomplish these tasks is legitimate. Government cannot legitimately involve itself in any other sphere: public charity á la Hobbes, is not a legitimate function and laws which would levy taxes to enforce such laws are not legitimate. The state, as Rawls has pointed out, in the libertarian point of view comes about "in the same way as other associations and its formation in the perfectly as-if [sic] just historical process is governed by the same principles"; the relationship of individuals to such a minimalist state is like that with any private association with which an agreement has been made.[20] Public law is replaced by a skein of private agreements. Likewise, individuals are mutually obligated to respect each other's freedom and, as a part of that, to scrupulously adhere to freely entered contracts. While they cannot harm each other and while mutual help may be a condition of a contract or a condition of membership in an enclave, individuals freely decided to enter, no general obligation of mutual help exists.

Libertarians certainly do not believe in an "absolute sovereign." However, libertarianism as it is conceived would inevitably give greater advantage to the more powerful, those with more wealth and those either with greater or with greater opportunity to develop equal talent. Such persons, as long as they did not directly interfere with the liberty of their fellow citizens, would be quite free to manipulate them to their advantage. The crass exploitation which untrammeled capitalism inflicts on many members of society is the obvious example. To argue that freedom is equal for all when the powerful are entirely free to arrogate ever more power to themselves as long as they do not directly prevent the weak from exercising a like freedom is, at the very least, disingenuous. In modern societies material conditions largely determine not only the power one will have but the power one will be able to arrogate to oneself. When, in such societies, freedom becomes an absolute so that restricting personal freedom can be done only when its exercise directly interferes with another's like freedom, the power of the haves to exploit the have-nots will inevitably increase and, thereby, institutionalize and enlarge powerlessness and poverty. I shall argue that even when one merely holds freedom to be a supreme value which generally but not invariably trumps all other values (instead of considering it to be an absolute), such a process is bound to happen. And many of us would argue that in reality and for those affected adversely, such a freedom is no freedom at all.

Although a view of asocial individuals "covenanting" and making an agreement of mutual non-harm is basic to Hobbes as well as the libertarians, there are basic differences. To the libertarians, individuals can always "opt out" of the association; in that sense libertarianism is not a social contract theory. The idea of making laws which would provide public charity, food inspection, or other public services (all of which imply taxation and, therefore, an incursion of individual freedom) is not, according to libertarians, legitimate. Libertarians see a minimal state as having come about in a relatively abundant state of nature. Provided private property was justly acquired, it cannot be limited. (This, of course, implies a particular vision of justice many of us would not share).

The shape of social association to Rousseau[21] was the key to morality.[22] He shared with Mill and with many others before and after him the belief that membership in society and the habits, customs, and beliefs that individuals grow up with critically shape their own individual beliefs. We are not and never can be "freestanding" individuals, self-made men and women.

Rousseau's concept of how societies formed differed markedly from Hobbes. Hobbes' view of the state of nature was one of a "war of all against all" "waged by a number of ferocious egoists each acting against his fellowmen in pursuance of his personal appetite for possession and power."[23] Rousseau saw humans in the "original state" as amoral and asocial animals whose morality was a product of social association. The idea of freestanding socially isolated individuals, however, remained. Rousseau, while he saw the state of nature as involving freestanding, socially isolated individuals who coalesced into families only to fulfill drives and needs, did not see such humans in the state of nature as intrinsically bent on harming each other. Nor did Rousseau regard the family as a stable association or as in the nature of a small community. Rather, he saw the family as being formed for the transitory needs and convenience of its members. The state of nature was not one in which terror reigned but rather one of amoral persons who would harm each other only when self-preservation dictated. This drive to self-preservation ("conservation de soi-même"), the strongest persistent drive, would dominate though modified by an innate primitive sense of pity or compassion present in all (normal) humans as well as in higher animals.

> I think I can perceive in it (the operation of the human soul) two principles prior to reason, one of them deeply interesting us in our own welfare and preservation, and the other exhibiting a natural repugnance at seeing any other sensible being, and particularly one of our species, suffer pain or death. It is

from the agreement and combination which the understanding is in a position to establish between these two principles, without its being necessary to introduce that of sociability, that all the rules of natural right appear to me to be derived—rules which our reason is afterward obliged to establish on other foundations, when by its successive developments it has been led to suppress nature itself.[24]

And again:

It is then certain that compassion is a natural feeling, which, by moderating the activity of love of self in each individual contributes to the preservation of the whole species. It is this compassion that hurries us without reflection to the relief of those who are in distress: it is this which in a state of nature supplies the place of laws, morals and virtues with the advantage that none are tempted to disobey its gentle voice: it is this which will always prevent a sturdy savage from robbing a weak child or a feeble old man of the sustenance they may have with pain and difficulty acquired, if he sees the possibility of providing for himself by other means.[25]

Rousseau holds that "generosity, clemency or humanity," indeed that benevolence and friendship are "only the effects of compassion, constantly set upon a particular object: for how is it different to wish that another person may not suffer pain and uneasiness and to wish him happy?"[26]

And compassion is not limited to human animals (who as Rousseau sees them are animals still):

I am speaking of compassion . . . that the very brutes themselves sometimes give evident proofs of it. Not to mention the tenderness of mothers to their offspring . . . One animal never passes by the dead body of another of its species without disquiet: some even give their fellows a sort of burial; while the mournful lowering of cattle when they enter the slaughter house show the impressions made on them by the horrible spectacle that meets them.[27]

"Amour de soi même" or regard for oneself (generally translated as "self-love" but perhaps better translated simply as self-regard or caring for oneself) is a natural human impulse (Emile) and the sense of self-preservation ("conservation de soi-même") vies with this primitive sense of compassion. It is the reason why, as a motivator for action, self-preservation will generally take precedence over the sense of pity. "Amour-propre" (also translatable as self-love), on the other hand, is quite another thing: it is a caricature of "amour de soi même," or "amour de soi même" taken to its extreme,[28] a degeneration of the individual which, according to Rousseau, is the result of aberrant social structure.[29]

Some persons seem not to be endowed with such a natural sense: they seem totally to lack pity or compassion for others. As I have mentioned in chapter one, such persons—if they exist and since this sense can, as we have seen, be crushed by external forces the reason for its apparent absence is conjectural—no more speak against the presence of such a sense naturally than does the fact that some persons are blind serve to deny that having sight is normal. Many will ask: where was and is the natural sense of pity, where was and is compassion in the horrors we have witnessed and continue to witness? How could slave keepers blithely keep slaves, how could whole tribes of Indians be decimated or exterminated, how could Nazi society operate, how can one group (as, for example, in Somalia or the former Yugoslavia) slaughter another if a sense of compassion were really a part of human nature? Rousseau, however, neither claimed that such a trait was universal (anymore than is the "trait" of sight or hearing) nor that it was inextinguishable or unopposed by other forces.

To speak about compassion as extinguished or opposed by other forces, we must, I think, differentiate between a feeling of compassion for another's suffering and acting upon such a feeling. First of all, as Rousseau clearly recognized, acting could be prevented by a sense of self-preservation: when acting out of compassion endangered one's existence, one might well feel compassion but might very well fail to act. When repeated, such a state of affairs could easily result in a blunting of feeling. Germans watching Jews being beaten or forced to wash the streets (and no one in Nazi Germany could entirely evade seeing this or something similar) may have been revolted or outraged: but knowing that to act or even to object too loudly would seriously endanger them, most shut their eyes or looked the other way. When one is treated to such a spectacle daily and when one fails to act, a habit is formed: a habit of averting one's eyes and, eventually, of no longer feeling uncomfortable. In a sense, experience (a powerful way of educating people) has served to diminish, if not altogether extinguish, this natural feeling. This is not far different from what many occupations experience: most butchers will tell you that killing animals was initially difficult but, as time went on, became easier until doing so no longer was associated with any negative sensation; medical students inevitably felt embarrassment, which soon vanished, when they first had to examine a patient of the opposite sex.

Nazi society was caught in a bind: on the one hand, it did all it could to extinguish such a sense of compassion, on the other it clearly recognized the social danger of accomplishing such a task. It did all it could to extinguish compassion in at least two ways. First of all it claimed that Slavs, Jews, Poles and, for that matter, all "non-Aryans" were "Untermenschen" (subhumans). Such persons counted less or not at all and when the nation claimed to be fighting for its very life, the interests of Untermenschen counted for far less. Secondly, it taught that certain persons were "enemies of the state" whose very existence threatened German existence. Some, like Jews or Gypsies, were not only inferior beings by virtue of belonging to such a group but were also enemies on a genetic basis: Jews were Jews and Gypsies were Gypsies no matter what they did. They could convert, even offer to serve, even do service; they could be infants, old, sick, or disabled: they were still enemies and had, therefore, to be done away with.

Despite all these attempts it was not possible to entirely extinguish compassion. The "final solution" posed more than merely administrative problems. Administrative problems could be—and largely were—overcome. The final solution posed overwhelming psychological problems for the Nazi state and its members.[30] First of all, it proved impossible to entirely crush a sense of compassion and, secondly, doing so was recognized as having potential social dangers. Even Himmler recognized this difficulty, even the "Einsatzgruppen" (those units of the German SS who followed the German advance into Russia and whose mission was on the spot extermination) were troubled.

In a speech Himmler held to his SS generals on 4 October 1943, in Posen (and quoted by Shirer), he gave expression to this problem:[31]

I also want to talk to you quite frankly on a very grave matter. Among ourselves it should be mentioned quite frankly, and yet we will never speak of it publicly.

"I mean . . . the extermination of the Jewish race . . . Most of you must know what it means when 100 corpses are lying side by side, or 500, or 1,000. To have stuck it out and at the same time—apart from exceptions caused by human weakness—to have remained decent fellows, that is what has made us hard. This is a page of glory in our history which has never been written and is never to be written.

This, for a number of reasons, is a revealing and complicated statement. First of all, it would appear that, perhaps among other things, "human weakness" consisted of revulsion or of failure to set aside one's sense of compassion. Strength, by implication, is the capacity to resist compassion. Secondly, the notion of "remaining a decent fellow" is peculiar for two reasons: it denotes that continuing to act in a socially acceptable manner and continuing to feel compassion in another sphere was recognized as desirable and it suggests that one can in fact "remain decent" at the same time as one brutally murders men, women, and children. And, peculiarly enough, this strange almost schizoid ability is historically documented. If one reads some of the cases documented by, among others, Simon Wiesenthal, one is struck again and again that some of the most brutal murderers after the war led perfectly "normal" social lives. They, it appears, returned to being able to be "decent fellows": albeit, and most astoundingly, decent fellows without any apparent regret for what they had done whatsoever.[32] Thirdly, it suggests that this "page of glory" is known to be shameful rather than glorious: why, otherwise "never speak about it?" It seems that even some of the most vicious officials had a glimmer of compassion or at least a recognition that totally extinguishing such a trait could have disastrous results at home. In the fall of 1941, the commander of the SS and head of the Einsatzgruppen, in the middle sector of Russia, ("Höhere SS- und Polizeiführer Russland Mitte") von dem Bach remarked to Himmler:

> One can see in the eyes of the men of this command how very upset they are! Such men are finished for their entire life. What kind of followers are we breeding here? Either psychiatrically ill persons or brutes![33]

The thousand year Reich lived a mere twelve: not enough, some might say, to permanently create "brutes." Here is not the place to discuss what actually happened or why it did: the failure to come to terms with the evil that had been committed, the shielding of known Nazi criminals (with, incidentally, the collusion and active help of the Vatican and the secret services of the United States) or the attempts to foil meaningful restitution to victims of Naziism. It may be the case that had the thousand year Reich endured a generation or two, education of the young might have resulted in crushing an innate sense of compassion. But at what a price! Deep down it is evident that even the Nazis recognized that to crush such a sense was ultimately socially destructive. Had the thousand year Reich endured a generation or two it might well have destroyed itself. A sense of compassion, I have argued, is evolutionarily a trait which, because it fosters communal solidarity and, therefore, supports communal survival, constitutes an important survival mechanism for the individual as well as for the species.

As we have seen, this sense of compassion which all (normal) humans (and most higher animals) possess can be fostered or extinguished. Fostering and channeling this impulse into socially useful and productive channels is one of education's most important tasks. Rousseau saw this "sense of compassion" or "sense of pity" as a critical feature and its extinction by unjust societies as one of the features which perpetuated such societies. Modern societies, according to Rousseau and what he says would hardly be inapplicable today, have stifled much of this primitive sense of compassion and have, in the process changed one's natural drive for self-preservation into an unbridled, often hedonistic, and frequently irresponsible sense of self-love. In the Nazi state, the sense of compassion (at least towards those not acknowledged to be members of the elite group) was deliberately suppressed so as to serve what were perceived to be communal interests; in starkly Capitalist nations the same is done so as to foster individualism and, thereby, perpetuate the system. In the long run, both will destroy solidarity and, eventually, destory the community itself.

Rousseau clearly claims that this sense of compassion (while innate) is socially conditioned. In highly individualist societies in which personal freedom and individual rights are either the condition for or the highest value of an ethical framework "amour propre" (self-love)—to Rousseau a pathological extension of the normal "conservation de soi même"—is inevitably stressed: a minimal ethic results in a steady attenuation and attrition of compassion until one ends up with similar results as pertained in the Nazi state. Americans of the middle class with poverty all around them who steadily deny the existence of poverty or, a step worse, blame the disadvantaged for their own disadvantaging likewise have learned to sublimate their innate compassion. (See also the section on "rational compassion" and "compassionate rationality" discussed first in chapters 4 and 5).

In the past, following Schopenhauer,[34] I have placed this sense of pity as central to the notion of morality itself: as the "Triebfeder" (or driving force), the trait without which the moral question would remain sterile and ethics would become merely another intellectual game.[35] Many others would deny the central role of pity in morality and would, indeed, argue strongly against it. Plato and Aristotle both considered pity to be an irrational (i.e., not reason bound) sentiment and in the sense of being an emotion necessarily as opposed to reason. The Stoics likewise felt that to act morally was to act dispassionately and without sentiment. Benign persons, motivated by reason alone, would act morally: leaving aside, of course, the question of how benignity without sentiment can come about. Likewise Mandeville, who held self-interest as central to morality, felt that pity was an extremely strong but essentially destructive force. When pity causes one to act (when for example pity prompts one to establish schools for the poor) societal instability is apt to result. In various ways and in different degrees Plato, Spinoza, and Mandeville viewed pity as essentially inimical to dispassionate cool reasoning and, therefore, opposed to making sound ethical decisions.[36] In general, more recent analysis has tended to assign a "morally neutral" position to compassion.[37]

Some have argued (wrongly, I think) that Kant's position towards the sentiment of compassion (or "Mitleid") was, likewise, largely negative. Kant's position towards compassion or Mitleid was, in many ways, positive. Nevertheless, to Kant, Mitleid is "pathological," that is, the product of emotion and not of pure reason. Although, as we shall see, he denies Mitleid a central or even critical place (and, as we shall see, denies that acting merely from pity or any other "inclination" can be meritorious), he does concede its place. In his Metaphysics of Morals he even goes as far as to consider the cultivation of compassion, while not a "perfect" ("unbedingte"), nevertheless an "imperfect" ("bedingte") duty.[38] In his *Doctrine of Virtues* Kant seems to consider this sentiment in a rather positive light.[39]

> Even though it is not in itself a duty to experience "Mitleid" (suffering because of the suffering of another) and so also "Mitfreude" (joy because of the joy of another), it is a duty to participate actively in the fate of another. Hence we have an imperfect duty to cultivate the sympathetic natural (aesthetic)

feeling in us and to use them as as so many means to participating from moral principles and from the feelings appropriate
to these principles.—Thus it is our duty: not to avoid places
where we shall find the poor who lack the most basic essentials, but rather to seek them out; not to shun sick-rooms or
debtor's prisons in order to avoid the painful sympathetic feelings that we cannot guard against. For this is still one of the
impulses which nature has implanted in us so that we may do
what the thought of duty alone would not accomplish.[40]

Kant here seems to be quite clear: one cannot have a duty to
experience a given sentiment and a natural sentiment cannot in and
of itself give moral direction. However, since the sentiment is natural and since it is our obligation to participate actively in the fate of
others (the notion of the "realm of ends" among many others makes
this clear), we have, as shall be mentioned again, an obligation to cultivate such a sentiment. Avoiding active participation with those
who arouse Mitleid is avoiding one's duty and will tend to blunt
our compassion. I would argue (and I think that Kant might agree)
that doing those things which nurture compassion and avoiding
those things which would tend to crush it is our obligation.

If pity is a passion (or a sentiment—at any rate something
innate and not under our control) can it have moral meaning or
force? It can, of course, cause us to act. But can one judge an action
caused by innate impulse or by sentiment to be good or bad? The separation between reason and sentiment (or "the passions" as Hume
calls them) are often seen as in natural and inevitable conflict with
each other or, at any rate, acting motivated by sentiment instead of
motivated by reason cannot be praiseworthy. To some (Hume) the
passions inevitably and properly triumph over reason:

> Reason is and ought only to be the slave of the passions and can
> never pretend to any other office than to serve and obey them.[41]

To Hume, therefore, shaping the sentiments and forming proper
habits was of primary importance. Reason "can never produce any
action or give rise to volition."[42] But sentiments and passions are
generally not universal, are to a large extent at least culturally conditioned, if not indeed determined, and cannot form a possible way of
enabling a dialogue and, therefore, of producing an ethic which is not
entirely empty. Contrary to the faith of the enlightenment in the
ultimate power of reason to produce a better and perhaps a more

moral world, are those who would deny its power (or emphasize its captivity) and those who like the libertarians would reduce it to a formal condition which can yield only a formalist ethic. Reason enables us to see that the only way we can live in peace is by absolutely respecting the freedom of others; reason cannot enable, let alone motivate us, to have other than this minimal and individualistic condition or principle.

But is there really this gulf between reason and sentiment? Are they truly opposed? Again, Rousseau seems to think otherwise:

> Whatever moralists may hold, the human understanding is greatly indebted to the passions, which, it is universally allowed, are also much indebted to the understanding. It is by the activity of the passions that our reason is improved; for we desire knowledge only because we wish to enjoy; and it is impossible to conceive any reason why a person who has neither fears nor desires should give himself the trouble of reasoning. The passions, again, originate in our wants, and their progress depends on that of our knowledge; for we cannot desire or fear anything, except from the idea we have of it, or from the simple impulse of nature.[43]

Certainly inclinations or sentiments or feelings cannot be allowed to dominate moral decision making. The contemporary preoccupation with what is called "care ethics" notwithstanding (a subject peripheral to our present discussion but which will be taken up later), our unguided emotions alone cannot substitute for reason.

This supposed dichotomy between sentiment and reason is, I would argue, an artificial dualistic construct. We cannot have feelings which somehow do not involve or even originate in what we understand by the concept "reason": having feelings about something or some situation implies at least some sort of right or wrong understanding. The concept of compassionate rationality or rational compassion (which I shall begin to develop in chapter 4) may begin to help to get us out of a dichotomy which sees one as "the slave" of the other. Briefly: in this concept compassion (emotion or sentiment) and rationality (reason) are seen as the mutually interactive components of a homeostatic relationship in which one modifies the urgings of the other in pursuit of a common goal. (See the sections on compassionate rationality and rational compassion in chapters 4 and 5).

The use of the word ought (a word which underlies much of our conversation when it comes to ethics) can be used in two distinctly different ways: it can be used in a prescriptive sense (as in "you ought not to steal" or "you ought to be charitable") or the word ought can be used as in a descriptive sense (as in "you ought to like peanut butter or Mozart"). An ought, in the prescriptive sense, cannot intelligibly be used when it comes to inclinations or feelings. Telling someone that they ought to feel a certain way is intelligible only in a predictive sense: since I know that you like Haydn and Beethoven, I can (fairly safely) predict that you ought to like Mozart; but it is possible that you will not and all my telling you that you ought to like Mozart will not convince you (one need but look at Glen Gould's, for me, incomprehensible attitude towards Mozart). This use of the moral and nonmoral ought can, however, become somewhat complicated when it comes to compassion. To say that one has an obligation to be compassionate (which Kant has been and easily could be misinterpreted as saying) is not coherent. However to claim, as I think that Kant does, that one has an obligation ("ought to" in its moral use) to use the natural inclination (or capacity which nature has implanted in us) of Mitleid (compassion) and, incidentally "Mitfreude" (an English word is lacking but it can be translated as deriving pleasure from the pleasure of others), to foster a sentiment of benevolence towards others will hold water. Whereas it is not possible to force oneself to have a given feeling, it is possible (and, therefore ought can properly be used in its moral sense) to try to cultivate and to foster, rather than to supress or to stifle, such a feeling. When Kant speaks of compassion as an obligation (albeit an imperfect one) he seems to (even if not as clearly as he usually does) differentiate the uses of ought here. We cannot prescribe the having of a feeling but we can prescribe using (and fostering) what nature has given us.

> Deriving pleasure from the pleasure of others and compassion (sympathia moralis) are feelings of pleasure or pain derived from the senses (and, therefore, may be called aesthetic) of pleasure or displeasure in the state of joy or sorrow of another (feeling with or participating in another's feelings). Nature has already planted susceptibility to such feelings in man. Using these feelings as a means of promoting active or rational benevolence is a particular, even if still a conditional duty. It is called the duty of humanity (humanitas) since man is here regarded not merely as a rational being but also as an animal equipped with reason. Humanity can be located either in the capacity and will to share in others feelings (humanitas practica) or

merely in the susceptibility, provided by nature itself, to feel joy and sadness in common with others (humanitas aesthetica). The capacity and will is free and is therefore called compassionate (communio sentiendi liberalis): it is based on practical reason. The mere susceptibility is not free (communio sentiendi illiberalis, servilis) and can be be called communicable (like susceptibility to warmth or to contagious disease) or also sympathetic or compassionate since it spreads naturally among men living near each other. Only the first is obligatory.[44]

In trying to assess the role of feeling or inclinations in morality, then, Kant distinguishes between these senses of the word ought. Nevertheless, he leaves us with a problem. There are really several ways of conceiving the spring of our actions: (1) we may act from pure inclination and these inclinations happen to accord with the moral law; (2) we may act purely from a sense of duty; (3) our sense of duty may run counter to our (strongest) inclinations; (4) our inclinations may be reinforced by our sense of duty; or (5) (similarly but not quite the same thing) our sense of duty may be reinforced by our inclinations. Acting from pure inclination where this accords with moral law (but where the fact that it does so is irrelevant to the motive of action) is morally neutral (a utilitarian would certainly argue otherwise). Acting would (to different degrees) be meritorious if duty played a significant role in the motivating force ("ground") of our action; blameworthy, if it contravened duty. The larger the role of duty as a driving force, the more merit. Inclinations, whether they incline us towards or away from an action, inevitably play a role in what we do; only the "supreme being," (in whom duty and inclination invariably coincide) can be conceived as acting only because of duty (albeit, as Kant has pointed out, speaking of inclinations or duty in the Supreme Being is really not possible). Kant pretty clearly seems to say that the greatest merit accrues to the person whose obedience to duty requires a strong struggle with his/her inclinations.

What is essential in the moral worth of actions is that the moral law should directly determine the will. If the determination of the will occurs in accordance with the moral law but only by means of a feeling of any kind whatsoever, which must be presupposed in order that the law may become a determining ground of the will, and if the action thus occurs not for the sake of the law, it has legality but not morality. Now, if by a

motivating force (elater animi) ["Triebfeder"—Kant] we understand a subjective determining ground of will whose reason
does not by its nature necessarily conform to the objective law,
it follows, first, that absolutely no motivating force can be
attributed to the divine will; and, second, that the [moral] motivating force of the human will (and of that of every created
rational being) can never be anything other than the moral law;
and, third, that the objective determining ground must at the
same time be the exclusive and subjectively sufficient determining ground of action if the latter is to fulfill not merely the
letter of the law but also the spirit.*

> *Of every action which conforms to the law but does not
> occur for the sake of the law, one may say that it is
> morally good in letter but not in spirit (in intention).[45]

Inclinations are motivated by feelings: we feel inclined to do
something even when we know that doing so may not be in our best
interest. Witness the persons who smoke, eat excess salt, or have
unprotected sex with strangers! Inclinations, therefore, cannot be
allowed to serve as our ethical guide. But that hardly solves the problem. Kant has been understood to think inclinations at the very least
suspect, if not indeed probably negative.

> Natural inclinations, considered in themselves, are good, that
> is, not a matter of reproach, and it is not only futile to want to
> extirpate them but to do so would also be harmful and blame-
> worthy. Rather, let them be tamed and instead of clashing with
> one another they can be brought into harmony in a wholeness
> which is called happiness. Now the reason which accomplishes
> this is termed prudence. But only what is opposed to the moral
> law is evil in itself, absolutely reprehensible, and must be com-
> pletely eradicated; and only a reason which teaches this truth,
> and more especially one which puts it into actual practice,
> alone deserves the name of wisdom. The vice corresponding
> to this may indeed be termed folly, but again only when reason
> feels itself strong enough not merely to hate vice as something
> to be feared, and to arm itself against, but to scorn vice with all
> its temptations.[46]

Kant, then—as he does when it comes to the question of
Mitleid—does not actually consider inclinations as bad. While he con-

siders acting merely motivated by inclinations morally neutral, he does not deny a legitimate place to inclinations and seems to consider nurturing proper inclinations (those which incline us to do our duty) as a moral obligation. Nevertheless, Kant is quite clear when he considers meritorous acting to be acting motivated by duty; acting merely according to inclination may be morally neutral if acting in this manner does not contravene the moral law; acting according to inclination when doing so contravenes the moral law is blameworthy; acting motivated by moral law when one's inclinations would suggest otherwise (in other words, suppressing "evil" inclinations) according to Kant would be the most meritorious (or praiseworthy) way of acting.

This interpretation still leaves some of us unsatisfied. Would one really say that a person who enjoyed helping his/her fellows was acting morally neutrally but that one who—against every desire and inclination—did so was meritorious? If that were so then the meritorious person who acted in the same way as the one acting morally neutrally would be meritorious precisely because of his or her evil inclinations. Could one argue that a Mother Theresa or an Albert Schweitzer were less meritorious than one who grudgingly and against every inclination contributed to a charity? So far Kant is less than convincing on this point.

One would have, I think, to analyze this problem more closely. It is true enough that persons who exert their energy to fight evil inclinations so as to act in accord with duty are meritorious and that, undoubtedly, they exert more energy (have to overcome more barriers) than do those whose inclinations correspond to what they conceive to be their duty. But it is likewise true that persons who consistently school themselves so as to educate their inclinations and who ultimately find that their inclinations and duties were no longer in strong opposition are no less meritorious. When we listen to our primitive sense of pity and allow it to raise the moral question rather than succumbing to self-love and taking "the easy road out," we are performing a moral act which forms the foundation of the acts which are to follow.

Kant does (partially at least) get out of the dilemma when he argues that feelings themselves can be caused by our moral reasoning.

> But he has reason for a yet higher purpose, namely, to consider also what is in itself good and evil, which pure and sensuously disinterested reason alone can judge, and furthermore to distinguish this estimation from a sensuous estimation and to make the former the supreme condition of good and evil.[49]

Therefore, in Kant's analysis, there must still be a feeling side to practice. So that we will care about acting as we should, we need to feel respect for the demands of morality.[48] And yet, ultimately, this feeling of respect must rely on our prior reason. To Kant there are two kinds of feeling: when we are interested in the consequences of our action our interests are "mediate;" when our actions are morally meritorious, our interest are "immediate," that is, they are regardless of the consequences brought about.[49]

> In order to will that which reason alone prescribes to the sensuously affected rational being as that which he ought to will, certainly there is required a power of reason to instill a feeling of pleasure or satisfaction in the fulfillment of duty, and hence there must be a causality of reason to determine the sensibility in accordance with its own principles. But it is wholly impossible to discern, i.e., to make a priori conceivable, how a mere thought containing nothing sensuous is to produce a sensation of pleasure or displeasure.[50]

But Kant, a little later in the same paragraph, goes on to show us that this feeling of satisfaction in fulfilling our duty is a very valid feeling indeed:

> Only this much is certain that it (the feeling of satisfaction) is valid for us not because it interests us (for that is heteronomy and dependence of practical reason on sensibility, i.e., on basic feeling, and thus it could never be morally legislative), but that it interests us because it is valid for us as men, inasmuch as it has arisen from our will as intelligence and hence from our genuine self . . .[51]

Kant seems to argue that this feeling is valid not because it is a feeling but because it is ultimately a product of our intellectual being. To Kant the feeling is valid and beneficial (in promoting proper behaviour) because it is a feeling which is, ultimately, the product of our power of reason.

Kant, I think, might argue that we have an obligation to consider our inclinations in the light of our duty and that our inclination to follow such a duty can be educated by the habit of examining our grounds of action in that fashion. Beyond this he seems to say, though not as clearly as one would like, that a sense of satisfaction which is felt when one does one's duty will provide an additional stimulus to act properly and that this feeling is an appopriate (even if not a necessary) component of moral education. At any rate, his extensive interest in ethical questions seems to have in part at least been fortified by his belief that by examining moral issues rationally man can learn not only to act more morally but also that rationality can serve to discipline man's inclinations.

To be blamed or praised for something, to be praiseworthy or blameworthy, we must have had choices and the ability to choose. If one is driving a car whose brakes suddenly and unexpectedly fail one can be legally held liable (one was, after all, causally responsible for what happened) but one cannot, provided one did all one could to maintain one's brakes and drive with care, be held to blame in a morally meaningful sense. It is only to the extent that we "freely choose" or "freely choose not to" that moral blame can be assessed. If our inclinations prompt us to do something we know to be wrong or if they prompt us to refrain from doing something we know to be morally compelling we could, provided we had the freedom to choose, be held to blame.

But things are not quite that simple. Freedom to choose implies a lack of coercion: external coercion exercised by someone or something as well as internal coercion which can be produced by fear as well as by strong desire. External coercion generally will stimulate internal coercion as when the fear of being shot "forces" us to do something we would not otherwise be inclined to do. And yet external coercion is far more often accepted as not only an explanation but as a justification of an act we would concede to be wrong than would be internal coercion. Are we really ever entirely "free" to act?

Kant would claim that a person who resists inclinations so as to act in accordance with duty is far more praiseworthy than one whose inclinations support such an action. In simple language, this would make the person who habitually and with a sense of pleasure acts dutifully (or in a fashion we would regard as good and right) less admirable than others whose impulses would drive them to act reprehensibly. Some persons get a great deal of personal satisfaction in helping the poor or in opposing what they deem to be injustice. Their inclinations reinforces their sense of duty. They act, in part at least, because they want to not because with clenched teeth they are opposing an inclination to do otherwise. It seems somewhat strange that such persons should be deemed less praiseworthy. Such persons have formed a habit that most of of us would count as a habit of virtue.

Those who follow their inclination to neglect their duty clearly can, to the extent that they are free to act, be held blameworthy. Trying to go beyond this seems to be fruitless. Perhaps the best that we can say is that both persons whose inclinations prompt them to follow their duty and do good and those who oppose their inclinations in order to follow their duty are meritorious albeit they are, perhaps, meritorious in different ways. Those who have freely chosen to school their inclinations, foster their sensitivities and hone their habits of acting dutifully deserve at least as much merit as those whose evil impulses are simply resisted one at a time.

Persons whose inclinations generally prompt them to follow their duty and who see in doing their duty more than merely an obligation are what, in popular parlance, we would generally consider to be "good persons": who can say how much of such inclinations have been formed by their social setting and how much is, whatever that means, "inborn?" Persons who habitually and successfully resist inclinations to act against their duty may ordinarily have the same effect. One can, however, easily imagine that such persons when confronted with circumstances in which they must act without great forethought or under great pressure may more easily forsake their obligation and follow their inclination. Perhaps this can be analogized to the problem people have driving in the United Kingdom (an apt analogy which was suggested to me in conversation with my wife): under ordinary circumstances persons will drive on the left and oppose their inclination to drive on the right. When they suddenly confront an unanticipated danger, however, they are likely to revert to their previous "appropriate" habits with disastrous consequences because these are "right sided" driving reflexes in a now "left sided" world.

This is only to demonstrate that inclinations are in great part, at least, conditioned by the social structure in which they develop. Compassion, as Rousseau has pointed out, is a "natural trait" one common to all higher creatures but one which like many other traits can be reinforced or attenuated by social forces. To the extent that we can be said to freely choose to develop our sense of compassion and school our inclinations we can be said to be praiseworthy; to the extent that we freely choose to oppose society's pressure to ignore the misery which surrounds us, we can be said to be blameworthy. Many of the German citizens under the Nazis were not as much guilty because they participated in the evident evils of a vile regime but because they chose (at what must have been considerable effort) to close their eyes to its evil; many of us who live in crassly

Capitalist societies today and who choose to live in middle-class comfort or in opulent luxury and avoid confrontation with the misery which surrounds us, do the very same thing: we allow our inclinations and our sense of compassion to become blunted. Both the opportunists in the Nazi era and those in "wealthy" societies today use much the same "excuses" and the same language. Both claim, on the one hand, that they do not or did not know about the evil in their society while, on the other hand, affirming that they were or are powerless to do anything about it: a curious thing, since any claim of ignorance must render the claim of impotence incoherent.

Resisting societal pressures is in many ways very similar to resisting inclination. Coercion, be it external or internal coercion, operates by forming our inclinations. Societal pressures likewise operate in part at least by modulating and forming our inclinations. In a later section of this chapter, I shall have reason to refer to Rousseau's "volenté general" (general will), to its formation and to its role in our thesis. Although Rousseau does not mention it, a part of such a general will may well be the formation of what one might call general inclination: the way in which a given collective fosters and shapes individual inclination. German society, already before the onset of Hitlerism, fostered habits of extreme nationalism and unthinking obedience to the law. Such habits, sometimes in part attributed to Kant's influence, in many ways run counter to Kant's basic message: in order to act morally we must be obedient to a law we have set for ourselves not to a law extrinsically (heteronomously) applied.

Inclination to do something is eventually expressed by one's intention. The intention to follow one's duty, for example, may include resisting an initial inclination: an initial inclination which may be analogized to the kind of reflex action one would take in a near accident when one has been conditioned to drive on the right side of the road. Here we have the typical case of two inclinations vying with each other and resulting, eventually, in an intention. When one has the time to reflect on the situation one may do "the right thing": whether that is to take a correct evasive action or to act consonant with one's duty in a different set of circumstances.

John Dewey has put this very well:

> A generalized sense of right is a support in time of temptation; it gives a reinforcing impetus in carrying us over a hard place in conduct. A mother is habitually attentive to the claims of her offspring. Nevertheless, cases arise when it is much easier for

her to put her own comfort first. A generalized sense of right and obligation is a great protection; it makes the general habit consciously available. But such a general sense as this grows out of occasion when the mother was faithful because she was actuated by direct affection for the child and direct interest in his welfare. A sense of duty is a weak staff when it is not the outcome of habit formed in wholehearted recognition of the value of the ties involved in concrete cases.[52]

Inclinations are shaped by the particulars of a given society as much as they are by the experiences and constitution of a particular individual. Societies produce general inclinations and these in turn produce general intentions and, eventually, a general will which is a community's expression of aim and direction. Such a process is not a one way street: personal inclinations, shaped by the society in which they evolved, eventually become part of a society's general inclinations; these in turn help form the general will and the nature of the general will in turn shapes or modifies the way in which personal and general inclinations express themselves in a general will. Basic inclinations, I shall argue, rest on our common realization of what I am calling our "existential a prioris."

When societies are "evil"—say Nazi, Bolshevik, or crassly Capitalist states—the particular will may be shaped in the image of such a society: many individuals may allow their primitive sense of pity or their compassion with others to atrophy. Such individuals may act from a sense of opportunism (in which case, while they are aware that their support of what they know to be basically evil rests on the expectation of personal gain, they, to further their own basically selfish ends, train themselves to avert their face) or they may indeed become "true believers" who have suppressed their sense of pity sufficiently so that it no longer intrudes. In such societies all that can be done to suppress a sense of man's common heritage and common framework of needs and ways of thinking is done. The amazing thing is that despite societal pressures and despite everyone's inclination to ultimately act to their own benefit, a large number of people will continue to resist what they perceive to be evil. Experience tells us that their perception of evil while it may appeal to a logical acceptance of universalizability is, in general and for the most part, driven by their unsuppressed sense of compassion and their visceral realization of those things which unite (rather than those which divide) all sentient beings: emotion generally comes first to be later reinforced, checked, and controlled by reason.

The problem remains: who decides what actions are "good," who says what course of action is "right." To Kant, the answer is obvious: the right course of action is that which accords with our duty, a duty which is logically derivable, which all rational beings would be forced to recognize and which, therefore, is universalizable. Most of us, as a formal condition, would have to agree with this. But while this may help and indeed may be most important as a "starter," it is, in a practical sense, not enough.

Something called the "care ethic" has been suggested as a corrective to a rule based type of ethic. It represents the antipode to Kant.[53] Kantian ethics juxtaposes inclinations against duty or obligation and insists that, to act morally, duty must win out. Kant regards inclinations with extreme suspicion. To act morally we must follow rules which accord to an overarching principle and to be praiseworthy we must resist our inclinations. Care ethics forwards the opposite claim: to act morally we must "care" and, ultimately follow our inclinations. Care ethics has been suggested as a step forward: away from a coldly analytical attempt to examine and resolve ethical problems and one that is best suited to being applied to concrete ethical problems.[54] "Care based" has been opposed to "justice based" reasoning.[55] According to the advocates of the care ethic justice based reasoning reasons along rule based lines and finds resolution for problems by an appeal to rules which in turn are based on some ethical theory. It is "cold," analytic and, somehow, not quite human. Care based reasoning evades this sterility: it looks at each situation with concern and caring and finds resolution by examining its own inclinations and instincts. Therefore, it supposedly lends itself far better to dealing with what are, after all, uniquely human, uniquely existential, and uniquely situational and contextual problems. Care-based ethics is doing what one's innermost instincts counsel one to do in a situation in which one is deeply involved instead of in a situation from which one stays remote: it is precisely following one's inclinations instead of following rules.

Care ethics takes a path quite opposite to Kantian ethics: do away with a formal framework and do what your inclination commands. The background assumption (a patently false one, I think) is that one's "natural" inclination will be to do "the right and good thing." Whereas Kantian ethics looks on human inclinations with a rather jaundiced eye, care ethics sees inclinations with rose coloured glasses. Since following one's gut feelings (the way "caring" plays itself out) rather than attending to (mere) formal principles takes place in a very distinct society which has already conditioned the way our gut will feel (take the "gut feelings" of a youthful member of a Nazi youth organization, that of a Christian fundamentalist, and that of a member of a Buddhist or Quaker group) it is a quite different thing.

One of the many problems with the care based ethic is that it never states what it is really supposed to be: is it a theory, a method, a way of thinking or feeling or is it none of these? Writings in the field fail to make clear or convincing distinctions and claim all of these (and, indeed, suggest more) at various times. It cannot be the case that an ethic based on caring alone is a theory unless that theory, pure and simple, were to be "act as your feelings (or instincts or 'guts') tell you"; but that is rather a direction of how to apply something than it is a theory. Is it a method then? But if a method, a method for what? For applying itself? It is difficult to see how a concept like caring can be more than a concept: an important concept, one which can make an ethic alive and breathing but a concept which in itself is neither a theory nor a method. At best, and not insignificantly, it would seem that what has been sketched is a tool to implement the making of choices and the carrying out of actions in existential human and in often very difficult situations. Searching for a resolution to an ethical quandary or problem without much caring about it or applying such a solution carelessly is surely not what we would want to see done: that makes caring an awfully important part of seeking or applying a good solution to a troubling problem but that does not make caring central to the resolution or to its application.

When we think about ethical problems we can approach them from a purely analytical point of view, a little like playing a dispassionate and purely cerebral game of chess. In such a game we do not care about the interests of the game but care about our interest in the game. When it comes to dealing with the real problems which real people face in a real world that may be helpful (may at times even be essential) but it is surely far from enough when it comes to dealing with real problems in their context. Caring should substitute a warm, feeling and human process for such a cold and analytic one and should, therefore, lend itself much better to dealing with concrete problems in real situations. But what is caring? Dictionary definitions include the notions of being engaged in something, being concerned even of sorrow as in "bent with care." It denotes an activity which means much to the one engaged in it: to be careless is simply not to be attentive or, in the vernacular, not to "give a damn." And caring is, in fact, "giving a damn."

On the other hand, when we care terribly much about the real problems real people have in a real world, when we are so concerned about them that we fail to carefully analyze, carefully draw distinctions and carefully search for solutions, we reduce such problems and the search for their solution to gut feelings, emotion, and sentimentality. This may, in fact, render us quite impotent to help: we may care so much that our reasoning is distorted and our action paralyzed. This is exactly why health-professionals or attorneys, while being very much concerned about their patient's or client's good, must keep a distance and in some sense act dispassionately. The agony of decision making may, as I have in the past claimed, very well be the measure of ethical involvement but in and of itself the agony cannot solve a problem, provide a solution or even act as a guide: it merely counsels us to be involved as humans, to think and act carefully and not merely to be involved as computers in the decisions we make.

Care ethics is moot about what caring should bring about or how to measure one caring against another: for people may, it is true, care quite differently about the same thing. Opposite to libertarianism (or at least Engelhardt's version of libertarianism) the care ethic in relying on caring and in assuming that persons care in very similar ways about issues, assumes not that we are moral strangers but rather that we are indeed "moral friends" sharing a very similar framework of interests and values. In assuming such a very similar framework, instead of in relying upon a framework constituted by basic interests but allowing much room for cultural diversity, a universally acceptable definition of what constitutes a good solution is assumed. Such a definition does not exist even within a culturally homogenous society let alone within a pluralist world.

Unless there is a prior framework of what does and what does not count as a good solution, caring itself cannot be a measure of the good. When caring becomes a measure of a good action, it can open the gates (and can open them very widely indeed) to some of the worst mischief mankind can conceive. Jesus, Ghandi, and King cared very much about the equality of humans, Schweitzer cared very much about all manners of life, Hitler cared very much about the sanctity and purity of German blood, and members of the KKK care very deeply indeed about white superiority. Physicians who override their patient's wishes care very much about doing as they feel "best": they have presumed to define and judge their patient's ultimate good because they truly care not because they really do not. And yet, we would hardly consider such caring to be an ethically proper thing to do. In many respects, the care ethic applied without a prior framework, opens the door wide to all manners of mischief including the crass paternalism of physician or nurse to patients and relatives. At least the technical paternalism practiced by physicians who override a competent patient's wishes so as to carry out treatment they consider necessary is predicated on empirically demonstrated and verifiable "facts," on the tacit assumption that "look, I know medicine and know the literature and, therefore, know that 'x' will work better than 'y'." And that is problematic enough. But the moral maternalism which would trump one caring by another is based on nothing but private emotion and personal sentiment.

The care ethic is basically antiintellectual. Since care ethics rejects any reasoning not based on emotion and emotionality ("I feel this way and I feel strongly, therefore what I do is right") it fails and indeed rejects all intellectual tests. In its antagonism to intellectual rigor as well as to rationally conceived and intelligently applied rules, in its insistence that when we "reason" we use "care-based reasoning" (i.e., reasoning based on the way we feel) it is antithetical to any intellectualization or dispassionate examination of problems. Now, I will be the first to agree that problems can be overintellectualized, that dispassion can easily be carried to the point of not caring (not giving a damn) about a person in an actual situation, and that in taking them out of their context and stripping problems of their individual nuances risks misreading and ultimately losing the problem itself. And I certainly am troubled by the assumption that at the very best acting when inclination and duty coincide is morally neutral. I will be the first to cry out against this sort of approach to the solving of real problems. But that does not mean that one has to flee from the one into the other danger: de-intellectualizing problems and reducing them to individual feeling and caring may be the far more dangerous of two most unpalatable extremes. At least intellectualization allows some weighing and judging before solutions are "applied": reducing problems to the emotions they engender and reducing praiseworthiness for moral excellence to the depth of people's feelings will, I think, open a Pandora's box of horrors.

What has been termed theoretical ethics, what has been called "justice-based reasoning" and what has been styled care-based reasoning when properly linked can form a useful model for dealing with ethical problems. Theoretical ethics develops theories of the good life, of what it is that constitutes an ethically proper framework and seeks to give convincing reasons for its recommendations. Examples of this are legion and the search even though hardly the solutions are common from Plato and Aristotle, through Bentham, Mill, Kant, Moore, Dewey, McIntyre, and Nozick: to name just a very few among hundreds. Indeed, there are few philosophers who have not at least had a few things to say about basic theories of morality. Our principles and rules are derived from such considerations. What has been called justice-based reasoning derives its rules of justice from some moral theory or way of looking at things. These rules, however, are not simply "derived" in a mathematical or linear sense: it is a to and fro adjustment in which rules and theory inform and correct each other. Analyzing an individual problem means laying it out in detail, drawing relevant distinctions, and examining various options in light of these considerations, in light of our rules and in light of the ethical theory to which they conform. Often this is a quite unconscious process and often such theory and principles are not consciously invoked until ideas clash and conflict occurs. Once possible options have been evolved and examined, the individual case (which has always explicitly or tacitly been part of the process) moves into center stage. Attempting to use the options in a fashion which is unmindful of context or individual peculiarity is applying it uncaringly and it is here that care-based reasoning finds its usefulness. Care, it is hoped, has been exerted right along: we have, one hopes, cared about what we are doing and we have undoubtedly hardly been free from examining our gut feelings about the case. *BUT*, and this is the major but, we have not leapt from feeling to adjudication, have used our feelings perhaps as a starting point and to help guide us and modulate but not to control our thinking. Applying what we have learned and fitting it to the individual case again is not a linearly derived activity and comes to us neither from looking to the options we have found nor from the feeling in our guts as to what we should do. Individualization in turn relates to justice based reasoning and theory in a critically interdependent fashion. As we deal with the individual case, we may call the options derived by justice-based reasoning and modulated by the way we feel about the case into doubt: we may correct, as it were, our justice-based reasoning just as our justice-based reasoning may correct our gut feelings. Somehow, in the real world with real problems justice as well as caring (both, as Nelson has pointed out, virtues but quite different ones[56]) are necessary elements in almost all ethical decisions: it is not that they are juxtaposed or somehow antagonistic but rather that they have to be meshed and jointly brought to bear on the problem at hand. This, since they are quite different virtues is not altogether impossible:

after all, virtues can as well be seen as reinforcing and not as competing with one another.

The relationship, it seems to me, is a homeostatic balance between these various forces all of which properly come into play not only in dealing with particular problems but likewise in thinking about "theory" and "justice" or care-based reasoning. Even the most abstract reasoning is informed by experience with or at least knowledge of concrete problems. To say that theory, justice, and caring are related in a linear fashion is to oversimplify a complicated and necessarily involved process. They are inevitably intertwined, interrelated, and mutually reinforcing and corrective. In dealing with real problems, in real situations or, for that matter, in speculating purely on ethical theory one cannot, in truth, say where one begins and the other ends. In chapters 4 and 5 I shall be suggesting that what I shall call compassionate rationality as well as (and not quite the same thing) what I shall call rational compassion can help mediate between both of these necessary components of a viable and humane ethics. Moreover, once a "solution" has been found or a rule or theory corrected, it is not conceived as a fixed solution, rule or theory valid in all such future cases but as a step in our future learning and growth. Having made an indeterminate situation more determinate (or perhaps merely made a quite indeterminate situation somewhat less indeterminate), we do not accept it as "fixed" or "certain" but rather as a new starting point for our quest.

Even many of those (myself included) who find an intellectual framework for ethical action to be essential, will have difficulty in accepting a "pure" Kantian (or a pure anything else, for that matter!) approach. We may accept Kant's very clear belief that morality cannot be (solely) drawn from experience (that an ought cannot be determined from an "is"); but we cannot simply relegate experience, inclination, and feeling to the sideline. Denying the role of experience (or the passions, emotion, or inclination) its role in forming judgment or denying the role of rationality to control and judge the probity of our passions but relying solely on pure rationality is unlikely to result in an ethic men can live with.

Dewey, likewise, would affirm the basic connectedness and indeed mutually supportive structure of each:

> . . . give us the key to the old controversy as to the respective place of desire and reason in conduct. It is notorious that some moralists have deplored the influence of desire; they have found the heart of the strife between good and evil in the conflict of

desire with reason, in which the former has force on its side and the latter authority. But reasonableness is in fact a quality of an effective relationship among desires rather than a thing opposed to desire. It signifies the order, perspective, proportion which is achieved, during deliberation, out of a diversity of earlier incompatible preferences.[57]

Asking what is ethically right (or proper) for Dewey was a form of inquiry not basically different from all other inquiry. Its methodology was similar to a hypothesis-forming scientific method.[58] Its answers were tentative, not absolute. Inquiry resulted in making indeterminate situations more determinate (or, some of us might say, making indeterminate situations somewhat less indeterminate) and the new form of determinativeness served as a springboard for further inquiry and, hopefully, better solutions.

This supposed tension between emotion (sentiment, desire, passion) and reason (rationality) is critical for what is to follow. It underlies, among other things, the way we look at justification: is justification a purely deductive exercise or is there more to logic than pure reason? The antipode of reason is not emotion, desire, or passion: the antipode of reason is reflex activity or irrationality and perhaps antiintellectualism (which itself relies on an exercise of—albeit shallow—reason and is made possible by the very thing it denies). Emotion or sentiment is what causes us to start to think; thinking is what refines and conditions our sentiments. The two are inevitably and organically related and mutually corrective. Both serve and exemplify homeostasis.

Both Rousseau and Darwin see a sense of compassion as innate to all higher animals. Even more emphatically than Rousseau, however, Darwin claimed (based on empirical observation) that altruism originating in compassion is not something unique to human animals:

> The following proposition seems to me in a high degree probable—namely, that any animal whatever, endowed with well-marked social instincts, would inevitably acquire a moral sense or conscience, as soon as its intellectual powers had become well developed, or nearly as well developed as in man. For, firstly, the social instincts lead an animal to take pleasure in the society of its fellows, to feel a certain amount of sympathy with them, and to perform services for them . . . Secondly, as soon as the mental faculties had become highly developed,

images of all past actions and motives would be incessantly passing through the brain of each individual; and that feeling of dissatisfaction which invariably results . . . from an unsatisfied instinct would arise as often as it was perceived that the enduring and always present social instinct had yielded to some other instinct. . . . Thirdly, after the power of language has been acquired and the wishes of the members of the same community could be distinctly expressed, the common opinion how each member ought to act . . . would become to a large extent the guide to action. . . . Lastly, habit in the individual would ultimately play a important part in guiding the conduct of each member; for the social instincts and impulses, like all other instincts, would be greatly strengthened by habit.[59]

Darwin sees the social instinct as prior to the possibility of developing moral qualities and moral qualities as inevitably developing when intellectual capacity manifested itself: admixing intellect with social instinct, in other words, produced a sense of ethics. To Darwin the naturalist, compassion as well as the social and moral qualities of man had survival value. To survive and to compete effectively, collectives require solidarity. Solidarity can only come about or comes about best when all individuals within a collective realize that others are concerned about them and will come to their aid—knowing only that others will not attack me, a distinctively different matter, helps to make me fear my neighbor a bit less but does not do much to foster a feeling of solidarity. Social instinct, intellect, and a moral sense are ultimately tools of survival.

To Darwin social instinct is prior to developing moral qualities. When animals with a social instinct developed intellectual powers a moral sense inevitably developed.[60] As a naturalist, able to make empirical observation and willing to draw conclusions from them, Darwin was quite ready to recognize that social instincts, intellect, and moral sense were—albeit perhaps most highly developed in human animals—not absent in nonhuman animals. As a naturalist he was able to observe clear instances of all of these and to see them moving from instinctive behavior beyond individual volition to behavior clearly selective and voluntary. Bees may have a social structure, but their intellect still does not permit variations in behavior which allow us to conclude that they "think" as individuals and not as a collective. Packs of dogs are quite a different matter. Higher animals are able to have friends, to form individual relationships and, with these, to develop a sense of obligation unique to a particular relationship.

In animals which appear to be largely motivated by instinct, solidarity can be considered to be an instinctive thing. Bees or ants seem to work together and to show a large "sense" of community without any true sense of themselves as individual beings with individual interests and individual "desires." They are unlikely to "compete" with one another and appear to "work together" in "unselfish" harmony. As one ascends in the evolutionary scale, the realization of oneself as an individual with individual interests and desires which may conflict with other members of the species becomes evident. Solidarity, which is necessary for group survival and ultimately for the survival of a given species, more and more depends upon individual and individually "chosen" behavior. A group of prairie dogs, each out only to safeguard his/her personal interests, would not long survive. As individuality emerges, solidarity is promoted by the development of this "primitive sense of compassion" which now forces the animal to see responding to the needs of another as in its own "interest." When individuals within a group not only not fear each other but know that they can "count on each other" for help, solidarity is strengthened and individual as well as group (and eventually species) survival is made more probable.

What has been called "social Darwinism" claims that society would be strengthened by getting rid of its weak or, at the very least, by not "artificially" supporting the poor or other weaker members so that their weakness can be perpetuated. Darwin claims nothing of the sort and to attribute this claim to Darwin is not only an unwarranted extension of his notion of "survival of the fittest" but in many ways directly the opposite of what Darwin claims. The claim that supporting the poor or the weak in society will ultimately weaken society is a claim made by those who have either crudely misinterpreted what Darwin has written or have confined their attention to the purely "physical" attributes of natural selection. (Darwin, incidentally, would along with many of us have difficulties in divorcing what is physical from what is "mental": mental processes—whether they lead to socialization or to anxiety neuroses—cannot be reduced to their physical substrate but are, in fact, unthinkable without it.) There are several interesting assumptions in the claim that society weakens itself and becomes less able to survive by supporting those less fortunate than others. Among these assumptions, three deserve mention: the assumption that societal survival depends above all on the sturdiness instead of also on the social connectedness of its individual members; the assumption that things which are counted as "weakness" (poverty, illiteracy, inability to finish school, or even criminality) are genetically transmittable; the assumption that having compassion for those less well off or handicapped is a sign of weakness or "loss of national fiber."

The assumption that societal survival depends above all on the sturdiness instead of also on the social connectedness of its individual members is not something Darwin would subscribe to. He argues that those factors promoting the cohesiveness of the group also promote its ability to survive. A group which feels connected to its members and individuals which see their goals as attainable best or even only in the context of a community will have far greater solidarity than one in which every individual member is out merely for his/her individual good. Seeing oneself as an individual with definable interests and goals as well as a member of a society whose very presence enables these goals can be viewed as a homeostatic, healthy and viable system. What is generally termed social Darwinism in not supporting those in need teaches the lesson that individuals cannot rely on the group: fair weather friends who know that they are fair weather friends cannot feel very close to one another.

The assumption that things which are counted as weakness (poverty, illiteracy, inability to finish school, or even criminality) are genetically transmittable is clearly wrong. (See also the discussion of this topic in chapter 5). Although there are family lines (especially in the United States with its still predominant ghettoization) in which poverty, unemployment, and even criminality are traditional, experience has demonstrated over and over again that it is the social setting and not the biological substrate which produces such situations: people are not born as poor or as criminal, albeit that they may be born into crime or into poverty. The assumption that such "weaknesses" are in some sense inherited can lead to a very handy evasion of responsibility: being "genetic" or "inherited" there is nothing we can and, therefore, nothing we must do. Such a belief carried into action and explicitly or tacitly conveyed to those who are or may be affected gnaws at and ultimately destroys solidarity.

There is, of course, another set of assumptions which underpin the assumption that such characteristics are transmittable. It is the assumption that such traits are, in and of themselves, weakness. While few would argue that crime or being criminally inclined is a weakness (or at least that it is a societally destructive force) such an argument can hardly be made for poverty. It is only a very material sort of valuing which equates poverty and societal weakness: did the presence of the likes of Mozart, Schubert or many other artists and thinkers who lived in poverty "weaken" society?

The assumption that having compassion for those less well off or handicapped is a sign of weakness or loss of national fiber, as well as the argument that inborn or developed illness weakens society, cannot hold water. Many of our physically ill (Stephen Hawkins, for example) and even of our mentally disturbed (Dostoevsky or van Gogh) have contributed to and enriched society. And once again: knowing that society will feel obligated to extend a helping hand should misfortune strike, makes individuals eager to be members and interested in the well-being of their society. There was no society more ready to actively practice so-called social Darwinism and foster what it conceived to be "societal strength" than the Nazi state.[61] And yet when the euthanasia program (a program to kill—not at all gently, by the way—"misfits": i.e, the mentally deficient, the insane, cripples or the hopelessly ill) became known to the public it had to be stopped. Stopped not as much because morality was affronted as because solidarity (and, therefore, the survival of the state itself) was threatened.

Not that having the poor, the cripples, the criminal, or whatever it is that society would define as a "misfit" necessarily strengthens society. There is no question that hordes of poor, hungry, or homeless or that having a large percentage of physically handicapped not to speak of criminals weakens societal structure. But such weakening does not speak against equitable programs for these unfortunates: on the contrary, it underlines the necessity for such programs. Throwing such persons overboard (as surely as "euthanizing" them!) conveys the message that those who fall on hard luck will be abandoned. As the Nazi state found out: such knowledge, rather than strengthening society, threatens its very existence.

When societies form (however they are seen to form) structures have to be established and laws proclaimed. Sooner or later all visions of social contract wind up with a "sovereign." In a Hobbesian view, such a sovereign is necessary to enforce the original contract and to him all powers are given by those united in such a contract. This, as we have seen, is a direct route to dictatorship and tyranny. To Rousseau, the sovereign is quite something else. The sovereign is not a person or institution but is the name Rousseau gives to the body politic when active.[62] In making a social compact:

> Each of us puts his person and all his power in common under the supreme direction of the general will, and, in our corporate capacity, we receive each member as an indivisible part of the whole.[63]

Such a subjugation of individual interests and motives, needs to be justified:

> In fact, each individual, as a man, may have a particular will contrary or dissimilar to the general will which he has as a citizen. His particular interest may speak to him quite differently from the common interest: his absolute and naturally independent existence may make him look upon what he owes to the common cause as a gratuitous contribution, the loss of which will do less harm to others than the payment of it is burdensome to himself; and regarding the corporate person which constitutes the State as a persona ficta, because not a man, he may wish to enjoy the rights of citizenship without being ready to fulfill the duties of a subject. The continuance of such an injustice could not but prove the undoing of the body politic.

> In order then that the social compact may not be an empty formula, it tacitly includes the undertaking, which alone can give force to the rest, that whoever refuses to obey the general will shall be compelled to do so by the whole body. This means nothing less than that he will be forced to be free; for this is the condition which, by giving each citizen to his country, secures him against all personal dependence. In this lies the key to the working of the political machine; this alone legitimizes civil undertakings, which, without it, would be absurd, tyrannical and liable to the most frightful abuses.[64]

The act of association, in other words, creates a corporate instead of a private identity. Such a corporate identity has a "will" which is not simply the sum of all individual wills but is something new and unique: perhaps, it is the realization by the individual wills that without the existence and flourishing of community their own private goals cannot be attained and that, therefore, these goals can only be realized within the context of the individual's conformity with the greater good.

The general will is above the vagaries of personal feeling. It is the result of civil association and it has a:

> rational quality, moral quality which . . . enables (the individual) not only to understand the reciprocal obligations which exist between himself and his fellow men, but also to see more clearly into his own fundamental nature. By identifying himself with the general will, the individual works for others as well as

for himself; but he does so in a way that raises him above merely petty interest, since his own well being is seen as part of the common good.[65]

To Rousseau, virtue (in a civic sense) is the conformity of the particular will to the general.

If you would have the general will accomplished, bring all the particular wills into conformity with it; in other words, as virtue is nothing more than this conformity of the particular wills with the general will, establish the reign of virtue.[67]

Such conformity has opened Rousseau to the charge of supporting absolutism and ultimately tyranny. Indeed, the concept of the General Will is difficult and never quite clear. But Rousseau, acknowledged to be the spiritual father of the French Revolution (during which persons were seen reading passages from Rousseau to the revolutionaries) hardly wished to stifle individuals or deprive them of freedom. Cole puts it very well:

The general will, then, is the application of human freedom to political institutions. . . . The freedom which is realized in the general will, we are told, is the freedom of the state as a whole; but the state exists to secure individual freedom for its members.[67]

Rousseau sees a properly used general will as the proper basis for the establishment of a just state. To Rousseau there is a world of difference between subjugating and ruling people. In a state in which rulers rule by force and in which the general will does not find expression, Rousseau sees a master-slave relationship: it is not an association but rather can be described as an aggregation of individuals. When the general will finds its expression in general law a true "social bond" (lien social) is formed and a just association and a proper relationship between the freely chosen ruler and the willing subjects can be formed. As different as Kant and Rousseau may seem at first blush, it is this fundamental belief which unites them. The formulation of Kant's Categorical Imperative which states "act so that the maxims of your will could at any time be considered valid as general law"[68] Kant in his formulations of the Categorical Imperative seems to have been very much influenced by Rousseau's conception of "moral liberty." As Rousseau writes:

moral liberty, which alone makes him truly master of himself; for the mere impulse of appetite is slavery, while obedience to a law which we prescribe to ourselves is liberty.[69]

In this statement, Rousseau closely approaches not only the idea of Kantian conceptions of autonomy and the Categorical Imperative but already dimly begins to presage Kant's realm of ends.

Rousseau's "volenté general" is a proper will formed by a society and an individual's subjugation of his personal into the general will is brought about through societal forces. I would suggest that it is not so much a subjugation by the general of the individual will as it is a dissolving of the individual into the general. Part of this is the result of a realization that personal ends can, in general and for the most part, only be conceived, enunciated, accomplished, and protected by and through the general will. It is a homeostatic blending, for society in turn understands that fostering individuality is critical to its own needs. Individual interests, inclinations, intention and will in a properly and dynamically functioning community thus are part of the general interest, inclination, intention, and will. They do not vie with each other but rather serve to shape and modulate each other. Kant's realm of ends—in which ideally all individual ends ultimately must correspond to a common end for all—makes a not too dissimilar point. Kant seems to feel that so as to act morally we must include (or, I think, at least accommodate) the aims (ends) of others among our own.

> The concept of each rational being as a being that must regard itself as giving universal law through all the maxims of its will, so that it may judge itself and its actions from this standpoint, leads to a very fruitful concept, namely that of a realm of ends.

> By "realm" I understand the systematic union of different rational beings through common laws. Because laws determine ends with regard to their universal validity, if we abstract from the personal difference of rational beings and thus from all content of their private ends, we can think of a hole of all ends in systematic connection, a whole of rational beings as ends in themselves as well as of the particular ends which each may set for himself. This is a realm of ends, which is possible on the aforesaid principles. For all rational beings stand under the law that each of them should treat himself and all others never

merely as a means but in every case also as an end in himself . . . what these laws have in view is just the relation of
these beings to each other as ends and means.[70]

The influence of Rousseau on Kant (and, perhaps quite telling,
Rousseau's picture was the only one in Kant's study) cannot be
denied.[71] Once again, Cole puts it well when he states that "In Kantian language the will is autonomous only when it is directed to a
universal end."[72] To Kant, the apostle of rationality, as to Rousseau
who has often been accused of sentimentality, individual freedom is
realizable only through active engagement with and participation
in a realm of ends. In the Categorical Imperative's second formulation (in which we are enjoined never to treat others *merely* as means
but always *also* as ends in themselves) as well as in the Kantian
realm of ends we recognize basic ideas of Rousseau's writing: the
insistence that all humans have innate personal dignity as well as
the "lien social" (or social bond) which enables the emergence of
the volenté general which is the product of our social contract and
permits us to formulate laws we are compelled to obey. However,
there seem to be some fundamental differences: Rousseau tends to
see morality as emerging from social association and, therefore, con-
ceivably quite different depending upon the nature of such an association; Kant appears to hold much more not only to a universalizable ground rule (something which, I think, would be acceptable to
Rousseau) but also to a universal, discoverable (rather than being
fashioned) and enduring ethic. Rousseau takes a far more jaundiced
view of what has happened in society: to Rousseau, social associations the way they existed then (and, one could, I think, safely
extrapolate, the way they largely exist today) were responsible for
creating a detrimental ethic: detrimental because it fostered inequality, deprived man of legitimate opportunities, and caused individuals
to act singly and in association in unacceptable ways. Furthermore,
Kant in more practical terms, would oppose revolution, even when
he saw its ends as just. Yet once revolution was successful, Kant
would, curiously enough, support the new regime. Not surprisingly,
seeing the differences in their cultural settings (Kant was German,
Rousseau French; Kant was a religious pietist, Rousseau a skeptic;
Kant rarely if ever left the environs of a small German town,
Rousseau lived in various large urban as well as small rural French
and Swiss areas) Kant is much more ready to rather rigidly obey
rules. Neither Kant nor Rousseau, however, see humans as estranged
from one another. To both Rousseau and Kant humans are social

beings and not isolated asocial entities whose only shared interest is in pursuing their own private lives in their own particular way. In a world of strangers no lien social and no volenté general will emerge as collectives form, albeit that individuals may, when they freely join collectives, recognize the common rules particular enclaves have fashioned for themselves. But that is a quite different thing indeed.

The importance of the concept of the general will to social philosophy and to Democracy has been recognized. The idea of a "general will" is, as John Dewey recognized, essential to community formation and to democracy:

> in his political writings he (Rousseau) advanced the idea that a Common Will is the source of legitimate political institutions; that freedom and law are one and the same thing in the operation of the Common Will, for it must act for the common good and hence for "real" or true Good of every individual.
>
> If the latter set up their purely personal desires against the General Will, it was accordingly legitimate (indeed necessary) to force them to be free. Rousseau intended his theory to state the foundations of self-governing institutions and majority rule.[73]

The role of Rousseau's general will (volenté general) is a critical element of my thesis. Although Rousseau did not originate the concept—indeed, its roots are religious rather than secular and it was first used in a secular sense by Montesquieu—he certainly used it in its most extensive manner. To Rousseau, a true general will develops only in a proper community. Proper communities, to Rousseau, were largely conceived as species of a well-functioning polis and the way the general will manifested itself was an expression of social structure. It is akin to Rousseau's concept of morality in which the moral sense arises from social structure and in which acceptable morality depends upon the integrity of such a social structure.

In this work I shall adapt the concept of the general will. Not only will it be understood as being one of the main tacit driving forces of communal action but also the general will should be seen as both formed by and forming a sense of personal and communal inclination; these inclinations, in turn, are helpful in forming communal intention and in motivating communal action. The general will should be understood not as some general feeling which somehow

arises mysteriously from mere association but must be understood as
the common interest to which persons, in any association, must be
willing to subordinate many of their personal inclinations, intentions, wills, and interests: properly seen, in other words, it is democracy at work.

Such a conception of the general will is quite different from a
merely personal will which prompts an individual to join a preexisting collective, accept its rules and, perhaps if he or she so
wishes, participate in fashioning new ones. The general will as used
here is conceived as an organic and developing entity, not only a
characteristic of each particular association but ultimately a lien
social (social bond) which unites different associations into a world
union. It is the dynamic recognition of common interests and the
dynamic formulation of common inclinations, common intentions
and a common or general will which makes communal and ultimately individual survival possible.

One obeys the promptings of the general will, rather than pursuing purely one's own particular personal and nonsocial inclinations, because the general will in a properly constituted and educated society is, in fact, central to what one recognizes as "one's
own" will. The general will has been internalized by every member
of a well-functioning community. Certainly, particular wills may, in
their desires, interests, and inclinations, not conform to the general. But acting in accordance with the general will, rather than in
accordance to one's particular will, is done because individuals
understand clearly that ultimately their particular will is realizable
only in the context of a dynamic, well-functioning community that
supports it. Such a point of view is one of the struts of the concept of
a homeostatic relationship between individuals, between individuals
and their community and among diverse world communities. In
many ways, such a concept creates the preconditions of a viable—as
contrasted to a merely formal—democracy.

The general will is a "civic will" which aims for the good of all
and which, ultimately (as I shall and have argued) is the necessary
condition for the possibility of attaining our individual goals or the
goals of lesser associations within greater ones. Rousseau's reason for
initial association is that humans found it impossible to lead satisfying lives unaided by others; not, as in Hobbes, that humans in terror of each other chose to make merely a compact of mutual non-
harm.

Some have argued that Rousseau's general will is a somewhat
mystic concept: vague, cloudy and, therefore, something one cannot

concretely work with. I would suggest that the general will, while not as demonstrable as a mathematical proposition or a physical law, is nevertheless something quite concrete and something we have all experienced. Anyone who has taught classes, soon realizes that each class has its own "character," its own way of going about things and its own particular interests which differ from those classes we have taught before and makes any particular class unique. Anyone who has sat on a committee and watched its workings, will have noticed the same thing. Members on a committee or students in a class begin to act differently than they would as single persons: they come to recognize that in order to meet their private goals a general goal needs to be pursued and they are willing to express this realization in actions which are aimed towards the general rather than merely towards their private goals and interests. Such a class or such a committee has solidarity. They have formed a working home-ostatic system and they exhibit, even if in a rudimentary form, a general will.

It is fashionable to see in Rousseau's work an antiquated glori-fication of what has been called "the noble savage." Rousseau does not glorify any more than Hobbes vilifies the original state: both try to use the idea of such a state as a conceptual and heuristic building block in shaping a workable society. They disagree sharply and emphatically in their conclusions but agree in the conceptual method. Rousseau must be understood (as must all writers and all events) in the context of his own culture, language and experience. As Cole, once again, put it so very well:

> He (Rousseau) failed, no doubt, to find the solution of many of his problems; but his approach to them all rested on a consis-tent belief in three things—the inalienability of human liberty, the natural propensity of man to goodness, and the necessity of basing political institutions on democratic sovereignty as the means of expression of the General Will.[74]

Rousseau clearly saw the function of the general will as it oper-ated in a given "polis." However, he did not (or certainly did not clearly) extend his concept of community or social collective beyond that. In this work I wish to adapt the concept of the general will and extend the concept: the relationship between the particular and the general will, I shall argue, forms not only within a given, rela-tively small society. Associations, be they institutions within a com-munity interrelating with other institutions or with the larger community or be they such associations or nations interrelating with each other so as to form a peaceful and dynamic whole, are more than the sum of their individual goals and interests. Within each there forms a general will, a will which serves its corporate interests and in which the individual will is submerged in some ways in order to be ultimately realized in others; such a general will, in turn, must be coordinated with the will of other associations with which the first shares a common area of interest or a common sphere of action. Ultimately, the individual wills of individuals or associations are realizable only within the embrace of the general social nexus and its will. And it is the social nexus which, in turn, is critical to shaping the general will. The relationship amongst these is a homeostatic one. It is not an association of moral strangers, for, indeed, moral strangers could not possibly be conceived as having more than a minimalist general will. It is not persons or "enclaves" who know no general facts except that they wish to live freely about each other; it is an association of individuals and groups who share a good number of very basic things with each other.

As this book proceeds, I will try to reintroduce and further develop and explicate the notion of existential a prioris. I am attempting to start to build a secular ethic which can be valid in more than particular (as Engelhardt calls them) "moral enclaves." Libertarians—though they claim that they would be happy to recognize a "canonical account of justice or morality" which could possibly be compelling in a pluralist society or world—despair of the possibility of building a content-full ethic. Their vision of what unites humans ultimately reduces itself to a respect for each other's freedom—a respect as near absolute as the safeguarding of everybody else's freedom can render it.

It is, of course, very true that an ethic in which every content is agreed upon, in which all of us agree on the particulars of abortion, euthanasia, or blood transfusion as well as agreeing on the particulars of interracial and economic justice, is not an ethic we can hope to forge. But why do we need to do this? Must ethics be an either/or proposition? If we cannot fashion an ethic whose every particular is tidily agreed upon, must we abandon the search for slowly fashioning a content we can all (or at least most of us) agree upon altogether?

The question reduces itself to our ability to form a workable society and to integrate it into the social circumstances of an entire planet. Such a task may be formidable and it is one which no one will or probably ever can accomplish. But again: does this mean that because the task will never be finished it cannot be started? Can we not try to move from the very imperfect to the less imperfect and perhaps even eventually towards the somewhat more perfect?

To accomplish such a task, we need something akin to the general or common will: not something which unites us in every particular but something which allows individuals to recognize that they can only be individuals inside a community and communities to recognize that they can only be individual communities in the context of a larger social nexus. A "general" or "common" will is nothing more than a capacity to communicate and to employ some common symbols. John Dewey put this very well:

> Events cannot be passed from one to another, but meanings may be shared by means of signs. Wants and impulses are then attached to common meanings. They are thereby transformed into desires and purposes, which, since they implicate a common or mutually understood meaning, present new ties, converting a conjoint activity into a community of interest and endeavor. Thus there is generated what, metaphorically, may be termed a general will and social consciousness: desire and choice on the part of individuals in behalf of activities that, by means of symbols, are communicable and shared by all concerned. A community thus presents an order of energies transmuted into one of the meanings which are appreciated and mutually referred by each to every other on the parts of those engaged in combined action. "Force" is not eliminated but is transformed in use and direction by ideas and sentiments made possible by means of symbols.[75]

Just as Rousseau basically shared a belief in the democratic ideal (even though some passages in Rousseau may cast doubt on this, one has to interpret the totality of his political writings as ultimately favoring democracy), Dewey saw in a working democracy and in its just processes the only hope for working out our problems. That idea is a moral idea and something that cannot be accomplished by the minimalist ethics of moral strangers. Since ultimately differing moral enclaves will interconnect, a merely minimalist world will not suffice. The idea of a general or common will and the notion that members who do not comply may, under some circumstances, be compelled to do so, is something to which libertarians will not agree. But without it, unity is not possible and solidarity a sham. Dewey speaks about:

the nature of the democratic ideal in its generic social sense. (1) From the standpoint of the individual, it consists in having a responsible share according to capacity in forming and directing the activities of the groups to which one belongs and in participating according to need in the values which the groups sustain. (2) From the standpoint of the groups, it demands liberation of the potentialities of members of a group in harmony with the interests and goods which are in common. Since every individual is a member of many groups, this specification cannot be fulfilled except when different groups interact flexibly and fully in connection with other groups.[76]

Democracy implies a willingness and an ability of persons, who share more than a minimalist conception to chart their own destiny. Moral strangers cannot form a functioning democracy if only, as I shall argue, because inevitably a world of moral strangers is one in which the powerful will be free to dominate the weak: an inevitable process because power will always be able to arrogate more power to itself. A democracy predicated on the notion of moral strangers is merely a caricature. Persons in such an association may be free but since there is no community obligated to assure their material and social necessities they are free to starve and to live in ignorance. They may be free to vote (nothing except their own socially induced ignorance and indolence stands in the way) but they will lack the education to do so meaningfully. Absolutism, on the other hand, likewise exploits people, albeit it does so more honestly and without pretense at "respecting liberty." A community which truly respects liberty and which wishes to form and to perpetuate a state of free persons will have to be interested in more than merely their theoretical capacity to participate in democratic process.

Regarded as an idea, democracy is not an alternative to other principles of associated life. It is the idea of community itself. It is an ideal in the only intelligible sense of an ideal: namely the tendency and movement of some thing which exists carried to its final limit, viewed as complete, perfected. Since things do not attain such fulfillment but are in actuality distracted and interfered with, democracy in this sense is not a fact and never will be. But neither in this sense is there or has there ever been anything which is a community in its full measure, a community unalloyed by alien elements. . . . The clear consciousness of a communal life, in all its applications, constitutes the idea of democracy.[77]

A democratic collective forms a public and ultimately a public forms a state. To go from an individual (if one can even conceive the concept "individual" outside a social nexus—something I would deny) to a public and ultimately a state requires something akin to a general will. An absolutist state, by propaganda as well as by other means, denigrates such a process. A libertarian state claiming to be democratic but which does not underwrite the necessary conditions for individual development makes a mockery of that very idea. Once again Dewey has formulated this rather neatly:

> If we look in the wrong place for the public we shall never locate the state. If we do not ask what are the conditions which promote and obstruct the organization of the public into a social group with definite functions, we shall never grasp the problem involved in the development and transformation of states. If we do not perceive that this organization is equivalent to the equipment of the public with official representatives to care for the interests of the public, we shall miss the clew to the nature of government . . . The state is not created as a direct result of organic contacts as offspring are conceived in the womb, nor by direct conscious intent as a machine is invented, nor by some brooding indwelling spirit, whether a personal deity or a metaphysical absolute will. When we seek . . . in such sources . . . a realistic regard for facts compels us to conclude that we find nothing but singular persons, you, they, me . . . But a community as a whole involves not merely a variety of associative ties which hold persons together in diverse ways, but an organization of all elements by an integrated principle [which] reinforce [s] our proposition that the perception of consequences which are projected in important ways beyond the person and associations directly concerned in them is the public; and that its organization into a state is effected by establishing special agencies to care for and regulate these consequences.[78]

In the last chapter I briefly alluded to what I think is an incoherent ontological question: does the community precede the individual or do individuals precede the community. Which, in other words, is the necessary condition for the other. The question, already since one is necessarily defined in terms of the other, linguistically strange, does not make much sense: individuals are necessarily defined in terms of community and communities cannot be defined apart from the individuals which constitute them.

In using the social contract as a basis for social structure and social morality and as using it so as to sketch some of our obligations the question has usually been tacitly answered: individuals form communities and are prior to them. The assumption that the social contract is a quasi-historical event which preceded the here and now is further made. Not that anyone (whether it is Hobbes, Rousseau, or any of the other social contractarians) believe that their sketching of the genesis of social contract is an actual historical happening: they use it as an heuristic device so as to understand where we are today and, perhaps, ultimately to prescribe for today's ills. Such assumptions look upon social contract as something that happened and to which our remote ancestors subscribed "in the original state." They presume a certain type of "human nature" and, therefore, a certain way of behaving. On the other hand, one can look at social contract as an ongoing association among individuals as well as among diverse collectives or states and ultimately as an evolving, dynamic social agreement in which the priority of one or the other is irrelevant: what matters, so to speak, is not the original constitution but the way we interpret and change it according to our needs today. Strict constructionists would derive their particular rules from their particular vision of a static and unchanging contract; others would look upon such speculations as interesting but would see the main task as one of interpretation, learning, and dynamic growth. The social contract would be viewed by those of us who subscribe to the latter idea as forever engaged in experimenting with change aimed at meeting the changing goals and needs of a dynamic community; and we would look at the general will in a quite similar fashion: not as something which is but as something which is in being and which is modulated by and in turn modulates the nature of the contract itself.

Individuals, in my view, cannot even begin to exist without a communal nexus. As infants, born helpless and unaware of our separate existence, we are critically dependent upon the support and nurturing of our environment; as adults and throughout adult life and more critically as societies increase in complexity and diversity, we cannot maintain our individuality apart from the community in which it is rooted. The public already is constituted of persons supported by and enmeshed in their community; the state (certainly in a democracy) in turn depends upon the support of the public. This is true even in rank dictatorships. Absolutist governments, so as to maintain their absolutism, spend vast amounts of money and cunning on propaganda so as to maintain at least a semblance of popular support. The individual develops his/her individuality in the embrace of communal support and beneficence; the public is nurtured by the state; and ultimately the state cannot hope to endure and flourish without the support of the world. What makes this possible is some sort of common purpose, some sort of general will, some sort of realization that we are interconnected and interdependent.

In what is to come, I hope to show that underlying every social contract and fundamental in shaping every general will is the tacit realization that we are united by a number of bio-psycho-social "facts" which are unavoidable and which are, even if only tacitly, known and understood by and among all of us. These I have called the existential a prioris. In what is to come, I hope to explicate these existential a prioris and to show that they make of us not moral strangers who are united in an ongoing social contract and inevitably, if we are to survive, share a general will. Furthermore, I intend to apply such a framework (for these a prioris are neither principles nor natural law but arc simply demonstrable conditions) not only in its relevance to particular communities and their members but likewise to the communities as corporate individuals who must relate to and with each other in a very similar way. Engelhardt is right: we live in a pluralist world in which our assumptions, habits, ways of looking at things and, therefore, moral ideas differ widely. He is likewise right when he says that unless we find common denominators which allow us to engage in meaningful dialogue with each other, any hope of forming an ethic is chimeric. He is, further, correct when he claims that all persons (and I would include higher animals here) wish to live freely, to shape their lives as they will, and that being left alone to do so is of universal importance to all. This, to Engelhardt, then becomes the necessary formal condition for living together at peace and no attempt to secure further content can be fruitful. Therefore, the idea that, except for this one thing we know about each other, we are moral strangers who do not share a common framework and therefore are unable to form a content-full ethic has initial merit. Where he and I differ is that he despairs in finding a content-full ethic either in religion, natural law, or rationality and sees no other possible areas of common interest except our desire to live freely. My claim is not that we are sufficiently well acquainted to form an all encompassing overarching ethic which would hold for all cultures, for all world views and for all times—for as I read Engelhardt and others like him the idea of shaping an ethic which is eternally true, while never expressed, is very much present. Rather, my claim is that such a minimalist project exempts one from looking for the common interests which can begin to provide some framework which will allow specific cultures to begin to craft their own ethics and to develop their own unique ways of living. In denying the possibility for ever finding more than a minimalist connection among peoples and cultures, the minimalist agenda forestalls inquiry.

3 Social Connectedness, Social Contract, A Prioris and Strangers

In the first chapter of this book I have briefly reviewed some of my previous work as it relates to the idea of using suffering as at least one of the crucial markers of moral relevance, argued that the capacity to suffer (with all this entails) gives moral standing and have shown that moral standing can be divided into three broad categories: (1) prior worth (or value): being, nature, and the future as the condition for all else; (2) primary worth (or value): an always positive property enjoyed by those who have the capacity to have a life (with the capacity to suffer as at least one of the markers for this condition); and (3) secondary worth (or value) divisible into material and symbolic, capable of being positive or negative with its value a reflective one: that is, it has value because of the valuing done by one of primary worth. I have shown that moral standing is prima facie and not absolute: to act so as to affect entities (or conditions, for many of the things which are of "prior worth" are not objects but conditions) of moral worth without their consent (or ability to consent or dissent) requires moral justification. Furthermore, I have suggested that ultimately the community must determine the way specific hierarchies are set so that the inevitable choices which arise when our obligations conflict can be made.

Beyond this, I have argued that the idea of suffering is inescapably tied to the way we see and structure community and that likewise our obligations to one another and to our community are a function of this concept. In beginning to discuss community, I have briefly introduced various general types of collectives and characterized them by their complexity and capacity to change, adapt, evolve and grow. At the same time and in trying to explain the structure of some of these collectives I have introduced and briefly discussed the concept of homeostasis and its applicability to our problem. I have spent some time reviewing some of the ideas of social contract and mutual obligation as seen by some key figures in the past and have suggested that there are other ways of conceptualizing such a structure.

In this work I have used and shall continue to use an analogy between the relationships of individuals and the relationships of "corporate individuals" with each other. Collectives in their acting with one another are corporate individuals; just as persons have a will which directs their acting and their relationships, corporate individuals are motivated by what Rousseau would term a general will. Persons must come to terms with each other if they and their community are to flourish; similarly corporate individuals must come to terms with each other if their association and the more complex association of which they are a part are to thrive. Therefore, as I have argued, a complex homeostatic relationship between these various persons, structures, and wills strives towards the goal of prosperity and survival for all, a survival which for any is made possible only by the solidarity and consequently the survival and prosperity of the world community.

In the second chapter, I have tried to contrast the libertarian notion of communal structure and of individual obligation with other conceptions. I have, in particular, tried to show both similarities and differences in the way community is envisaged by Hobbes on the one and libertarians on the other hand and have contrasted both these views with those of Rousseau. In setting a foundation for what is to come, I have tried to address the problem of the relationship among emotion, inclination, and duty. I have tried to show that Kant's essential discounting of (if not, indeed Kant's apparent downright hostility to) inclination and inclination's role in acting morally, is not only far too formalistic but unrealistic and problematic. Kant, as I have discussed, while remaining skeptical of sentiment, does at times seem to acknowledge the importance of fostering moral sentiments. In Rousseauean and Humean terms, it is the shaping of these inclinations (in other words, the formation of habit) which is central to moral action. Such "shaping" is, furthermore, quite consistent with John Dewey's conception of morality as a dynamic social rather than as a strictly asocial individual concept. End points (ends) to Dewey are not fixed but rather are flexible and shaped by the interaction of community and individual. The general will to Rousseau is the outcome of social shaping and in a proper society the general will is the will to which individual wills (so that their own ends and goals can be met) must eventually conform. I have tried to show that the concept of the general will is central to our thesis and shall, therefore, continue to use it. But I have extended the concept to show that when properly operating a general will is an expression of homeostatic forces aimed at communal as well as at individual survival, flourishing, growth and understanding.

To Kant, as Nagel has pointed out the "basic feature of the agent's metaphysical conception of himself" is freedom.[1] To Nagel— as to the thesis of this book—the basic metaphysical conception of oneself is as "person(s) among others equally real." To me both views are critical to any conception of the moral agent—whether the moral agent is conceived as an individual person or a corporate self. Without the notion of freedom the very idea of responsible choice vanishes; without the insight that we are necessarily connected social beings (person[s] among others equally real) the notion of responsibility (to whom if not to others with whom we are connected?) is obscured. These two metaphysical notions point out what is to me the absurdity of seeing the idea of freedom and the idea of social connectedness as somehow opposed to one another: freedom, to be meaningful, implies others just as surely as responsible choice implies not only others but the freedom to choose.

In the present chapter I will extend my vision of a different ontology of collectives and of a different dynamic notion of social contract. I hope to show that the whole notion of freestanding asocial individuals is untenable for very fundamental psycho-socio-biological reasons and that social connectedness rather than social separation is one of the necessary conditions of individual existence. The concept "individual," I have argued and shall argue further, requires the concept of community just as the concept "community" is not intelligible without the notion of the individual. The notion of freestanding asocial individuals is as incoherent as is the notion of community without awareness of its particular parts. The attempt to envision bodies without being aware of the organ systems, the organs, and ultimately the cells of which they are composed is as unintelligible as trying to understand cells, organs, or organ systems out of context with each other. The attempt to understand the functioning of such bodies, organs, organ systems, and cells as in competition with each other rather than as balancing each other in a homeostatic balance in which a common good is pursued (a sort of "realm of ends" or general will, if you will) leads to a very impoverished view of physiology. Understanding the interrelationship of organic structures and their components is, I think, best done when we employ the concept of homeostasis.

Looking at communities and their individual component parts (institutional as well as individual) as in competition with each other is equally unsatisfactory. Communities in which individuals are or feel themselves in competition with the whole of which they are an inevitable part are unhealthy associations, lacking cohesion and, therefore, lacking viability. Cells are the components of any tissue just as individuals are the components of any collective. Cells which are in competition with the tissue of which they are a part are almost by definition cells run amuck: they are cancer cells and will ultimately destroy tissue and organism. Tissues, in turn, make up organs just as less complicated collectives join to make up larger and more complicated societies. Ultimately, cells, organs, and tissues together make up a functioning body just as a variety of societies eventually form a world community. The needs of the cells cannot be ignored if healthy tissues are to result: it is in the "interest" of the cell to have a healthy tissue of which to be a part just as it is the interest of the tissue to have healthy cells. Likewise, the goals, needs, and aims of the individual cannot be long ignored if the collective of which he/she is a part is to endure; equally, the collective's needs, aims, and goals are crucial if individual's are to accomplish theirs. Needs, aims, and goals will differ and a balancing of interests among all the component parts will occur: but such a balancing is not an aggressive competition in which the interests of one will predominate and eventually extinguish the other. It is not a "zero sum game" in which there are "winners" and "losers." When such balancing functions well it is to everyone's ultimate interest. It is a social example of a well ordered and functioning homeostatic system.

Employing Hobbes' notion of social contract or communal structure or using a libertarian approach to the formation of collectives and to the mutual, supposedly only minimal, obligation their members have to each other and to their association is, I believe, not only wrong-headed but is also destructive to the continued peace which the Hobbesian vision of social contract is allegedly aimed at sustaining. It is wrong-headed for a number of reasons: first of all, so-called freestanding asocial individuals, by virtue of being individuals at all, are already inextricably enmeshed in a social nexus which by its very being already entails obligations beyond the minimal; secondly, because no collective based entirely on mutual terror can ever truly come about; and thirdly, because the more complicated our world has become, the more do we need the aid of community to enable our living free and individually satisfying lives. Kant argues that one of the essentials of the moral life is to share in a realm of ends; Rousseau sees social life as the necessary condition of morality itself and the formation of a "volenté general" as a sustaining force of communal existence. Even libertarians agree that there must be a realm of ends: that is, they recognize that certain social preconditions must be met if freedom and peace are to be sustained. In recognizing the need for a minimal ethic of at least mutual non-harm, they have inevitably conceded the need of at least some social connection. The problem of the libertarian position among others, I think, is their failure to recognize that a notion of basic bio-psycho-social facts which precludes the notion of asocial individuals necessarily precedes the concept of such "individuals."

I would, furthermore, argue that in practice the libertarian belief in merely minimal obligations if maximal freedom for all is to be vouchsafed, inevitably leads to a constriction of individual liberty and, eventually, must lead to the control of the weak by the strong. The idea of "moral strangers" who know nothing about each other beyond the fact that they want to live as freely as possible, is necessary if one is to sustain the claim that we, as humans, are unable to forge a content-full ethic. So as to be clearly understood here, I will reiterate what I have said before: I agree that an ethic in which all or even most of us agree about all or even most aspects is neither possible nor, in my view, desirable. But that does not mean that an ethic in which at least most of us agree on basic conditions of mutual obligations and respect is not only very much needed but, indeed, that it is quite achievable. In what is to come I shall argue that such an ethic can rest on a recognition of a shared and mutually at least tacitly understood bio-psycho-social framework.

At this point I will reintroduce and extend my notion of "existential a prioris." I will go on and discuss the individual "a prioris" and illustrate their at least in part lexical interdependence and their inevitable interconnectedness by giving examples of contemporary problems. In chapter 4 I will begin to sketch out a framework of a dynamic ethic by reintroducing the notion of homeostasis and will introduce the idea of "compassionate rationality." Finally, in the last chapter, I will show the adaptability of some of these notions to a few contemporary problems in our society.

In the last two chapters, I have suggested that the whole question of whether individuals precede community or whether community precedes the individual is an idle and pointless question. Indeed, the question is more than merely idle and pointless: without helping advance anyone's argument, it deflects us from doing real work in shaping our community and grappling with crucial questions of relationships. Since the term individual implies the existence of community just as the term community implies individuals which constitute it, either argument is ontologically circular. The argument is likewise an idle one from an evolutionary point of view: species, capacities, ecosystems, and societies did not spring full blown but evolved and continue to be in a constant state of evolution. Biologically we know that there was substrate long before there was life, that there were cells and later organelles within cells long before there were organisms and organs and that the build-up proceeded from the less to the more complex. But this does not imply much for the eventual social organization of organisms: when individuals which can as self-conscious beings be allowed that status, ultimately evolved they did not evolve as single entities but were born into a community of like or at the very least of very similar creatures. What matters to us today (and what matters in the point of view we assume towards mutual obligations) is that throughout the imaginable history of higher nonhuman as well as human animals, there has been interdependence between collective and individual with one being, in many if not in truth in most respects, critically dependent upon the function of the other.

As species and eventually as human societies became more complex, this interdependence became more evident, more complex, and more critical. Indeed, if one looks at the world today one will see not only the simple interdependence between and among individuals and their particular community but just as certainly the present and evergrowing interdependence between societies and their particular institutions and ultimately among the different societies and cultures themselves. Each individual has a will and each individual adjusts his private will consistent with the general will if the collective he or she belongs to is to succeed. This is, of course, least marked in what I have called the "Verein," most noticeable in what I have called the "Gemeinschaft" and it is caricaturized in what I have called the "monastic community." (see chapter 1) But we have to look beyond this in the world today: each collective exists within other collectives of which, to a greater or lesser extent, it is a functional unit. In that sense, it is a corporate individual and its "general will" then can, in relation to the larger collective of which it is a part, be looked upon as an "individual will." So as to fit into and work with other collectives towards a common goal, such an individual corporate will (analogous to Rousseau's volenté general) must adjust its own will to that of the other collectives. Thus, ultimately, all individual wills (be they the wills of individual or of corporate members) have to take on some of the willing (in other words, some of the aims, goals, and values) of a far more broadly conceived and in today's world global general will. It is a complex version of a realm of ends.

If we accept that institutions or collectives within communities, different enclaves within societies, and different societies throughout the world have corporate individuality, we can readily see that the same problem in their interrelationship as exists in the interrelationship between individuals and their particular collectives exists here also. Just as one of the problems encountered in individual relationships today is the tendency to view the individual as asocial, so likewise one of the problems encountered in relationships among institutions, collectives and societies is the tendency to view them as "asocial": to see them as torn from their inevitable larger social nexus and to exist as entities able to be understood or even conceived outside such a social nexus. Just as we tend to look at an individual's particular problem as though it existed outside a social nexus (as though it were merely his/her own), we tend to speak of the "problem in our health-care system" or of the "problem of India or Pakistan" as though such a problem could be understood—much less dealt with—outside its larger social context. Each individual has a personal will which needs to be reconciled and fulfilled within a general will, just as each corporate entity has a corporate will which in turn must, if it is to be realized, be reconciled with the more general will of the larger community of which it is a part.

This concept is one which, while utilizing Rousseau's insights, adapts and extends these insights beyond his work. It is, after all, hardly surprising that Rousseau, to whom I owe much, was unable to see this interconnection: not only was Bourbon France in such a mess that solving its problems within such a large unit seemed hopeless but the world and its interconnections were quite different. To Rousseau, a general will which was a true general will, required a much smaller Polis to manifest itself. Even Geneva, which was a rather small town in those days, at times, seemed a bit large! Interdependence and interconnectedness (including material interconnectedness as we take it for granted today) was far less developed, albeit it that it certainly was evident. I shall argue that we do not need to go to either extreme: on the one hand, we need not (indeed we cannot since the very attempt would be foolish) flee backward into small, isolated, polis-like communities; on the other hand, we need not (indeed, as I shall argue we must not if we hope to thrive) aim at establishing the kind of volenté general which results in a largely homogenous collective. Our various individual or corporately individual wills need not be entirely submerged by and eventually subsumed into a global general will: indeed such homogeneity would stifle all progress and, therefore, would be self-defeating. What needs to be done is to see our individual as well as our individual corporate will as interconnected and interdependent and, consequently, to adapt our individual as well as our individual corporate wills to the larger and ultimately global but quite multifaceted general will. Just like the general will of a society, if it is to function, must allow sufficient playroom for individual differences, such a general will is one which would perforce have to allow sufficient playroom for the expression of a variety of societal and cultural wills. We need to do this so that smooth interaction and cooperation aimed at assuring some mutually agreed upon broad goals can be achieved. As conditions change, new goals can be tentatively developed and tried. Doing so does not reduce the capacity of the individual or the corporate will: indeed, just as personal will requires the nexus of a community to express itself and flourish, the corporate will of a given collective requires the larger collective of which it is a part to in turn express itself and flourish. Such a concept is, of course, not possible in a world of strangers.

Let me briefly recapitulate and somewhat extend what I conceive to be the genesis and the roots of all human social existence, obligation, and association. I have previously briefly stated that we are born as helpless infants, only poorly aware of our separate, individual existence and that we are critically dependent upon the support and nurture of others in our environment. We now know— what Hobbes, Rousseau, Kant, and others could not have known—that infants are born not only helpless and absolutely dependent upon the support of others but also that they are born without a realization of being a "self." Hard as it may be to imagine, at birth we and the world about us are all of one piece and it will be some months before we will slowly discern our personal borders and establish our own sense of personal identity. What is psychologically true is, interestingly enough, likewise true immunologicaly: the newborn only poorly distinguishes between self and nonself.

A newborn creature in the sense of having personal self-knowing identity, then, is not yet an individual in his/her own right. We—observing this being from outside—recognize its individuality as distinct and separate and, therefore, endow it with singularity: with name, identity, and social as well as legal standing. But such singularity is something which we personally, socially, and ultimately legally endow such a creature with and it is something which (so that such a being can become an individual in its own eyes) we feel compelled to foster.[2] To become an individual necessarily implies having been the recipient of beneficence and nurture. No creature, no matter how miserably treated at the very beginning of life, can possibly survive to become mindful of its separate existence without such nurture: even the poorest ghetto child who survives must have experienced such minimal beneficence; merely not being harmed does not suffice. The possibility of autonomy, therefore, necessarily develops in the embrace of beneficence. Thus all human animals (and perhaps all higher animals) develop a sense of trust in an environment which necessarily had sustained them: necessarily because without such nurture or beneficence such creatures could not reach the place where they were persons who could develop trust. A feeling of security and trust precedes the inevitable disappointments and hurts: indeed, without having had trust, there would have been nothing to violate and, therefore, nothing to disappoint. This puts the question of ontology and priority into a new light: to ask whether the individual which cannot be an individual without prior communal support or the community which cannot be a community without individual members came first, is irrelevant and ultimately deflects us from what we should, in fact, be examining.

It is true that the nurture of infants is not, in itself or solely, a "moral" or even a deliberate thing but rather that such nurturing rests upon biological drives, instincts, and an inborn primitive sense of pity or compassion; all of which, since they are drives, instincts, and senses, are, in themselves, morally neutral. And yet, even though we cannot, since they are inbuilt senses, instincts, or drives, legitimately call the experience of nurture or the primitive sense of pity moral, we would almost all feel that hurting or failing to nurture such a being when nurture is needed was not only a violation of something that we felt we were inclined to do but was, in fact, morally impermissible. Thus we are confronted with a situation in which doing something was, on the one hand, morally neutral: not harming and indeed nurturing such a being was "natural." It was impelled by instinct and, one might perhaps even claim, accorded at least with normal biological inclination. Violating such a natural activity—not nurturing or even harming such a being—would, on the other hand, be seen as morally blameworthy because, at least in part, it violated these supposedly morally neutral forces. This is not to argue that what is or is not moral can be derived from nature. Once again I want to be quite clear: I am not reducing morality to biology and not committing what has been called the naturalistic fallacy. I merely argue that separating such considerations entirely— looking down upon what is natural in the same way as Kant looks down upon what is inclination—is artificial and in practice not possible to carry out. Nor am I trying to say that we "ought" to do all those things which nature or inclination suggests: an ought cannot be that simply extracted from an is. What, as I have said before (see chapter 2), I do suggest is that our rational behavior perforce must express itself mindful of the natural conditions with and in which we feel, think, reason, interrelate, and ultimately shape our communities and adopt a sense of mutual obligation. To claim that this can be otherwise is a fallacy which, since it splits "nature" from reason and morality from inclination, is at least as grievous as what has been called the "naturalistic fallacy." It is a fallacy we might, in a sense, label as a "dualistic fallacy." Further, I shall argue that while a natural sentiment cannot in itself be moral, nurturing or at least not crushing or inhibiting sentiments which support moral actions is an individual and societal obligation.

As humans grow older and as they further develop their individual being they are less, or at least less absolutely, dependent upon a beneficence which directly supplies them with their daily needs, cares for them, and protects them. They can begin to explore on their own and begin to do many things for themselves. But this does not change the fact that beneficence, albeit of a more sophisticated kind, continues to be essential for human survival, growth, and development. In modern society humans continue to be dependent upon the nurture of others, even when such nurture is now of a different kind. And this is true not only for children or young persons: albeit in different ways, we are throughout our lives dependent upon the physical, emotional, and intellectual support of others. No individual can achieve or maintain true individuality without interacting with others. Such interaction takes different forms but the help that such interaction provides to any individual is critical to that individual's capacity to be truly an individual: a distinct being with particular interests, capacities, and talents which, to be expressed and developed require a community of others to be expressed and developed.

The poor (at least in Capitalist states such as the United States which lack a social safety net guaranteeing basic necessities, education, and health care for all) never can fully develop their potential and, therefore, never can really become individuals. To be an individual implies at least a fair chance to develop one's interests and talents to the extent of one's ability: something which when one is hungry, homeless, or lacks full and equal educational opportunities for all is not possible. The poor—especially the poor in the United States or in many underdeveloped and exploited countries—have an inherited and traditional type of poverty. To them, meaningful beneficence, and consequently meaningful individuality, has been denied.

The very wealthy who are able to live in aimless luxury in crassly or predominantly capitalist-oriented societies, do so by virtue of their past and ongoing exploitation of others: such aimless luxury requires a society structured so that such a state of affairs can be achieved, a society which tolerates it and a society in which such aimless luxury can play itself out. Members of the middle class who while they may work hard live very well indeed and have ample opportunity to develop their talents and follow their inclinations likewise can only do so in a society which supports such a state of affairs. Inevitably they too are the beneficiaries of past as well as ongoing exploitation of the underclass. The well to do person who belittles the waiter who (God forbid!) does not immediately supply his every need (a clear violation of the Kantian or any other conceivable idea of respect for persons) could not have gotten where he is and could not maintain his rudeness without a society structured so as to permit and to continue permitting such behavior. That kind of society—like the Bourbon France of which Rousseau writes—is a society in which large numbers are powerless to prevent their own exploitation. Power has been allowed to pass into the hands of a few: it is a society in which the general will since it excludes any consideration of the wills of the exploited has been perverted and has been suborned to the interest of those in power, one in which the general will has been crushed or, and perhaps worst of all, it is a society in which the general will can be safely ignored. Worst of all, ignoring the general will is either done openly or the fact that it is being ignored is hidden by hypocritical appeals to ill-conceived and unsubstantiated national pride.

When persons are poor or when they cannot develop their natural talents true democracy is not possible. By fostering an emphasis on individualist values and through an educational system which indoctrinates more than it educates, the electorate has been deluded and as a consequence the general will is seen as a summing of individual wills instead of as a general will in the sense of Rousseau.

Such societies tend to attempt to condition the individual will by a process of seduction: success, seen as mainly material, is promised as a result of merely individual effort and is touted as a possibility for all who will subscribe to the individualist ethos. The idea of moral strangers and of minimal obligations is stressed. In more autocratic states—be they autocracies of the right or of the left—a general will is, by those wielding power, stifled, or simply ignored. In such autocratic societies rape rather than the seduction which occurs in freer capitalist societies is what breaks or defeats the formation of such a will. Rather than touting the idea of moral strangers, the philosophy of automatons rather than individuals united to serve an all powerful and all knowing state is stressed. Ultimately, I shall argue, both of these extremes must and will fail. History has amply shown that societies of either sort cannot and do not long endure.

But even in the crassest autocracies or the starkest capitalist systems, those who survive—be they the exploited or the exploiter—depend upon some, even if only minimal, communal support. They are not freestanding, asocial individuals and they are well aware of that fact. Exploiters need those they can exploit; those who are exploited still need sufficient support so as to enable them to survive (and, of course, so as to make their exploitation possible). Slaves on American plantations had basic needs met and slave workers in Nazi camps had to receive minimal support of basic needs or—as many of them did—they would cease to be exploitable. But just as the collective called a plantation or the collective called a concentration camp is hardly a "Verein," let alone a "Gesellschaft" or a "Gemeinschaft" in our sense, such support can hardly be termed beneficent: it is, at best, self-serving and calculated. It does not constitute a well-working collective, lacks a homeostatic balance with common goals and dynamic interactions and ultimately cannot develop, adapt, grow, or survive. Such collectives lack a general will. But even such collectives have social connectedness of each with each, of each with particular institutions, of institutions and their individual members with a larger society and, ultimately, such societies must directly or indirectly, be socially connected with and to all others. Even the Nazi attempt to isolate their concentration and especially their extermination camps was not possible.

To be connected, to be a member of a social group or, as a corporate entity to realize one's connectedness with individual or corporate others presupposes a tacit or explicit understanding of shared interests. Libertarians will—along with Hobbes—claim that only one such interest is truly shared: it is the interest of living as one pleases. Since being entirely free to do as one pleases could, and very likely would, result in interfering with the same interest in others and since others would then defend themselves, a shared interest in maintaining peace and, therefore, a shared interest in respecting each other's freedom emerges. A minimalist ethic results. We are, according to this philosophy, moral strangers who can share merely this one interest and who are, therefore, unable to build more than this most minimal ethical framework. To show that sentient beings have obligations beyond these minimal ones, requires that one shows shared interests enabling a fruitful moral dialogue. While I agree that a basis for dialogue cannot be found in any particular religion (or even in the idea of religiosity itself), I shall argue that such a ground can be shown to exist in very basic and fundamental capacities and realities of existence. Beyond this, I shall claim that these capacities and realities (which I have called the existential a prioris of ethics) can be used as a starting point to shape a dynamic ethic.

Throughout I have insisted on the importance of meaningful dialogue. Meaningful dialogue has been tacitly assumed to be a necessary even if not sufficient condition for living together and for creating ethical frameworks. The alternative is brute force: individually, socially, and internationally. Meaningful dialogue is, of course, part of the democratic idea, an idea which as Dewey clearly recognized is not merely a political but likewise a social, economic, and industrial one. Indeed, as I along with Dewey shall argue, the political presupposes the others. Dewey puts this quite clearly:

> From the standpoint of the individual, it (the democratic idea) consists in having a responsible share according to capacity in forming and directing the activities of the group to which one belongs and in participating according to need in the values which the groups sustain. From the standpoint of the groups, it demands liberation of the potentialities of members of a group in harmony with the interests and goods which are common.
>
> Regarded as an idea, democracy is not an alternative to other principles of the associated life. It is the idea of community itself.[3]

But even if democracy is more than merely political, if democracy is likewise social, personal, and economic (or, as Dewey puts it, "industrial"), what, in fact is democracy? Again, from his essay "Creative Democracy, the Task Before Us" Dewey has put the difficult-to-define general idea of democracy very well:

Democracy is a way of personal life controlled not merely by faith in human nature in general but by faith in the capacity of human beings for intelligent judgment and action if proper conditions are furnished.[4]

. . . democracy is belief in the ability of human experience to generate the aims and methods by which further experience will grow in ordered richness. Every other moral and social faith rests upon the idea that experience must be subjected at some point or other to some form of external control; to some "authority" alleged to exist outside the process of experience.

If one asks what is meant by experience in this connection, my reply is that it is the free interaction of individual human beings with surrounding conditions, especially the human surroundings, which develops and satisfies need and desire by increasing knowledge of things as they are. Knowledge of conditions as they are is the only solid ground for communication and sharing; all other communication means the subjection of some persons to the personal opinions of other persons.[5]

. . . democracy as a way of life is controlled by personal faith in personal day-by-day working with others. Democracy is the belief that even when needs and ends or consequences are different for each individual, the habit of amicable cooperation— which may include, as in sport, rivalry and competition—is itself a priceless addition to life. To take as far as possible every conflict which arises—and they are bound to arise out of the athmosphere and medium of force, of violence as a means of settlement into that of discussion and of intelligence is to treat those who disagree—even profoundly—with us as those from whom we may learn, and in so far, as friends.[6]

To have meaningful dialogue, to sustain a viable democracy, to recognize a necessary framework and to tentatively begin to fill in such a framework (i.e., to build an ethic most of us would be willing to subscribe to and live with) certain tacitly or explicitly agreed upon common denominators are needed. There are, in other words, certain interests and capacities we must all share, certain capacities and interests we must all know that we share and certain capacities and interests we must all acknowledge freely that we share. The libertarian point of view recognizes this: without shared interests there can be no meaningful dialogue. Dialogue is the necessary condition for reaching any agreement: without communicating with each other no agreement is possible. Dialogue is necessary even to merely reach the agreement to keep the peace and prevent what Hobbes called "a war of all against all." Dialogue is the necessary condition of reaching any (even a minimalist) agreement. Dialogue presupposes a framework of shared interests and capacities all could and do in fact (explicitly or implicitly) recognize. If we are to get on with our individual lives such a framework of shared capacities and interests recognized by all (or—in the libertarian view—one of a single overriding interest) is needed. While different persons and different cultures may, at times, share a multitude of interests and commitments, many other interests and commitments are not shared and are the result of personal belief. According to libertarian belief, there are many persons and many cultures which share no interests and commitments other than the single universal desire to develop their own lives or cultures as they see fit. Such persons or groups may radically differ in their interests, commitments and beliefs and "when God is silent and reason impotent" will find a shared interest only in keeping the peace and, therefore, in a framework of absolute mutual respect for personal freedom.[7] A minimalist ethic and an inevitably contentless framework results.

It bears reiterating: I do not claim that a detailed universal ethic to which all can subscribe can be constructed. I do not believe that such an ethic or way of life is either possible or desirable. While I do agree that "God is silent" (or, at least, that if we believe in God's existence that we all inevitably hear God in different ways), I do not believe that reason is "impotent" and, for that matter, neither do the libertarians for their argument for a minimalist ethic squarely rests on reason. Neither do I deny the importance of personal freedom nor the essential dignity of all sentient beings. On the contrary, in insisting on dialogue and an all-embracing democracy, I celebrate it. But I celebrate it not as an asocial event but as occurring in the embrace of others and of community with others who inevitably share such a framework. Forging an ethic, even a minimalist ethic, is a social task. Viewing persons as asocial beings and as moral strangers and denying the ultimate power of rationality ultimately must defeat any—even a libertarian—attempt to justify their point of view.

I claim that the undoubted fact that we cannot—and ought not, in my view—forge a detailed ethic to which all could subscribe (that we cannot settle the abortion question or agree on a "proper" type of physician-patient relationship) does not mean that we cannot begin to fashion some tentative common ways of looking at and dealing with common problems. The fallacy that if a complete explanation cannot be given or a complete task accomplished that no explanation or task is possible is often appealed to: in being either "black" or "white" this "all or nothing fallacy" is, in its nature, a basically absolutist one. Libertarians in their insistence on individual freedom would deny meaningful democratic process: they would, for example, insist that even if a large majority agreed that taxes were necessary to help feed the hungry or provide health care for the poor, no single individual could be forced to participate. When an educated, well-informed, and intelligent electorate makes a choice, there will always be some who oppose it. Since the basis of a democratic community is a willingness of individuals to share their individuality with others (since, in other words, receiving benefits implies a willingness, when able, to contribute) it is obvious that the most minimal coercion possible to attain truly, democratically chosen ends is justified. Such compulsion, however, is not coercion in the usual sense: in forming and joining democratic institutions or collectives all members have agreed to abide by certain agreed upon conventions. These include the decision to abide by a free, democratic process in order to forge the rules of a given society and to accept agreed upon sanctions when one fails to adhere to such rules. The fact that America today lacks an educated, well-informed, and participatory electorate speaks not against the democratic process nor supports the idea of moral strangers but speaks rather for creating the necessary economic and social conditions so that such an electorate—and with it a meaningful democracy—can emerge.

Leaving aside the claim that "rationality is impotent" (if it is, all discussion is quite useless), I challenge the libertarian claim of asocial beings, of moral strangers who can find common ground for creating an ethic only in strict individualism or in an association grounded on some idiosyncratic belief system. There are, I claim, other vital and inevitable conditions—shared interests and, therefore, inevitably shared commitments—which make the forging of an ethic possible. I find these in what I have called the existential a prioris of ethics.

The phrase existential a prioris of ethics needs explaining. By "existential" I mean that what I call a prioris are conditions dealing with existence and known by experience. This at once opens me to the criticism that my ethic is an entirely "empirical" one and that, fundamentally, it is empiricist. But that is not the case: these so-called a prioris do not provide an ethic but form what I consider to be the necessary conditions for mutual understanding, dialogue and, ultimately, for forging an ethic. No matter how we reason: to reason at all, some sort of prior experience is needed. To reason requires experience and to have meaningful experience requires the faculty of reason: to claim otherwise is inevitably to appeal to an unwarranted dualism. In saying existential then, I claim that these a prioris are things we not only innately have but that these are things we know, and take for granted, about each other from everyday common human experience.

The "a priori" in existential a prioris refers to what I believe to be a fact: while we know from experience that these conditions exist, the conditions themselves are the "givens" of our existence, the conditions with which and within which we inevitably operate. They form not only the necessary but indeed the inevitable conditions which allow us to reason, to participate in collectives and in community and, ultimately, to forge those rules for common living which we term an "ethic." They are, as it were, the conditions for experience (and for reasoning) itself. We have and interpret our experience in the context of these bio-psycho-social givens of our existence.

These a prioris do not, however, stand alone: we are not autonomous asocial individuals who, using our understanding of these a prioris decide to form collectives and ultimately communities. Our very existence and the possibility for recognizing, satisfying, and fleshing out these a prioris rests on our membership and ultimately in our participation in community. If one can show that these a prioris and their necessary social connection are universal for sentient beings, the idea of moral strangers and of asocial beings cannot maintain itself. One is well along the way of moving from "moral stranger" to "moral acquaintance." To be moral friends requires more: it requires that we share with those whom we choose to call friends vastly more common social interests. To be moral friends requires shared tastes, experiences, common outlooks as well as compatible temperaments and a shared sense of humor. That is more than one could expect and, indeed, more than one would desire from most individuals we come in contact with or know about. If we were all moral friends, homogenized peoples and cultures would result and progress would be stifled. It suffices—indeed it may be desirable—that we remain as moral acquaintances.

These a prioris are not a sort of metaphysical reality. They are not "out there" but are rooted in the human condition and in that of all sentient beings. They are not the a prioris of all possible worlds but they are the a prioris of our earthly existence. Knowing them is a matter of experience (if you will it is "a posteriori"); having them is the inevitable material condition for our being and, in that sense, is a priori. It is a priori not in a metaphysical sense, not as something which is out there for us to discover and know, but as the basis for our knowing, thinking, and experiencing.

Nor is what I suggest some variation of a "natural law" point of view. These existential a prioris are not laws: they are the necessary bio-psycho-social framework within which ethical precepts or "laws" as well as anything else which humans as biological beings undertake to do are forged. Natural law pretends to be a "law" discoverable by humans. In that it does not much differ from "revelation" for the mere claim that something is a "law of nature" does not and cannot prove it to those who do not agree. What I suggest is demonstrable by simple introspection and experience with a variety of other sentient beings. To deny the existence of these shared existential a prioris is to deny the obvious foundations of our own existence.

What is the functional role of these existential a prioris? In later chapters I will try to show that they have served to underwrite all human thought and actions, have enabled religions to form and have allowed various forms of government to emerge. They form the conditions for history itself. A failure to recognize their existence in others, a belief in the moral strangerhood of others, may very well not result in personal freedom but may, since the powerful and wealthy are at liberty to use their freedom effectively to stifle the weak and the poor, eventuate in injustice and tyranny. No one who recognizes the existence of such a prioris in others can run roughshod over them without violating the basic framework of ethical action itself. Persons who ask "why is it wrong to ignore these mutual interests" fail in the very basis of ethical behavior: under like conditions they would permit themselves to do what they would deny to others. Persons who ask this question recognize neither a realm of ends nor a general will. Despite their inevitable connectedness, they hold themselves to be asocial and unconnected.

Even if one acknowledges that these existential a prioris are a fact of sentient existence, one is left with justifying how they can serve as a basis for shaping an ethic. I say "shaping" rather than "finding" an ethic. Ethics, to some, is not a matter of social creation but a matter of discovery. Leaving aside those who insist that a universal ethics can be derived from religion (naturally from their particular religion!), there are many who believe that somehow "truth" (even if not revealed) not only exists but is accessible to us: truth is out there and to be discovered. Once found, of course, such truth is unchanging and immutable. Justification, for such persons, (if it is not justification by revelation) is strictly and merely logical and deductive. I do not deny the importance of logic in shaping an ethic; indeed I hold basic logic to be one of the existential a prioris, a necessary condition for meaningful dialogue and for allowing us to build an ethic. Logic as well as reason are necessary but logic and reason can operate only within the framework of experience. (In chapter 4 I shall develop the notion of "compassionate rationality" or and not quite the same thing, "rational compassion"). Logic and reason are essential but not sufficient tools we use in crafting our daily lives and the ethic we live by. In shaping ethics—a social task with social roots and ultimately social consequences—dialogue, mutual tolerance and willingness to listen to and engage with other points of view are needed. We use dialogue and hopefully mutual tolerance in dealing with problems in science and politics. Why should ethics differ? Dewey, once again, puts it rather well:

> The real trouble is that there is an intrinsic split in our habitual attitude when we profess to depend upon discussion and persuasion in politics and then systematically depend upon other methods in reaching conclusions in matters of morals and religion, or in anything where we depend upon a person or group possessed of "authority." We do not have to go to theological matters to find examples.[8]

A universally accepted ethic spelling out in detail how we should or should not behave in our relations with others and with our community has never been found or, if it has, has never been agreed upon. Nor can it be. What we must seek is a framework for dialogue and democratic process within which we can then proceed to shape an ethic. Such a framework, I believe, is one we all necessarily share and which we all, explicitly or tacitly, use when we proceed to dialogue.

I have claimed that a framework for shaping an ethic can be found in what I have called the six existential a prioris. There may be more than these. Further, I have claimed that these existential a prioris are in lexical order: that is, one rides piggyback on another. Without satisfying the first, the second is not possible. Insentient life forms are endowed with some but not with all of these. Insentient beings, by definition, cannot know about themselves and, therefore, cannot recognize such a prioris in themselves or in their fellows. I would argue that higher nonhuman animals (birds, mammals and, perhaps, some fish) have similar, even if perhaps more rudimentary, a prioris as do human animals. Even though some of their a prioris may be more rudimentary, they are similar in nature; only the more advanced among them may recognize such a prioris in themselves or in others. Evolution is evident here. Lower life forms have some but not others, somewhat higher life forms are endowed with similar but perhaps more primitive a prioris than even higher nonhuman animals and only very advanced nonhuman animals tacitly recognize the existence of these a prioris first in themselves and then in others. We slowly move from instinct through more primitive to higher forms of rationality. Claiming that rationality is reserved to the human species (claiming that some function such as rationality appeared suddenly and without precedent) is a basically "creationist" argument which flies in the face of experience; claiming that all feeling nonhuman animals have, qualitatively and quantitatively, the same capacities as do human animals, appeals to sentimentality. Such a point of view neither denies "rights" to nonhuman animals nor makes them coequal to humans. But it does provide very definite moral standing to such nonhuman animals, moral standing which can be seen to increase as do their capacities.

What, then, are these existential a prioris? I shall discuss, although there may well be more, six: (1) being or existence; (2) biological needs; (3) social needs; (4) a desire to avoid suffering; (5) a basic sense of logic; (6) the desire to live freely and to pursue our own interests. In this chapter it remains to describe and elucidate them.

By "being" I do not mean some mystical concept. I mean existing, being alive, maintaining one's individual or corporate self. Existence is the first drive all biological beings have and guarding as well as perpetuating one's existence is, primitively speaking, the first priority of every life form. The question "why should one be" or "why should one (extraordinary circumstances not withstanding) value being" is biologically and existentially incoherent. In the first chapter, I briefly developed the notion of "prior worth": something (being, nature, community) which is the necessary condition for the existence of valuing. Similarly being is basic: without existing all else (including all the other existential a prioris) is not possible.

In sentient beings this drive to exist is expressed in the drive to self-preservation ("conservation de soi-même") of which Rousseau speaks and which may prevent one from acting on one's (likewise innate) sense of compassion. "Amour de soi même" or regard for oneself (generally translated as "self-love" but perhaps better translated simply as self-regard or caring for oneself) is a natural human impulse (Emile) and the sense of self-preservation (conservation de soi-même) is balanced and shaped by the primitive sense of compassion.

Amour de soi même (wrongly, I think, translated as self-love but better called "self-regard" or caring for oneself) is, in a sense, merely an expression of our drive for self-preservation. On the other hand, "Amour-propre" (also and, I think more properly, translated as self-love) is quite another thing: as I have mentioned, it is a caricature of amour de soi même, amour de soi même taken to its extreme. While we are endowed with an innate sense of compassion, education, social structure, or deliberate conditioning can amplify and help develop as well as help reduce and finally crush our sense of compassion. Upbringing, social structure, and deliberate conditioning can, likewise, transform amour de soi même into amour-propre. While not quite as readily educable, the sense for self-preservation also can be increased or decreased by social forces: in training military personnel, an attempt to do this is evident. Amour-propre is egotistical self-love: amour-propre would cause one to allow often trivial considerations of self-interest to override virtually all other, even all other crucial, considerations. Amour-propre tends to stifle compassion in the pursuit of its own (narrowly conceived) interests. In the long run, of course, since a sense of compassion seems important for communal survival and since communal survival ultimately must underwrite individual success, amour-propre can, by fostering crass opportunism, work to defeat not only what most would call ethical behavior but, eventually, even amour de soi même itself.

Kant, similar to Rousseau, differentiates between amour de soi même (which he calls "benevolence towards oneself" or "philautia") and amour-propre (which he terms self-conceit). He calls the one "Selbstliebe" (self-love but again, like with Rousseau better translated as self-regard) and self-conceit (which he calls either "Wohlgefallen an sich selbst" or "Eigendünkel"). There are some important differences: to Kant the moral law which "strikes down self-conceit" is a given; to Rousseau, the moral law is something emerging from the nature and development of societal structure.

All inclinations taken together (which can be brought into a fairly tolerable system, whereupon their satisfaction is called happiness) constitutes self-regard (solipsismus). This consists either of self-love, which is a predominant benevolence towards oneself (philautia) or of self-satisfaction (arrogantia). The former is called more particularly love of oneself; the latter self-conceit. Pure practical reason merely checks self-regard, for self-regard as natural and active is in us even prior to the moral law; when this is done, self-regard is called rational self-love. But it strikes self-conceit down, since all claims of self-esteem which precede conformity to the moral law are null and void . . . the propensity to self-esteem, so long as it rests only on the sensibility, is one of the inclinations which the moral law checks. Therefore, the moral law strikes down self-conceit.[9]

The drive for being, expressed in amour de soi même (self-regard) and the "primitive sense of pity" (or compassion) are, as I have previously indicated, helpful, if not indeed necessary, for individual as well as for communal survival. Compassion for others ultimately tends towards self-preservation since compassion for others, as we have seen, fosters solidarity and communal cohesion. And individuals, without the support of their community, cannot thrive or develop their individuality. The primitive sense of pity (or compassion) is not always pitted against but rather may, at times, support the drive for self-preservation.

Both the sense of compassion and the urge for self-preservation are ultimately necessary if existence (being) is to be preserved, that is if individuals and their community are to thrive and endure. They interact and are, therefore, conditioned by the context of their community. The interplay between our sense of compassion and our sense of self-preservation takes place and is, at all levels, conditioned by the collectives to which an individual belongs: membership in family, in religious or social organizations and in the society or community, all play their role. In turn, societies have a sense of self-preservation: if they are to thrive the general will in the long run has to be properly formed so as to be conducive to survival. The way forces within a given society structure that society to a large extent determines how such a society will attempt to structure individuals. Individualistic societies in which the doctrine of individualism favors those in power will tend to change a natural sense for self-preservation into one of individual self-love and, in the process, will tend to stifle compassion.

If existence is to be possible, biological needs must be met. No organism whose biological needs are not met can long endure. Our drive for being and our sense of self-preservation will see to it that we—under almost all circumstances—will do all we can possibly undertake to assure access to those things necessary for our existence. Such things as a source of food, water, and air are universally necessary for the existence of all biological beings and some sort of shelter (including clothing for humans) is needed by virtually all higher animals. The finer details of what is needed may differ: some of us are omnivores, others herbivores, and still others facultative carnivores; some of us, depending on the climate we inhabit and the biological constitution we have inherited, may require little shelter and certainly little clothing. But for a given species the general needs (modified by environment and society) are, nevertheless, virtually identical. Humans need—and know of each other that they need—food, water, air, shelter, and (in most climates) at least some clothing. To say that we have biological needs seems platitudinous; to say that we know this about each other seems obvious; to derive, therefore, an obligation to see (if that is at all possible) that all have ample access is another matter. The justification of obligations has been briefly discussed before and will be further discussed later on. Here I do not (as yet, albeit I will later) wish to make this claim. Here I merely want to establish that having ample access is an interest we all share and that having access to ample biological needs is part of a possible (and I would argue necessary) framework for mutual understanding.

Communities, just as individuals, have biological needs. If they are to endure, such needs (the material circumstances of their existence) must be met. When such needs are inadequately met an impoverished nation, and an impoverished people, results. Although I will, I do not as yet make the claim that the global community has an obligation to—as far as that is possible—assure proper access to all its partners, nor will I as yet claim that on this basis alone affluent nations have an obligation to their less fortunate neighbors. Here I simply want to show that all communities know this and understand it about each other.

All higher, intellectually more than primitively developed nonhuman as well as human animals have social needs. These needs differ: the social needs of polar bears are not those of prairie dogs or starlings; the social needs of Australian bushmen are not those of Norwegian fishermen. But while they differ markedly from species to species, from culture to culture and even from individual to individual within a given culture, they remain social needs. Likewise, as I shall argue, all societies—at least all societies today—have social needs which can be met only by and through other societies.

In human animals such social needs are more fully developed and perhaps more extensive than they are in lower species and differ far more markedly from person to person and from culture to culture. Some lower animals, for example, have little need for more than the most rudimentary education and what education is needed for survival is more a perpetuation or reinforcing of innate instincts than it is a deliberate shaping of habits. Such animals also do not, in a meaningful sense, seem to know this about each other: they react as they have been programed. Higher animals, however, have a need for more education than that: while teaching a lion cub to hunt may be a programed activity, teaching it the details of this skill seems more deliberate than it is in lower forms and has to be adapted by the teacher to environment and circumstance. Humans, however, especially humans in less than entirely primitive societies, must have education beyond such rudimentary survival skills. So as to optimize their different lives and develop their highly variable inclinations and talents, humans need far more elaborate education. Without education, their skills remain undeveloped and their talents perforce will lie fallow; their ability to be functioning and, therefore, contributing individuals within a community made thriving by that fact critically depends upon free access to education. Humans, furthermore, know about each other that they all have social needs.

Communities, likewise and especially under today's circumstances, have social needs which they can only fulfill by mutual interaction. In today's world, no community can stand alone. Whether we like to admit this or not, it is a fact hard to deny. I shall, as this work progresses, argue that an obligation to aid other less developed communities to meet social needs like education, emerges not only from the fact that social needs are a part of the existential a prioris but likewise from the fact that such communities have often (indeed almost invariably) been the victims of those more fortunate (or, perhaps, luckier or more rapacious) and more powerful.

In the first chapter and based on previous works,[10] I have briefly reviewed what I conceive to be the role of suffering in shaping an ethic.[11] Here suffering is used in the same sense but as part of an existential a priori framework: as I have previously defined suffering, it is inevitably negative and something all beings will seek to avoid. Our primitive sense of pity or compassion, furthermore, allows us to know not only that others are suffering but permits us to care about the suffering of others. Without being, without existence, there is (except perhaps in a spiritual or religious sense) no suffering. If biological needs go unmet, suffering—while intense—will not long endure. When social needs go unmet, suffering will endure and will be intense. Persons unable to develop their talents and unable to develop their individual social selves to the fullest will be frustrated, unsatisfied, and disgruntled: they will have an often lifelong sense of suffering. Such a state of affairs is not rare in our society: the poor—especially the traditionally poor or those penned up in a Ghetto—lack even proper primary education not to speak of their lack of truly equal access to higher forms. This deprivation—a frustration of interests, talents, and capacities—results in frustration and suffering. Persons denied necessary health care are likewise apt to suffer. Such suffering is not merely physical: such suffering in many instances is needless (amelioration or cure could be affected) and it being needless is known to the victim who suffers more because of the needlessness of his/her suffering. Furthermore, persons without proper health care are often unable to develop their talents or pursue their interests (the person with poor vision, the diabetic as well as almost all afflicted with chronic disabilities), are consequently frustrated and through this knowledge suffer all their lives. Suffering—whatever its source—tends to turn the eye inward and make it focus on oneself and one's suffering to the exclusion of all else: just like the amour de soi même of pampered persons may turn into amour-propre, the legitimate amour de soi même of the chronically suffering can, when circumstances are right, turn into amour-propre. Such persons can—if driven to the limit—become socially destructive and dangerous.

Our desire to avoid suffering together with our realization that all other sentient creatures have the same desire—the knowledge that while and because suffering is a universal experience no one wants to suffer—is what underwrites what Rousseau has called the primitive sense of pity or compassion. Since all sentient beings, at least all sentient beings we consider to be normal, have this innate drive we all, to a greater or lesser extent, are discomfited by the suffering of others. Our sense of self-preservation tries to keep our own suffering to a minimum and part of this "keeping to a minimum" depends upon our neighbor's and our community's sense of compassion which would have them keep everyone's suffering to a minimum. That fact and our realization that others care about our suffering and will, when possible, come to our aid is important for all of us. In that sense acting as a result of compassion is not opposed but is indeed motivated by this same sense of self-preservation: we know that if we expect others to act to minimize and ameliorate our suffering we too are obligated to act in such a way. It is only when our so acting would severely jeopardize our own welfare that self-preservation may counsel us not to act. The way we conceive our "welfare," however, is largely a social construct: in a society in which material gain and profit—even gain and profit beyond the amount needed to live a comfortable life—are of paramount importance what appears to be callousness towards the suffering of others may indeed be a product of a peculiar kind of socialization. Stark individualism which holds to merely minimal obligations of mutual non-harm and which ultimately is destructive of individualism itself easily results.

Communities who are deprived of ample material or social resources suffer. As we have seen, the general will is not simply the summing of all individual wills but rather is the tacit or explicit realization by individuals that their flourishing is made possible and limited by the community. Well-functioning members of well-functioning communities, realizing that their personal will can only be effective in the context of such a community will adapt their personal to the general will just as ultimately the general will (while not the sum of individual wills) must be willing to accommodate a broad spectrum of individual wills. Suffering members when deprived of ample access to necessary material and social resources by inadequately functioning communities will see their individual wills thwarted and will see little purpose in accommodating such a will to that of their community. Whether one can, in such communities, even speak of a general will is questionable. What will there is, is not as much a will formed by the smooth interaction of personal as well as communal accommodation but one imposed by those with the resources to maintain their power.

I have laid great stress on a democratic process in which reasoning together allows persons to grapple with common problems. So as to reason together, a common denominator of reasoning must exist; if it does not, reasoning together is a sham. Kant, when he spoke of the common structure of our mind which enables us to order objects of perception into categories, was getting at the same thing. Our ability to perceive and then deal with our perceptions as well as our capacity to communicate our thoughts to one another requires a common ground of reasoning. Such a common ground of reasoning is one of the building blocks of a framework of shared interests and capacities. A common sense of basic logic (a common ground of reasoning) is present in all sentient beings. I do not mean a detailed, complicated, or elaborate common logic but a logic which enables us to deal with our environment successfully. If we lacked this common sense of logic, we would be unable to successfully accomplish even elementary tasks. Dealing with our environment in a way which would not assure our destruction, requires that we either approach it through pure instinct or by reason. The higher in the evolutionary scale, the more does reason appear to supplement, even if not completely replace, instinct. And the better our ability to reason, the better will be our ability to deal with, adapt to, and successfully manipulate our environment and survive. Animals which (whether by instinct or by reason supplementing instinct) were unable to deal successfully with their environment would, literally, shortly die. Furthermore, the very fact that we attempt to communicate with others and to engage them in dialogue, presupposes not only such a capacity but that we all know that we all share it.

Societies, in a sense, express their common sense of basic logic through the general will. It is the tacit given of any interaction between different societies as it is the tacit given of dialogue among individuals. Unless basic reason were presumed, an exchange of views, an agreement or even a bitter disagreement would be incoherent.

Societies just like individuals have a desire to live freely and according to their own culture and traditions. Shaped by their material conditions, societies have and will continue to evolve different values, different ways of looking at things and different ways of living. Even in fairly contiguous nations, great differences exist. Growing up in a given culture generally conditions the individual to feel comfortable and "at home" in it. This societal desire for freedom finds tacit expression in the general will of that society. Societies, just like individuals, have amour de soi même: they wish to preserve their existence, to prosper, and to thrive. Political forces within a society may seek to use this healthy expression of self-regard and transmute it for their own interests into a form of national amour-propre, a national self-love which then becomes nationalism and, eventually, chauvinism. Just as individual amour de soi même is an expression of the drive for self-preservation and allows individuals to feel comfortable with themselves, national amour de soi même is an expression of society's desire to preserve itself and to feel comfortable with its culture. National amour de soi même does not claim superiority to other societies; it does not seek to impose its own way of life on its neighbors or hold itself to be the frame of reference. National amour-propre does.

The desire to live freely and to pursue our own interests is undoubtedly one of the critical driving forces of our individual as well as of our societal lives. Libertarians maintain that this desire is not only one of the driving forces we all share but that it is the one and only common interest different persons and different cultures can reliably know about each other. It is not a component of a wider framework enabling mutual understanding, dialogue and, eventually, the crafting of an ethic: it is the complete and only possible framework shared by all. Those who share other particular interests or who have particular beliefs are united in separate and separable moral enclaves and may well be able to craft a particular but idiosyncratic ethic for and binding only for themselves.[12] Although not explicitly stated, it is remarkable that Engelhardt in *Secular Humanism* seems to find such "moral enclaves" merely, or at least for the most part, in adherence to a particular religious point of view. It seems that to him secular uniting forces are necessarily weak and cannot be relied upon to share common interests. Such a state of affairs is, however, hardly the case. Well-functioning communities may not share a complete set of values and interests but well-functioning communities share enough of these to go about shaping their destiny.

Democratic societies which function through a method of mutual respect and common arbitration certainly share an interest in the democratic nature of their community. They understand that being part of such a community implies an accommodation of at least some personal to corporate interests. Inevitably such an accommodation eventuates in regulations and laws; inevitably, such regulations or laws can operate only if they are enforced. To libertarians the general will (expressed through the mutual recognition by all of every members right to a full set of liberties) is a very narrow and essentially bodiless concept but it is a concept to which all must accommodate. Fleshing out such a general will and having it result in meaningful rules, regulations, and laws is, according to libertarians, possible only in particular, freely subscribed to collectives. To libertarians regulations or laws beyond those assuring everyone of their personal freedom can only—even in a democratic community—be binding on those willing to accept such regulations or laws; all else is unjustified coercion and an infringement on personal liberty. Although one would be tempted to say that they fail to recognize that shared interests and a shared framework with its resulting regulations and laws is necessary if we are to live peacefully, such is not the case. In claiming that laws which limit freedom are legitimate, that, indeed, they are necessary so as to assure to all others equal freedom, they have accepted at least enough coercion to accomplish such a purpose. They have, at least, accepted a common framework of interest. Libertarianism is not anarchy; not quite.

These six existential a prioris are, in general, in lexical order: that is one depends upon and, so to speak, rides piggyback on the one or ones before it. To live freely and to shape our individual lives requires that we can operate with a sense of logic, that our suffering (including the suffering we have because of inadequate access to basic biological and social needs) is minimized, that our social needs (including, among others, education, health care and the freedom to pick our own friends and associates) are not stifled, our basic biological needs met, and our being underwritten. Without existence (being) the other a prioris are moot.

In the chapters that follow, I will show that these existential a prioris relate not only lexically but dynamically and will show how they can serve as a framework for some agreements about justifiable basic ethical precepts. In this chapter it remains to reiterate: what I have called the existential a prioris of ethics are neither principles, nor rules. By themselves they cannot serve either as an ethic or as its principles. My claim is threefold: first, that these six (and there may well be more) existential a prioris of ethics form the inevitable, necessary framework within which we must do all we wish to accomplish; secondly, that we as individual sentient human beings at least tacitly know of others, even when their cultures and interests differ, that they inevitably share with us the same general sort of existential a prioris; and thirdly, that societies and communities as corporate beings have (and know about each other that they have) the same set. It remains to show the connection of these existential a prioris with each other and to show how a justifiable (even if a far from complete) ethic can be crafted within their embrace.

4   Crafting an Ethic

In what has gone before, I have reviewed some of the arguments supporting (and some of those opposing) the libertarian notion of moral strangers and the consequent notion that, in an inevitably pluralist world and society, we can forge no ethic with any binding content except one based on strict respect for individual freedom. A minimalist ethic, in which no obligations of beneficence exist and respect for autonomy is not only a high value but indeed the necessary condition of morality, follows. In essence, the libertarian position of "moral strangers" sees us unable to form a contentful ethic because persons from different backgrounds, beliefs and cultures supposedly know only that they wish to pursue their own lives and values in their own way. The libertarian position would have us believe that except when we voluntarily join into associations (Engelhardt calls them enclaves) and voluntarily subscribe to a set of rules as conditions for membership, we totally lack sufficient knowledge about each other to engage in meaningful dialogue about the moral issues which divide us. According to this position such a dialogue about moral issues and the crafting of a contentful ethic is possible only within specific enclaves which accept specific ground rules beyond the respecting of each other's liberty. From this view it follows that such enclaves—unless they were to voluntarily and with the consent of every single member join up with other enclaves—would have no way of holding a dialogue or crafting a universally acceptable ethic.

While very few persons would accept the radical claim of some libertarians that we, therefore, must respect individual freedom to the extent that individual and communal ethical obligations of beneficence vanish and only obligations of mutual non-harm remain, capitalist societies are built on a somewhat less radical but still crassly individualistic version. Such a version which considers individual freedom (economic as well as other personal freedoms) to have a much greater value than do other values will grudgingly per-

haps but nevertheless still recognize some obligations of beneficence. Such a position results in a society willing to inhibit personal freedom (including personal economic freedom) only sufficiently to prevent utter societal chaos, dissolution, or collapse.
Therefore, taxation to provide adequately for the poor, let alone taxation to provide full educational services or equitable health care
for all, is opposed or only grudgingly given. Even when such societies
cannot strictly be called "libertarian," they are constructed on a
model which borrows its philosophy of individualism by adapting
the libertarian point of view.

In previous chapters, I briefly discussed the notion of suffering applied to ethics and examined various notions of social contract and community. I stressed the importance of two innate traits:
the primitive sense of pity or compassion and the drive for self-
preservation. Both the primitive sense of pity or compassion and
the drive for self-preservation are believed to have an important role
to play in the way we lead our lives and formulate our ethics. Further, I have briefly reviewed and shown some connections among
various thinkers who have dealt with issues central to my thesis: the
thesis that we are not moral strangers and that we share sufficient
interests, desires and capacities to allow us to dialogue about moral
issues and to begin to shape an ethic most, even if not all of us,
would agree to. Such an ethic, while far from complete, is a far richer
one than libertarians envision. Lastly, I briefly elaborated what I
have called the six (there may be more) "existential a prioris" of
ethics: those implicitly understood shared interests, desires, and
capacities which are the necessary conditions of all human experience and of all human activity including the activity of philosophizing and crafting an ethic. Being mindful of these existential a prioris allows us to get on with our task, a task I envision as the forging
of a basic and ever evolving ethical understanding which allows us to
begin to work out some of our problems and improve the lives and
lot of all of us on this earth.

When the natural sense of compassion which all (normal)
higher creatures possess is blunted or suppressed, not cruelty but
indifference results. Indifference, not hatred, is the opposite of love
and indifference, not cruelty, is the opposite of compassion. Love,
hatred, compassion, and cruelty denote an emotional investment: to
hate or to love, to feel compassion or to be cruel denotes an emotional investment, whereas indifference denotes a lack of such
involvement. When we hate, love, feel compassion, or act cruelly we
necessarily recognize the existence of another who we assume shares

the capacity for such human feelings with us: we recognize that such a person or creature at least to some extent shares our existential a prioris. When we are indifferent such sharing is either not recognized or is irrelevant to us. To the moral life indifference may, in the long run, be more dangerous than is hatred or purposeful cruelty.

Indifference can come about in a number of ways. Indifference, however it comes about, implies that one's natural sense of pity or compassion has been suppressed, set aside, or, as it rarely may be, is entirely lacking. In part, such a suppression may be a personal protective device which allows one to proceed with what one conceives to be the job at hand. It is, for example, the way physicians may learn to protect themselves when they, so as to ultimately benefit their patients, are forced to do things which seem disgusting or cruel: when they must deal with pus, excreta, or when they must inflict injury or pain. Such apparent indifference, however, is often not really indifference: insensitivity is not the cause, at least not the initial cause, of such indifference. Rather such apparent insensitivity is actually the result of truly caring, the result of caring enough to overcome an innate emotion so as to accomplish a task seen crucial for the other's welfare. It is not reason as the slave of the passions but rather it is passion modulated and directed by reason. Allowing a person to come to harm because of one's own emotions which find what one has to do to prevent ultimate harm distasteful, unsavory, or personally painful, is not an expression of sensitivity but of sensitivity carried to sentimentality. In a sense, doing so conflates the symbol of caring with the reality which true caring implies. Compassionate rationality or, and not quite the same thing, rational compassion—as I shall call the combination of reason with compassion which, as I shall argue, is a necessary part of making ethical judgments—is not only a way of mediating between the sentimentality which would prevent or refrain from causing immediate pain or suffering and reason which would counsel one to lift one's eyes beyond the immediate situation but likewise counsels one to go beyond the crafting and application of a blindly rule-based ethic. Traditionally, there has been a dichotomy between sentiment and reason. (See chapter 2 in which the relationship between reason and sentiment also is briefly addressed.) The concept of compassionate rationality or rational compassion (in that compassion [emotion or sentiment] and rationality [reason] are seen as the mutually interactive, components of a homeostatic relationship in which one modifies the urgings of the other in pursuit of a common goal) gets us out of a dichotomy which sees one as "the slave" of the other.

The concept of rational compassion is not quite the same as the concept of compassionate rationality. The emphasis is different: in the first instance compassion is seen as modified or controlled by rationality; in the second, rationality is modified by compassion. In both cases, it is an example of a homeostatic system at work, of forces which are not competitive, antagonistic or adversarial but rather of forces which balance each other towards a common goal: that of crafting a just and acceptable ethic and of applying it to individual situations and cases. Moral strangers, although they can apparently (and despite the fact that reason has, allegedly been discredited!) be rational, may but cannot truly be expected to be compassionate and a society based on such moral strangers can have no obligation to foster compassion: when moral strangers are willing or able to put themselves into the shoes of another, their so doing is a quite private affair. Compassion in such a system, while perhaps nice in an aesthetic sense, would have no moral force.

"Compassionate rationality" or "rational compassion," of course, hearkens back to our discussion of the interplay between emotion and obligation (conceived in Kantian terms as "rational"). In chapter 2 we noted several ways that these may interact including that (1) our inclinations may be reinforced or modulated by our sense of duty; or (2) (similarly but not quite the same thing) our sense of duty may be modulated reinforced by our inclinations. The first of these is similar to the way in which I am using rational compassion; the second is similar to what I mean by compassionate rationality.

By compassionate rationality as well as by rational compassion, then, I mean the process by which cold and impersonal reasoning is modified by compassion. Reason without compassion can easily be cold, analytic, and basically not only inhumane but, given the natural occurrence of the "primitive sense of pity" (or compassion) unhuman. Reason alone, for example, might tell me that I had little obligation to give money to a hungry person who approached me on the street and asked for money to eat. Rationality alone might cause me to hesitate a moment but reason alone could not persuade me that I had any obligation to help: indeed, pure cold reason might well cause me to simply walk away. Cold reason, unfortified by any feeling of compassion, would be unlikely to cause me to reach into my pocket. But compassionate rationality would strengthen my momentary hesitation by accentuating and moving center stage my feeling that we who are well off by virtue of shared humanity and by virtue of being members of the same community owe each other such support. When one falls on hard times, those of us who are reasonably well off are obliged not simply to shrug our shoulders and walk away. That obligation, argued throughout this book, is one grounded not only in the moral need for a realm of ends and, therefore, in an obligation to include a stranger's goals among my own but likewise in our common human experience, our capacity to reason and our interest in preserving communal solidarity. If, however, compassion unleavened by reason were my only motivating force, I might well act impulsively, foolishly, and ultimately destructively or perhaps even unethically. Giving all the money I had to a hungry man and allowing my own family to starve or giving such money when a bit of reflection or inquiry might show me that the person begging was not in fact hungry would likewise be morally questionable. Our actions must steer between the Scylla of callousness and the Charybdis of sentimentality. A sense of rational compassion may help us chart this difficult route.

Compassion, as I have used the term here, is related to altruism but is not quite the same thing. Altruism is defined rather satisfactorily by Blum (a definition I will use here) as "regard for the good of another person for his own sake, or conduct motivated by such a regard."[1] Altruism in the first sense (regard for the good of another) is rather close to benevolence; in the latter or conduct sense, it bears a strong family resemblance to beneficence. Altruism in the sense I use it here (similar to the sense in which Professor Nagel uses it in his *The Possibility of Altruism*) does not denote some form of self-sacrificing activity. It means an activity which is entirely or partly motivated by our regard for the good of others. Altruism may be related to self-interest, may run counter to it or may, in fact, have nothing to do with it. Warning someone that they have a flat tyre is unrelated to self-interest; stopping to help him change the tyre, since it consumes time we wanted to spend doing something else, runs counter to it; and doing so because we hope the other will, in turn and directly, help push our car out of a ditch serves our self-interest. All, however, are altruistic activities. Their common denominator is help for another; their initial stimulus, even if not necessarily the sole or even main final motivator of our action, is our sense of compassion.

In Kantian terms, acting motivated solely by altruism would, since altruism is an emotion, be morally neutral. For Kant, acting morally is above all a product of reason: the adherence to and following of universally binding duties. A dualistic point of view which sees reason and emotion as entirely separate and not, in ordinary life, necessarily interconnected results in necessarily juxtaposing one against another and often as seeing them opposed to one another. We can see this in Kant's jaundiced view of inclinations, of Hume's belief that emotions dominate reason and, of course, in the "care ethic" which looks, instead of at inclination, at reason with a jaundiced eye. While Kant distrusts inclinations, he does (as we have seen) acknowledge the positive role of compassion and, therefore, the obligation to foster this sentiment. In daily practice (and the purpose of ethics is ultimately as a guide to our and our communities' daily lives) it is rare that a single motive motivates any action as complicated as that of making ethical choices.

I have considered compassion, or the primitive sense of pity to be the "Triebfeder" or driving force of ethics. In Blum's definition, altruistic feelings are quite similar to benevolence; altruistic actions similar to beneficence. Although I would think that it does not frequently occur, one could, at least in theory, be beneficent or act altruistically without the emotive part (altruistic feeling or benevolence) merely by recognizing that to act in this way is a duty. A world in which such actions, while undoubtedly meritorious, were merely motivated by a sense of duty would not be a safe or a desirable world anymore than would a world in which pure emotion (even benevolent or altruistic emotion) decided action by itself: unless the obligation to act is reinforced by an appropriate sentiment and the sentiment is held in check by appropriate reason action may not occur or may be inappropriate to the actual situation and need. A dualistic concept of reason and sentiment, rather than a viewpoint in which one properly reinforces the other, seems to be not only an impoverished concept but a concept about a situation which in reality does not exist. Our motives for action are rarely or virtually never solitary motives: they are multiple motives and they often are hard to dissociate from one another. The more complex our action, the more complicated are the actual motives informing it. When it comes to crafting an ethic or dealing with an ethical problem in real life our motives are complex and varied. Neither reason not tempered by compassion nor compassion unbridled by reason can serve.

We cannot—and, I believe, ought not—craft a complete ethic that will satisfy all or at least most of us who come from various cultures and belief systems. However, I believe, that we can begin to craft an ethic whose questions are more intelligible and which has sufficient content to make basic forms of personal, cultural, and societal interrelationship possible. Compassionate rationality and rational compassion can play a significant role in mediating between emotion and reason and, therefore, in crafting an ethic. Indeed, in moral reasoning, reason and emotion are, in the view I am suggesting here, not conceived as juxtaposed but seen as synergistic: the relationship is a homeostatic one in which both reason and emotion seek to find a workable and fair solution for actual or theoretical moral problems. Moral education, in that viewpoint, must emphasize and foster compassion as well as training reason: one without the other won't do. A world in which only reason—reason not stimulated, modulated and "softened" as it were by compassion—determined what we ought to do would be a sterile, cold, and inhumane (as well as unhuman) world: unhuman because compassion is a normal part of the human make-up; a world in which merely emotion—not corrected and directed by reason—decided our course of action would be one in which no way of judging such a course of action outside the sentiment that motivated it is possible and one which easily could deteriorate into one of dangerous and ultimately destructive sentimentality.

By rational compassion, I mean that our compassion to be effective and to be effectively targeted, needs to be controlled and modified by our reason. Compassion without reason could easily change reasonable and effective action into incontinent sentimentality. Compassion alone might move us to give all we have to the man who stops us on the street to ask for money; reason might modify this impulse by telling us that we not only could not afford this without depriving ourselves and our family of what we ourselves found necessary to our well-being, but also that doing so would deprive us of our ability to help others and, therefore, would make little sense.

Not only do we have an obligation to allow our reason to be tempered by compassion; we have, I would argue, an obligation to temper our compassion by reason. The distinction here is that since compassion is a natural trait (one which, at least initially we may or [rarely] may not have), an obligation to use a trait we may not have cannot exist: but fostering and using this trait if we (like most normal humans) are equipped with it, is, I would argue, obligatory. More often than being actually absent, our natural sense of compassion may, at times, be blunted or suppressed. It may be blunted by societal forces: in the United States a failure to educate people to the appalling social conditions which exist and, indeed, a widely spread attempt to deny them gradually results in a blunting of this sense of compassion. Persons whose sense of compassion is blunted will often be able to pass through poverty areas and "not see" them. The sense of compassion, furthermore, may be suppressed by our self-interest: voicing one's compassion for poverty and trying to bring about consequent action to make a change or going against the majority view of a committee because compassion counsels us to recommend another course of action is hardly a popular thing to do. We have an obligation to allow what compassion we have to play a role and beyond this to foster this sentiment in ourselves, in others and in our community. On the other hand, since reasoning is an ability all rational creatures (by definition) have, an obligation to hone and use this skill and to temper and control compassion by reason likewise exists.

Such considerations, of course, hearken back to the prior discussion (chapter 2) in which the whole question of the interaction between reason and emotion was discussed. Here, I would like to show that in going about crafting an ethic what I have called compassionate rationality turns out to be a vital tool. I have argued before (see chapter 2) that one of our obligations as individuals and as a society is the fostering of our sense of compassion and that fostering compassion is intimately related not only to the ethical choices we ultimately make but to the ethical questions we recognize and are willing to entertain.

The use of compassionate rationality can be defended in various ways: Similar to the way in which Kant deals with beneficence, one could argue that willing a world in which rationality were not modified by compassion, while logically possible, is difficult to will: inevitably, we have and will continue to have need for the compassion of others in our daily lives; willing a world in which compassion did not exist (even, I would think willing one in which compassion played no role in moral action) would, using Kantian language "cause the will to conflict with itself." Furthermore, and again within the framework of Kantian ethics, one can argue that the very process of including the ends of others among our own (that is, the very necessity for having a Kantian realm of ends) implies compassionate rationality; without compassion I would be unlikely not only to know but to seriously care about the ends others might have.

While such justifications of compassionate rationality are helpful, they tend to leave one somewhat unfulfilled. I would argue that, in order to preserve rationality itself, rationality must be tempered by compassion. Kant, Wittgenstein, Dewey, and others have pointed out that ultimately reasoning is a social function. We cannot know, reason or understand without a framework within which the activity of knowing, reasoning, and understanding takes place: and such a framework is inevitably social. So as to reason effectively, we need a community of reasoners.[2] One of the necessary conditions for reasoning, then, is a community of others within and in which we can reason. I want to be clearly understood: I do not mean to suggest that ultimately most of us who "think" (whether such thinking is expressed in writing or speaking about ethics or in painting, composing, sculpting, writing a novel, or solving scientific problems) will not do so in privacy and peace. Indeed, many if not most of us would be unable to think clearly, compose effectively, sculpt, write a novel, or solve a scientific problem in the immediate company of others. But our ideas, our "contact with reality," our aesthetic sense and our perception of what a scientific problem is, is inevitably shaped by past, present, or the imagination of future social contact. Unless we can know what others have thought and unless we can hone our thoughts through some sort of interaction with the thoughts of others, our thinking remains unclear and muddled. Even hermits who have withdrawn to contemplate, pray or, perhaps, work on a work of art have that prior social experience to fall back on.

If community is critical so that reasoning can take place, the preservation of a community of thinkers and of a larger community in which this community of thinkers is embedded, in which it can thrive and without which it is impossible, becomes crucial to the reasoning process itself. I have, prior to this, argued that a sturdy and viable community can exist only when sufficient cohesion within it fosters firm solidarity. Without our knowing that others feel compassion for us and will have a sense of obligation which causes them to come to our help when possible and needed, our sense of solidarity with others will, at best, be tenuous. For that reason, I have argued, community has what I have called "prior worth": that is, as the necessary condition for our individual and corporate being, community itself has a high moral value, a value which we are obligated to attempt to preserve.

Although to care about another's joy and suffering or to have compassion—since caring and compassion are sentiments and as such cannot be conceived as moral "oughts" (see chapter 2)—cannot be an obligation, doing those things which will foster such sentiments and refraining from doing those things which might crush them might very well be and, in the thesis defended here, are. It is an obligation because without compassion the concept of community and with it the other myriad lives and activities which individuals wish to pursue stand moot. Compassion, as I have stated above, is moreover necessary if rationality itself is to be maintained. Without compassion reason ultimately must defeat itself. Maintaining community, I have argued, must be a transcendent goal both for the community itself and for the individuals within it. Unless community is maintained, the individuals within it will be unable to exist in a meaningful way and will be unable to assert and maintain their individuality. Communities which have little compassion for and do little to support and assist their members, tend to produce individuals who likewise have little compassion for one another. In such a community, solidarity is woefully lacking and the community sooner or later (and usually considerably sooner) will perish. Reasoning in a shattered community is defective if not—when the community disintegrates altogether—impossible. Compassion, then, is necessary to support the prior value which I have argued community has.

It is not sufficient to only have compassion with persons whose fate immediately touches us, whom we actually see or to have compassion about situations which we ourselves have experienced. We must lift our eyes beyond our immediate selves and the experience our immediate selves have had and begin to have empathy and compassion with persons and situations unfamiliar to us. As a male, I have never had the experience of pregnancy or childbirth and it is quite possible that I myself might never have become personally familiar in a meaningful way with that situation in another. I have never lived in a Ghetto or, for that matter, had to flee Haiti in a leaky boat. And yet as a human and as a human who has, as all humans more or less must, experienced at least pain if not, indeed, suffering I should—with a little imagination—do at least tentatively and partially that which I cannot ever do completely: put myself into the shoes of another. The capacity that allows me to do this is moral curiosity and moral imagination. Like compassion—and as a necessary accessory to compassion—moral curiosity and imagination are, I believe, inborn traits and ones which all higher animals share. Curiosity, an inborn trait, causes us to investigate our external (and, I would argue, internal) world. Curiosity enables imagination, imagination serves to activate compassion. Without curiosity, we would not stop to investigate; without imagination we could not see ourselves in another's shoes; without compassion we would not care.

Imagination implies the ability to extrapolate from a series of things known or experienced by myself to a quite different set of facts or experiences: every scientific inquiry which goes beyond established data necessitates the exercise of this "what if" capacity; every artistic endeavour (whether it be in the performing or the producing arts) requires imagination as well as talent; and every dealing with moral issues, likewise, means that somehow we allow our imagination to go beyond what is the case here and today to what may be the case elsewhere and in the future. When a non-human or human animal shows fear or anticipation it exhibits this trait. Being curious as well as having an imagination—and having the capacity to temper curiosity and imagination with reason—further-more has survival value: we do not fail to investigate situations which affect us and we do not tend to blunder into an unanticipated situation heedlessly.

As a natural capacity or trait, being curious or having an imag-ination cannot be an obligation any more than having compassion can be; but, like compassion, curiosity and imagination are capacities all (normal) persons share. Curiosity and imagination, like compas-sion, must be tempered by reason: runaway curiosity or runaway imagination can easily lead one to build castles in the air, to roman-ticize real situations and, eventually to embrace a form of mysti-cism. Curiosity about a situation I have never experienced (or could—like pregnancy—ever experience) and with which I am in reality or thought confronted and imagining myself in such a situa-tion is necessary so as to be able to feel compassion with another's situation; reason is necessary to keep this imagination within the limits of reality and to enable one to do those things necessary and possible to help. A community consists of many varied and different life stories (both individual and corporate life stories) which must be understood. Solidarity is achieved by mutual understanding and will-ingness to help each other. While being curious or having an imagi-nation cannot be an obligation, doing those things which fosters curiosity and imagination and refraining from doing those things which might crush it are important if community is to maintain itself and flourish: in that sense, doing those things which foster and refraining from doing those things which crush rational imagi-nation become an obligation. Similarly, the ability to reason—an innate ability—cannot be an obligation; but educating and doing all not to crush that innate capacity and showing how it relates to curiosity, imagination, and compassion may well be. In a society which allegedly treasures freedom and democratic process educa-tion should be aimed at nurturing these capacities.

General as contrasted to individual problems are largely what has been termed problems of "unidentified" lives. Such problems are problems in which, for example, allocation issues or issue of communal justice must be dealt with: who or what group is and under what circumstances entitled to what. Here imagination informs compassion which, in turn, must temper reason. Without imagination unidentified lives will not become real to us and without becoming real such lives are unlikely to engage our compassion. When dealing with such situations, one must truly and fully realize that these so-called unidentified lives are (like those we identify) very much individual lives and that the decisions we make (remote as we may be and remote as they may seem) are apt to critically affect them and those for whom they are indeed "identified." These decisions ultimately are apt to affect many more individuals than are decisions made concerning a particular individual in a particular situation. An example from medicine may help: such choices and decisions frequently concern allocation (whether the allocation of the last bed in the intensive care unit, the allocation of organs or, ultimately, the allocation of communal resources for medical care). When physicians must deal with individual ethical problems in medicine (end-of-life decisions, truth telling, or whether to do an abortion are examples) such decisions involve far fewer persons than do these prior problems of allocation and justice. Without the imagination to realize that such decisions affect many individuals and without compassion tempering reason, we are apt to let nonhuman rather than human considerations guide our hands. Not allowing reason to temper compassion, on the other hand, would make us allow capricious, arbitrary, and ultimately unjust exceptions for persons whom we happen to know or whom we have happened to get to know.

It is not difficult—indeed it is natural if one is to believe Rousseau and Darwin—that we should feel pity or compassion when directly confronted with the suffering of another. These others in such a situation and readily apparent to us are "identified lives": not only lives which directly affect and impinge on us but lives with which, in turn, we readily identify. It seems to be more difficult to identify with and feel compassion for people we do not directly and personally see, know about or are in contact with. That, however, makes such persons no less real. Such persons and their problems may be less immediate and, therefore, less "real" to us but their individuality, their needs and their suffering are not, therefore, any less genuine. What connects unidentified with identified lives is imagination: our ability to transport ourselves beyond what directly and immediately concerns us. So as to engage our compassionate rationality, imagination is needed. When we choose to ignore unidentified in favor of identified lives and fail to temper our compassion with reason, we are pandering to our emotions and, in truth, taking the easy way out.

It has been said that a crying grandmother on a television screen can undo all allocation schemes: in pleading her particular case and asking for an exception she engages our attention and tries to strip reason from our compassion. If we have made such allocation schemes guided by compassionate rationality, making an exception will use up funds which another would, in consequence, lose. We have allowed sentimentality to replace sentiment and have stripped the component of reason from both compassionate rationality and rational compassion. In truth, what we have done is pandered to our own feelings: so as to make ourselves feel good we have caved in to a form of blackmail. In allowing an exception for a person immediately known to us and who has managed to engage our attention and uncontrolled pity we have done an injustice—by our own definition of the justice we used to set up the allocation scheme—to another whom we happen not to know or for another who is more phlegmatic or less "pushy." It is a policy in which, ultimately, the quiet, the considerate and the cooperative will be shortchanged in favor of those willing and able to make the most, the most dramatic and the most flamboyant noise: a true case of the squeaky wheel getting the grease.

If compassion is to be preserved, compassion must be tempered by reason. Not only is compassion without reasoning a potentially dangerous thing (see section on "care ethics" in chapter 2) since, among other things, a framework of judging whose compassion is valid is lacking but compassion (like imagination) without the discipline of reason defeats itself. Runaway compassion tends not only to stop one from acting when one, in fact, ought morally to act but when compassion alone and without reasoning controls our actions sentimentality rules and reality loses. In the name of being compassionate, we may easily refrain from doing those things which are morally essential. Functionally being truly indifferent and allowing oneself to be purely controlled by compassion can in many critical ways have the same outcome: meaningful activity to ameliorate the problems of individual or corporate others fails to be accomplished.

Indifference, if it is truly indifference, results from insensitivity. When habit fortifies and extends indifference, indifference turns to callousness. But not all of what at first blush appears to be indifference or even callousness truly is indifference or callousness. Such apparent indifference is not necessarily the result of insensitivity (it is not that the suffering of another simply is not recognized) but rather is sensitivity suppressed by reason in the service of what could be viewed as sensitivity to a greater end. It is what I have called rational compassion at work. The immediate suffering of another is recognized but it is recognized in the context of an overall assessment. Compassion for the immediate suffering of a person takes place in the context of compassion for the entire person and for his/her situation and possibilities. Acting on one's compassion for immediate suffering could, in some cases, jeopardize such a person's greater good. Such apparent indifference or even what may appear as callousness is not, as I shall discuss, the product of self-love but rather is the result of rational compassion: compassion which not only tempers reason but reason for which compassion is a true Triebfeder or "driving force."

A story may illustrate the point. A physician I know was walking through the emergency room. Three simultaneous attempts to resuscitate patients were going on—a rare but not unheard of situation. This left each team short-staffed and not optimally equipped. The physician was asked to help with one of the cases, a gentleman who each time resuscitation seemed to succeed, would proceed to struggle and with his free left arm flail about. Several attempts at restraining the patient had been unsuccessful. He had torn out all intravenous lines so that no sedation could be given. It was obvious that the patient would shortly succeed in making his resuscitation impossible and that, as a result, he would die. After various further short attempts to restrain the patient's arm, the physician picked up the arm and broke it across his knee. There was no further flailing about, no further interference and resuscitation went to a successful conclusion. The patient ended up alive but with a broken arm which needed a temporary cast. Incidentally, the care of the patient was assumed by that physician, the patient was told about what had happened and was more than grateful. Such a process did not denote insensitivity or indifference: it denoted a suppression of sentiment by reason. It is rational compassion at work. Refusing to take what was—rightly or wrongly—seen as the only way to get on with the task of attempting to save a life would have sacrificed true sentiment for sentimentality. There is, of course, another reason why persons may prefer to act on initial, unreflective rather than on rational compassion: injuring another—when one is normally endowed with a sense of compassion—is painful. Sparing oneself this pain by sparing another immediate suffering—even when such immediate suffering may be seen as necessary to achieve the person's ultimate best interest—is sentimentality compounded by self-interest.

Indifference, as in the above example, may be situational: it may know of the suffering of another or others but may, for the sake of accomplishing an ethically acceptable goal which cannot otherwise be accomplished, set one's innate compassion rationally but temporarily aside. In such a circumstance, it is not that the suffering of another is not recognized and deeply felt. It is deeply felt: deeply felt enough so that rational compassion rather than an immediate impulse of pity can control action.

There is, of course, the danger that what starts out as rational compassion may, as dealing with pain and suffering becomes a daily event, eventuate in callousness. What starts out as a protective device which permits one to overcome one's immediate sense of pity ends up as attenuating (and even at times almost obliterating) the sense of pity. When suppressing immediate compassion becomes a habit, immediate compassion may vanish. There is no doubt that this can and does happen. That does not speak against rational compassion but suggests that one must be fully aware of the danger. Rational compassion itself—by causing one to focus on the totality of another's suffering rather than upon his/her immediate suffering and one's own circumscribed reaction—can prevent the development of such callousness.

Apparent indifference, however, may have other roots. Concentration camp guards or members of an Einsatzgruppe seemed indifferent to the fate of their victims. Such indifference may be due to a suppression of compassion not because a higher compassion forces it but because doing so serves a number of other goals. Suppressing compassion sufficiently and even acting in what appears to be a cruel manner towards someone so as to help them is quite a different matter than suppressing compassion so as to serve oneself, the state or others than the person themselves. Unless one were to claim that all of the members of a Nazi Einsatzgruppe were psychopaths congenitally bereft of a sense of compassion (which in many if not most cases on record they clearly were not), the indifference which such people showed towards exterminating dozens, hundreds, or thousands of human beings is still the product of suppressing a natural sense of pity; but it is suppressing compassion for quite different reasons. Two different and perhaps at times intertwined motives may have been operating: on the one hand (misbegotten or not) a guard or member of the Einsatzgruppe may truly have believed that the extermination of such undesirables was a morally necessary goal; on the other hand, opportunism may have been the controlling factor. But in either case, compassion was set aside not to help the person directly involved (members of the Einsatzgruppe hardly killed their victims out of compassion for them!) but in the service of oneself and/or of the state.

Professor Midgley makes the point that in the "moral vacuum" which she—I think correctly—claims Nazism was, the hatred of the Jew formed the only recognizable (albeit terrible) "ethic."[3] And while there were, in higher circles as well as among those who were "in the trenches," undoubtedly some who wholeheartedly and unconditionally subscribed to this philosophy, many did not. One could argue that for those who truly subscribed to this warped morality, suppressing immediate compassion was done so as to serve a larger goal: still, even here, that "larger goal" was not a goal whose ultimate aim was to help the person or persons being acted upon. Certainly here also, reason controlled emotion. But there is a great difference. In part, that difference is that the "indifference" of physicians acting so as to inflict pain or suffering is done so as to serve a widely recognized ethically defensible goal, a goal which ultimately is believed to be in the best interest of the one suffering; in part it is that the goal of the Nazis had nothing to do with the interest of the sufferer (however conceived) and most importantly that these actions contravened all possible widely if not universally accepted standards of morality. Exterminating Jews was seen as ethically unacceptable even by many if not by most of those involved and was even acknowledged to be ethically unacceptable by the perpetrators themselves; one need only refer to Himmler's remarks quoted in chapter 2 (pp. 49–50).

There can be no doubt that opportunism rather than the actions of the true believer motivated most who actively or passively participated in Nazi evil and that opportunism is the motivating factor in most other circumstances in which evil is participated in, allowed to occur or ignored. Although not generally called opportunism, being forced to do something at gunpoint or because loved ones are held hostage really is a form, albeit an extreme and certainly understandable if not indeed condonable form, of opportunism: it is doing something one could refrain from doing because one's most primitive interests are at stake. It is self-preservation (not self-love) swamping compassion. From such an extreme (and under many circumstances morally at least difficult to judge type of opportunism) a straight line leads to doing or not doing things because doing or not doing them serves our less vital self-interest. There is, however, a difference: when, forced at gunpoint, self-preservation triumphs over compassion, it is, purely and simply, rape. When, however and despite their sense of compassion, persons do or do not do something so as to serve lesser interests, self-love rather than self-preservation motivates such a choice. As one moves from the starker form at which one's life is at stake to the more subtle forms at which one's comfort is at issue, seduction rather than rape is an ever closer analogy.

Our primitive sense of pity, as Rousseau has pointed out, is balanced by our sense of self-preservation or "conservation de soi-même": we refrain from acting on what we feel because doing so could destroy us. Few will leap into a raging torrent to try to save a child when doing so is very likely to mean their death: some will, but such persons are heroes and their action would be seen as unquestionably supererogatory. There are those, however, who, because doing so would be merely inconvenient, would not rescue a child when rescue was easy. Time and again one reads of persons who could have rescued another at relatively small, and at times at virtually no, risk but who have refrained from doing so. Acting might not be dangerous but it is seen as inconvenient: one might lose time, get wet or, God forbid, catch a cold! Here it is not self-preservation but a pathological self-love (what Rousseau refers to as "amour-pro-pre") which vies with and subdues compassion. It is normal regard for oneself (which, Rousseau terms "amour de soi même" and which is also unfortunately often translated as "self-love" but would be better translated as self-regard) caricaturized and taken to its extreme. According to Rousseau[4]—and I think he is undoubtedly right—such caricaturization is the result of aberrant social forces.[5] Many of us find this form of self-love morally unacceptable and would argue that an obligation to help another in distress when such help poses little risk to oneself exists. To the libertarian, rescuing another, even when rescuing them is easy and danger free, is a supererogatory act: it may be nice to rescue such a person, and undoubtedly many libertarians would do so but persons who failed to act would not be acting immorally. The motive of action of those who did rescue such a person would not be a moral but essentially an aesthetic motive: they would—perhaps because an innate sense of compassion is built into all of us—find not acting unpleasing.

Habitually giving in to our sense of self-love, like any other habit, results in acting in certain ways without thinking and often without feeling. It results in an insensitivity which starting by purposely ignoring the suffering of others ends up by truly failing to even see it. In Nazi Germany or in capitalist nations with a high incidence of poverty, hunger, and homelessness (the United States is unfortunately a good example) such insensitivity is, furthermore, encouraged by the state. Here insensitivity is a melange: it is a protective device for individuals which allows them to enjoy their own opulence free of a sense of guilt, it is a device for reducing personal pain and one's personal (and impotent) sense of guilt but it is also a method of reducing the pressure for change which those who profit in and from such a system and who hold power fear. Many Germans who lived in the Nazi period avoided seeing what was before their eyes: for one who lived in Nazi Germany and saw what was going on with his own eyes this is almost unbelievable; but perhaps there were some who really did not see it. Most Germans, however, probably chose to ignore what was going on until ignoring became a habit and not seeing became the order of the day. (The interesting statement, heard even today, is that, on the one hand "we didn't know what was going on" and on the other hand—and uttered at the same time—"we couldn't do anything about it.") Others withdrew themselves into their daily tasks, and chose not to hear, not to see or, for that matter, often not to smell. The statement that "I only made railroad schedules" when some of these schedules were schedules of trains which either went to or had to be routed together with trains carrying victims to concentration camps, is a form of insensitivity leading to parochial indifference.

While the Nazi or Bolshevik states make excellent examples of this problem, the problem of insensitivity, indifference, and callousness is hardly limited to such examples. The very horrors of the Nazi or Bolshevik State made them readily visible and readily recognizable: it was difficult if not impossible to claim ignorance of what was going on or to defend it. Absolutism, in its many forms, rapes; and rape is easier to condemn and, in a sense, easier to fight than is seduction. In the United States today, insensitivity and indifference are considerably easier to explain than they were in Nazi Germany: it is easy to ignore the hunger, misery, and hopelessness of American poverty areas, especially since, despite their prevalence, we have taken care to exclude them rather successfully from our everyday experience. That could not and was not the case in Nazi Germany.

Further, arguments which justify the current state of affairs are, even if no more convincing, a bit easier to make. Foremost among these arguments are the blaming of the victim itself: after all, persons could, if they would, pull themselves "up by the bootstraps." The poor, furthermore, by virtue of being poor are often considered to be at fault. This feeling—irrational as it seems to many of us—has well accepted historic roots in the reformation and the rise of Protestantism.[6] Material prosperity was taken as a sign of God's grace and as a reward for virtue; poverty, by inversion, was soon seen as part of God's well deserved wrath: the poor, at least in large part, were poor because they deserved to be. To libertarians, our particular lot is a result of the "natural lottery" (a term unfortunately coined by Rawls who is hardly a libertarian): whether we are rich or poor, ugly or beautiful, intelligent or stupid or whether we are healthy, ill, or deformed is no one's doing and, therefore, no one's obligation to help remedy.[7] Blaming the victim may become habitual enough so that one's sense of compassion diminishes until it is ineffective. In many cases such victim blaming effectively acts as a sop to one's conscience and serves one's sense of self-love.

We (whether individuals or nations) who are well off are inevitably advantaged by the persistent disadvantaging of others: when resources are finite and distribution is inequitable, white males (or industrialized countries), whether they like to be or not, are inevitably advantaged by the disadvantaging of minorities, women, and impoverished nations. Such a state of affairs cannot simply be blamed on a natural lottery. Such a state of affairs is the inevitable result of prior exploitation: of the way we have structured our society or our world. When persons or nations allow such a state of affairs to persist, when they do not do what they can to oppose it, they become culpable for allowing it to continue. It is this fact which makes affirmative action a moral imperative.[8]

When we are personally well off, when we stay at gaudy hotels, drive expensive cars, and frequent gourmet restaurants, we easily lose sight of those scrounging in garbage cans, hobbling with rags around their feet down the street or searching out a grate on which to sleep for the night. To ignore the poor, the hungry, or the cold is in our interest: ignoring the poor, the hungry, and the cold keeps us comfortable. Likewise, the industrialized nations (exploiters of yesterday and quite willing to continue exploitation today) will disregard the misery of less fortunate nations. We suppress our compassion for such persons or nations and become insensitive because doing so caters to our self-interest and, ultimately, to our self-love. A tactical initial indifference (tactical because it consciously serves us and allows us to do what we find most agreeable), soon yields to an actual one and eventuates in callousness. Many Germans to this day claim that (1) they did not know what was going on; (2) could do nothing about "it" (the "it" they did not know was going on); and, ultimately, may (3) try to blame their victims either for some nebulous evil-doing or for not better defending themselves. Americans often argue precisely the same: first, they attempt to deny the existence of conditions like stark and traditional poverty, racism, and injustice; then, when incontrovertible proof is given, they will claim to be impotent to change conditions and ultimately they will end up by blaming the victim for laziness, lack of gumption or, as we shall discuss in chapter 5, defective genes.

In the United States today the poor, the homeless, and the hungry are all around us. Institutionalized unemployment and poverty (poverty which has been present for generations and shows no hope of relief), racism, sexism, and prejudice are part of the American culture—as American, I fear, as apple pie and baseball— and yet a large number of persons either deny that such conditions exist or flee into blaming the victims. Such insensitivity is not only convenient for the individual but likewise is often in the short-range interest of those who hold the real power. When the poor can be kept powerless and the better off can be kept blind the status quo and with it those who are well-off and powerful are apt to be protected.

Things, however, have changed. At one time an exploitable underclass was necessary or at least desirable for a capitalist society. Body slavery—because it was no longer profitable—was replaced by a form of wage slavery. Today this formerly exploitable class has proven not even to be very exploitable: through generations of hopelessness and poverty the United States has developed a growing underclass which threatens to become unmanageable instead of exploitable. The kind of labor formerly done by this class, furthermore, is not the kind of labor much needed by society today. The situation is the fruit of our human indifference, the product of our studied callousness, and the just desert (just not for the victims but just for those of us who have—wittingly or unwittingly—been among the exploiters) of our lack of true community. Even if arguments of justice would not persuade us to embrace some form of effective affirmative action, prudence should.

Insensitivity is often the result of social forces. Persons who claim "never to see the poor or homelessness" on America's streets may (if they truly do not see instead of pretending not to see) have been taught the habit of not seeing by careful socialization into a system of stark individualism, a system in which the belief that we are basically moral strangers with little which connects us and with minimal obligations to one another is perhaps not explicitly recognized but certainly widespread. Such socialization starts in a family which in turn was socialized into a similar set of beliefs and is continued by a school system which teaches patriotic myths and loyalty to the status quo, often stifles inquiry and is generally reinforced by the media. All of these social forces, make, teach and subtly reaffirm a number of basic assumptions about human nature in general and American life in particular which, when repeated often enough, are believed. Among these myths is that humans "by nature" are greedy, selfish, and individualistic, that America is the "greatest country in the world," a "land of opportunity" for all, a country always ready to provide a haven to the suppressed of the world (what I have called the "huddled masses" myth) and one in which class, race, religion, and ethnic origin do not matter.

When indifference becomes a habit, callousness may result. The physician who in a dire emergency breaks another's arm to save that person's life could, if the inflicting of pain became a daily event, become insensitive and, eventually, quite callous. Nazi members of the Einsatzgruppen had evidently achieved that state. Many Americans, in dealing or not dealing with the social misery surrounding them, are rapidly moving in the same direction. If we accept compassion as a driving force for ethical inquiry and action and if we accept the role of compassionate rationality, such callousness must be seen as destructive to the possibility of crafting an ethic we all can live with. Persons who are callous may, at some level, be aware of the interests which connect all beings on this earth, may—when such interests are pointed out—agree that the existential a prioris in fact exist but may fail to draw any conclusions from this. Their callousness has re-inforced their self-love and their self-love has reinforced their callousness.

It is essential that we begin a dialogue and start to craft an ethic which while not complete is an ethic which allows us to deal with our very real problems and to get on with our lives. This is only possible if indifference to each other's interests is prevented and compassionate rationality is promoted. Without a sense of compassion, without Rousseau's primitive and innate sense of pity, the existential a prioris of ethics will be denied by or meaningless to those who are well-off. In today's world we must extend such a dialogue and begin to craft such an ethic not only within narrow national borders or among culturally similar societies. All of us (as individuals as well as societies) need to reach out to all others in this effort. And yet, the argument for holding such a dialogue is not one based entirely on compassion or even on moral considerations: self-preservation (individual self-preservation as well as national self-preservation and ultimately the preservation of the world community) and prudence would counsel such a move. Insensitivity towards the problems of others has long ago ceased to be a protective device; indifference towards our neighbors—be they our neighbors within our borders or our neighbors across the seas—is not only morally problematic but has become self-destructive. To be sensitive and not to be indifferent in today's world is not only ethically appropriate but has become a tool for our own self-preservation. Self-preservation not only may be more powerful than compassion; self-preservation—if it is to act to truly preserve oneself—should be more powerful than a self-love which inevitably would lead to its own destruction.

The claim that the only framework for shaping an ethic is respect for each other's ways of living as long as such ways of living do not directly inhibit the equal right of all others to live freely and that, therefore, we cannot craft a contentful ethic can, I believe, be shown to be wrong-headed. As I progress in this chapter, I will discuss and give some justification for the use of these existential a prioris in building a framework for some agreements about basic ethical precepts. I claim that while we (except in particular moral enclaves) most certainly are not "moral friends" and while there are many differing beliefs, customs, and ethical points of view we cannot hope to reconcile among us, we are, at the very least, sufficiently morally acquainted to begin crafting a more contentful ethic than the minimalist. We are morally acquainted because we share a far richer framework than is provided by the minimalist ethic.

I do not maintain that an ethic using what I have called the existential a prioris as a framework can produce a complete ethical system nor that producing a complete ethical system is either a necessary or even a desirable condition of interdependent living. In point of fact, I would claim that a complete ethical system all would adhere to would result in a homogenized world in which the forces of homeostasis which promote evolution and progress would be severely weakened and ultimately stifled. Progress and evolution depend upon free and democratic dialogue among persons and cultures with various beliefs but with deep and democratic respect for each other's customs and beliefs. Diversity (personal as well as cultural) rather than being bemoaned should, I think, be celebrated and used as a tool of inquiry in our ongoing effort to build a better world. What I do claim is that we, as inevitably interconnected humans who are inevitably enmeshed in this framework, share sufficient interests and know sufficient basic things about each other so that we can begin to shape an ethic we all can live and thrive with. In this work an ethic is not seen as being static, as somehow having an eternal and, as it were, external existence outside the human frame of experience. I use the term ethics not as something discoverable but as something which we in the human condition are compelled to craft for ourselves. Ethics, like all other human activity, is seen as an evolving construct among men of different backgrounds, cultures, beliefs, and temperaments who yet inevitably have much in common. If humans and with them human dignity, freedom and possibilities are to survive, more of a framework than is offered by the libertarians is needed.

The six existential a prioris I have previously discussed are, since they are the common condition and experience of sentient human existence, things that all of us recognize. They constitute our inevitable bio-psycho-social framework. While we cannot and must not reduce humans (or higher nonhuman animals) to their bio-psycho-social condition, we cannot escape the fact that all our striving, thinking, acting, and philosophizing is possible only within the embrace of our bio-psycho-social reality. The way societies are shaped, cultures developed and ethics crafted occurs within such a framework. The development of cultures and societies in turn helps shape the way these bio-psycho-social conditions will express themselves.

To reiterate: humans (and to some extent nonhuman animals) inevitably share certain conditions which must be met if we are not only to live but to live in a way which allows us to develop our potentials as fully as our cultural context will permit. Furthermore, as sentient humans we all know that other sentient beings share these same conditions with us. These six existential a prioris which constitute the necessary framework in which we act and which, I have argued, are in lexical order are our (1) drive for being or existence; (2) biological needs; (3) social needs; (4) a desire to avoid suffering; (5) a basic sense of logic; and (6) a desire to live freely and to pursue our own interests.

As higher animals we all, to a greater or lesser extent, inevitably share these interests, capacities, and conditions. Sentient humans (and perhaps higher sentient nonhuman animals) are aware that the same conditions apply to others. I may not know the habits of Fiji islanders or the social and ethical structure of Eskimo life, but I do know that Eskimos and Fiji islanders share with me the same existential a priori framework. As sentient beings in our particular world we are inevitably saddled with these conditions as a framework within all we can experience or think must take place. Together with the material and social conditions in which humans find themselves, such a framework, in the sense of being one of the necessary conditions, is prior to their culture and ethical structure. Cultures, ethical structures (and I would argue religions) are necessarily shaped and crafted by their particular material conditions within the context of such a framework. In turn, the way cultures and ethical structures are crafted will influence the way in which the particulars of the framework will express themselves.

Even when their details may differ greatly and even if they are differently defined and differently played out, certain ethical precepts are common to all cultures and religions. Even if we wish to hew to a revealed religion, this religion was revealed to us and received as well as interpreted by us in the necessary context these a prioris provide. As biological beings, and as biological beings who are human, no other possibility could rationally be imagined. Although the terms may be defined differently in different cultures and by different belief systems, none of these cultures or belief systems look upon murder, theft or lying as desirable and all, in different ways, concede that helping others is commendable and, under some circumstances morally required.

Pointing to the Ba Mbuti[9]—a tribe of impoverished African natives whose existence has been rendered precarious by systematic western exploitation—to claim, as Engelhardt does, that some societies lack any sense of beneficence defeats the very point Engelhardt is trying to make. The Ba Mbuti are not a "normal society"[10] anymore than the inmates of Auschwitz were a normal community.[11] In both the sense of compassion (the primitive sense of pity) was largely swamped by the need for self-preservation. And even among the Ba Mbuti as in Nazi concentration camps some vestige of a sense of beneficence and with it some sense of caring for each other, survived. Far from proving that normal societies without beneficence exist, Engelhardt's Ba Mbuti (or the experience in Nazi concentration camps) illustrate that the sense of compassion and the obligations for beneficence felt by us diminishes but does not vanish altogether when conditions are pathological. That the sense of beneficence, compassion and caring for each other diminishes should come as less of a surprise than that any vestige of it survives.

In the last chapter, I argued that these existential a prioris are in lexical order since each to be viable depends on those which have gone before. But their order is not merely lexical: they are connected, interrelated, and interwoven in a far more complicated way. It is evident that to have biological needs one must be alive but to be alive one has to have one's biological needs met. Not quite as evident is not only that one must have minimal biological needs met so as to have social needs but that, likewise and in turn, social needs influence our biological ones. Having our biological needs met depends upon social forces. Since man cannot live alone without some sort of social support this is true in virtually all circumstances. The more complex our social structures and the more advanced our technology, the more interdependent humans become and the more do these needs interrelate. Likewise, our ability to escape suffering, our common sense of basic logic and finally our drive to shape our lives freely and in accord with our tastes and talents is related to all the other conditions mentioned. The interrelationship is far more subtle than my initial claim that they "ride piggyback" and the degree of interrelationship varies from culture to culture and from situation to situation. One can envision the relationship as an interwoven network in which such an interrelation (varying with time and circumstance) is far more than the mere sum of the parts. An attempt to provide some content within such a framework does not leave the framework untouched. Content and framework interrelate and modify each other.

In the last chapter I also briefly made the point that what I call our drive for being or existence fuels our drive for self-preservation and that our capacity to suffer as well as our knowledge that all other sentient beings share such a capacity and seek to avoid suffering is intimately related to what Rousseau calls the primitive sense of pity or compassion. In general, our sense of self-preservation is seen as giving pause to our compassion: we may hesitate to act compassionately because doing so might jeopardize something of great value for us. On the other hand, and at least in part, we act on our sense of compassion precisely because our sense of self-preservation (which counsels us to choose means appropriate to what we conceive to be our self-interest) counsels us to do so: seeing another's suffering leaves us uneasy and not quite able to enjoy our own good fortune. I am not saying here that acting morally is always done out of (pure) self-interest; I am saying that in part widely defined self-interest at the very least plays a role in all, including in our moral, thinking and doing. Narrowly defined self-interest sees our own interest as bounded by our personal self and our acting controlled by whether that personal self is directly and materially served by our action; wider self-interest sees our selves as part of a community of others so that separating my own from my neighbor's welfare, or from my neighbor's interest, is no longer entirely possible. However, like any unbridled passion not controlled by reason, compassion alone is an unsafe motivator of action. It may cause us to act in an ill-considered fashion and ultimately in a way which defeats our aims and goals. If it is not to be sentimentality, compassion has to be modulated by reason. Ethics, if it is to be anything, at the very least is the application of compassionate rationality to our choices of options and actions insofar as doing so affects others.

If such a concept is at least partly accepted, the motivation for our acting is seen to be most complicated. Acting ethically, as conceived here, is partly motivated by an innate emotion (compassion) which at that point can be seen to be an inclination already modulated by considerations of self-preservation and partly controlled by our capacity to apply logical thinking to our willing action. Inclination, in such a definition, is not seen as something opposing but as something which, when properly educated, can support moral action. Social structure, Rousseau has insisted, produces the moral complexion of a particular civilization or society. I would argue that social structure—the way we choose to structure our society—likewise plays a significant role in determining our inclinations. Our social structure, then, determines how we, as individuals inevitably conditioned by the society in which we live, shall utilize our framework of existential a prioris: the separate particulars of the framework do not change but the way they and the framework itself are explicitly acknowledged, what is emphasized and the kind of role it is allowed to play in our structuring inevitably differs.

Even if we grant the presence of these existential a prioris and even if we acknowledge their fundamental importance to all our activities, it does not follow that such "a prioris" by themselves have moral force. Nor do I claim that by themselves they do. As I have discussed in previous chapters, no attempt to shape an "ought" from an "is" is intended. I claim not that these existential a prioris have moral force but that, along with our innate sense of compassion and our balancing drive for self-preservation, they are the necessary common conditions for shaping a widely agreed upon ethic that we can all live (and thrive) with. Therefore, while these existential a prioris by themselves lack moral force they do critically bear upon any ethic which will be shaped by man.

The is—ought distinction has been rightly much made of. I heartily concur that, in a simplistic sense, one cannot extract an ought from an is: merely because something is the case does not mean that it ought to be the case. But having once again stated this rather obvious point hardly exhausts the issue. Without an is all oughts stand moot: it is the case that we and all nature about us exist and that, likewise, a natural thrust for being is a fundamental driving force. To ask whether this ought to be the case or why this ought to be the case is in a biological sense incoherent: and, since we all inevitably are biological creatures, we need to accept this being and our drive for it as (barring a few exceptions) a universally valid proposition on which we then perforce must ground all else we undertake to do. If we acknowledge that what I have called the existential a prioris exist, they form an extension of such an is and, perforce, constitute the necessary and inevitable framework of all we do.

Some libertarians may even more or less readily accept the notion of existential a prioris and might even agree that they were lexically related. They would, however, argue that so as to keep the peace the only one which merits moral status would be our common desire to live freely and to shape our lives in our own way. Such an argument would base itself on the necessity of keeping the peace if one is to accomplish such an aim and, therefore, the necessity to agree on strict respect for each other's freedoms, including economic freedoms. The same argument cannot be made for the other a prioris: not seeing to it that others had the same existential a prioris met would not of necessity and in the short haul disturb our individual enjoyment of what we had in the same way in which not assuring full freedom for others might destroy our own ability to pursue our own interests and lives. To a libertarian, persons who are unable to get sufficient food, shelter, education, or health care because they lack money do not lack access: it is only personal circumstances and not the action of others which interferes with their ability to avail themselves of what they need or want.

A framework, even though it does not determine the material, pattern or other particulars of a piece of woven cloth, inevitably shapes its final structure: while the final product may be infinitely varied in texture and color and while one may appear quite different from another on superficial examination, all things woven on that framework inevitably have a basic structure in common. Their differences relate to the material conditions of the substrate chosen (color, texture, etc.) and the particular taste (pattern, design, etc.) of the weaver. Our preference for the one over the other is an aesthetic one and not one based on the quality of the cloth itself. The moral principles and precepts we form within the context of these existential a prioris, then, come in part from the framework itself which allows a family resemblance among the various principles, moral rules, and ethical beliefs of a given culture and the particular material possibilities as well as the history of the society in which these moral precepts are formed. Our justification for these moral precepts depends, as I have mentioned in chapter one, on a "compost heap" of justifications and such precepts or principles are tested and ultimately justified (until a better one can be developed by further work) in experience within a given cultural context. The way they may express themselves—as the way in which different types of cloth can be formed from the same material—may appear quite different even when the underlying material is not changed. Our preference for one over the other, likewise, is one associated with our particular cultural and personal point of view. As mentioned in the first chapter, justification is an ongoing process of learning and growth so that ultimately it can become a tool in our evolution and survival.

Such a claim should not be understood to be a defense of relativism: I am not saying that there "is no right and wrong" and that, therefore, anything which has come into being in a given culture "goes." Oftentimes, as Rousseau has pointed out, a defective social structure will produce a defective ethic: that is, an ethic which in fact ignores those conditions all men share so as to favour the interests of the few who have established themselves in power. Such an ethic will be defective because it fails to do what an ethic is supposed to do: advance peace, promote understanding and help all humans who live within their particular community as well as in the global community live more satisfying, fuller, better, and more fulfilling lives. A minimalist libertarian ethic which sees personal individual freedom as an absolute condition of morality instead of seeing freedom as one part of a framework of interests and values within which an ethic is shaped, favors the emergence of a strong elite who by holding power manage to establish rules and regulations which serve to aid their own, narrowly conceived personal advantage. If an ethic is to advance peace, promote understanding and help all humans live fuller, better lives, the minimalist ethic of libertarianism falls far short of the mark.

The framework of common interests and values which I have called the existential a prioris are, as I have mentioned, interrelated. In being interests and values they are not only mutually dependent upon each other but, at times, will be seen to conflict. It is only when they are united into a common and dynamic weave that they can be understood. Everyone's desire to live as freely as possible may readily conflict with everyone's desire to have social needs—

like full access to educational opportunities and health care which a society may offer—met. The drive to avoid suffering by one, may conflict with the exercise of full liberty in another. Only our common, basic sense of logic can help us arbitrate, only our innate sense of compassion (balanced by our natural drive for self-preservation) can allow us to care whether the things common to all are also available to all. If we were to shrug off or even entirely fail to recognize another's need, our drive to formulate a viable ethic would falter. Instead of being an exercise in compassionate rationality, ethics would become a sterile, scholastic amusement for a few instead of as something intimately connected with acting must necessarily be: a controlling force in the lives of all.

I have claimed that in many ways, the interrelationship among the various a prioris and of these existential a prioris with our innate sense of compassion modified by our drive for self-preservation, is not merely lexical but can be conceived as homeostatic. Interests and values must be adjusted to and balanced with each other so as to form a framework which, at the same time, is stable and dynamic. As I discussed in chapter 1, homeostatic balance is conceived as the dynamic equilibrium between various forces each of which seeks to maintain a balance and each of which can continue only within the context of the whole. Homeostasis is not competitive: it is not a zero sum game and one interest or value does not seek to trump the other but rather seeks its rightful place in the context of the whole; a place which is "rightful" because it serves not only a particular value or interest but the values, interests, and goals of the whole. The basic constituents of the framework of existential a prioris remain the same (the fact that we have biological and social needs, seek to avoid suffering, share a basic sense of logic, and wish to live freely do not change) but the pattern into which the components of this framework are woven will be an ever-changing whole and will differ depending upon time, circumstance, and material condition.

A good symphony orchestra consists of many instruments, each of which seeks to be heard. But if an instrument is to be effectively heard, it must be heard in the context of and balanced by all others. Only thus can it achieve its full effect. When, as sometimes unfortunately happens, one instrument or group of instruments predominates, when one instrument seeks to drown out the other in an attempt to assert itself, a bad performance and one in which not even the predominant instrument or group of instruments is heard to its best advantage, results. When orchestras continue to perform in such a way, not only is music not done justice but the survival of the orchestra and the role of each individual instrument within the orchestra is jeopardized. Each conductor, furthermore, will interpret the specific role of each instrument differently, giving more emphasis here or more emphasis there. A great symphony orchestra conducted by a great conductor will interpret a given piece of work quite differently from the way another orchestra with another equally great conductor might render it; in fact, interpretations, even when given by the same conductor with the same orchestra but at a different time, will vary from each other. Instruments and tonalities, to fit the particular mood and circumstance, will never be managed precisely the same. A Beethoven symphony performed by the Cleveland Orchestra and conducted by George Szell will be quite different from the same symphony conducted by von Karajan and a Berlin Philharmonic performance of a Beethoven symphony conducted by von Karajan in 1960 will be different from one done by the same group of performers some years later. One is not better than another; they are, to fit mood, setting, and circumstance, different. A concerto is not—if it is to be well done—a competition between soloist and orchestra: it is a smooth blending of all the forces to serve a greater goal. Whenever more than a single person is involved in a performance, it is not only the performance of each individual but the cooperative and smooth interaction of all which makes a good performance good and a great performance superb.

When we come to craft an ethic, when we come to try to create some content within our inevitable human framework of a prioris, we must do so in view of existing and perhaps today rather altered circumstances. Hans Jonas in his "Prinzip Verantwortung" ("The Imperative of Responsibility") suggests that the capacities of modern technology have changed ethics itself.[12] In former times, scientific and technical advances were slow to appear and change proceeded at a leisurely pace. Today that is not the case: while, because of our technical tools, the future has become more readily predictable in one sense, it has, because of the rapidity of change, become much more difficult if not impossible to predict in another. The only thing we can be certain of is that tomorrow will be almost unrecognizably different from today.

Furthermore, scientific advances and the technology which follows may not only have highly and as often as not unforeseen undesirable consequences but these consequences may devastate not merely a few persons or a small region but being itself. And, for Jonas, being is the first and necessary condition for all else and, therefore, its preservation becomes an ethical imperative. Being, as an imperative, is not something which needs to be argued for: the imperative of being is deeply within the marrow of all living things and, therefore, the question "why should I strive to be" or "why should we as humans have an obligation to exist" (or at least not to extinguish ourselves) is, at least in a biological sense, incoherent. If we agree that while ethics cannot be reduced to biology, biology nevertheless inevitably forms the necessary framework for ethics, the connection with ethics is made.

Such considerations (the primacy of being, scientific and technical possibilities and the uncertainty of the future) lead Professor Jonas to formulate what he calls the imperative of responsibility: "Handele so, dasz auch in Zukunft noch verantwortliches Handeln möglich ist" (act so that the capacity for responsible action is also preserved in the future).[13] His concern is that human actions today should not preclude the possibility of human actions tomorrow, that we do not, for the sake of a short range and immediate good obliterate the possibility of future existence. Jonas admits that there is nothing intrinsically illogical in choosing immediate satisfaction over long-range existence. Such a choice—a choice which risks permanence for the sake of a temporary advantage—may be a logically possible choice for an individual: I may choose to risk my future life for the sake of an immediate satisfaction or pleasure. But that is quite another thing than choosing my immediate satisfaction or pleasure at the risk of future others. We may, it is true, choose our own destruction but we are not equally free to choose the destruction of others and even less to choose the destruction of the conditions which make it possible for others to exist.

Professor Jonas is not as much concerned with the bringing about of "good"—with creating an ethic of progress through the harnessing of human knowledge and skill—as he is with the prevention of harm. This, from the perspective of his own life experience should not be surprising: having escaped from the hell of Hitlerism and seen the perversion of what was once conceived as "progress," his basic concern about, above all, preventing harm is easy to understand. Not unjustifiably, Professor Jonas feels that many scientific, technical and perhaps social "advances" run a heavy risk of jeopardizing the future itself. Therefore, he feels, scientific, technical, and perhaps social advances need to be evaluated pessimistically: the negative or possibly negative consequences of technical developments need to be considered as more important than the positive or possibly positive ones. The possible danger of such an "advance" should be given a heavier weight than the possible good the advance might bring about.

This basically conservative attitude would place a much higher value on not bringing about any harm than it would on producing good. All things considered, however, such an attitude would favor the maintenance of the status quo. Professor Jonas' pessimism about advances and progress goes further: the question to Jonas is how, in a world in which the concept of the Holy has been thoroughly discredited by science, an ethic which controls the effects of scientific and technical advances is possible. For Jonas, only theology (which has lost much of its force) can give a true fundament to responsible action.

From this basically pessimistic philosophy (I have sometimes, tongue in cheek, called it "logical negativism") a quite different world-view than the libertarian emerges. It is a world-view which certainly opposes the notion of "freedom as a side-constraint" and, in a way, puts "being as a side constraint" in its place. But this philosophy too, since it views the possibility of creating a binding ethic outside of theology skeptically, leaves us little with which to dialogue. Basically Engelhardt and Jonas might agree that religion has been discredited and they even might come close to agreeing that reason, or at least reason alone, has also. One (Jonas) is skeptical of creating any sense of responsibility for each other outside theology; the other (Engelhardt) denies that any responsibility, other than that of respecting each others freedom, can be agreed upon at all. I certainly agree with part of Professor Jonas' thesis. In a world in which the advances and consequent power of technology have outstripped advances in human understanding, technology poses a grave risk. Disregarding the effect our advances may have in the long run is neither prudent nor ethically defensible. The importance of preserving being (I have termed it "prior worth" and discussed it in past chapters) in any ethic seems self-evident: without being, there can be no ethic. "Handele so, dasz auch in Zukunft noch verantwortliches Handeln möglich ist" ("act so that the capacity for responsible action is also preserved in the future") is an essential imperative if tomorrow and with it human possibility including the possibility of having an ethic are to be preserved. There can be no ethic if there are none to share it. Those who would argue that strict logic and deductive reasoning cannot prove such a proposition are probably correct. But they presume two things: (1) that only deductive reasoning and logic, rather than a whole host of other methods, can prove propositions; and (2) that proof is something absolute and not merely sufficient to warrant action and to serve as a basis for further improvement and learning. In a sense, those who would insist that only strict logic and deductive reasoning can be compelling, insist on absolute truth before proceeding to act. With Dewey, I would claim that truth is not an absolute but is itself a tentative proposition which we can use to act and which, furthermore, will serve us as a starting point for further improving and refining.

Further, I agree with Professor Jonas (who would not, the evidence is all around us!) that scientific and technological advances have caused our future to be both more and less predictable. Our future is not only unpredictable in terms of our scientific possibilities: it is likewise, and perhaps even more importantly, unpredictable in a social sense. To a large part, this social change and attendant uncertainty are the result of our technical possibilities. This state of affairs has given a new dimension to all of our acting, has as Professor Jonas argues, given knowledge itself a moral dimension. Immediate communication, as well as rapid travel, has brought with it ever-growing economic interdependence; permanently comatose persons who formerly would have peacefully died at home now linger on in nursing homes. Social customs, which formerly changed slowly and which were predictable from generation to generation, change rapidly and drastically. While in one sense different cultures know and understand more about each other than they ever have before and while we have become far more interdependent, we have paradoxically and at the same time become more alienated and, therefore, more isolated from our immediate family and neighbors.

I agree with both Professor Jonas and Professor Engelhardt that religion has been discredited as a method of creating a contentful ethic which can unite disparate belief systems. I believe that the concept of the Holy (especially the concept of a specific Holy) is a concept which in a pluralist and largely secular world can, if it ever could, no longer be relied upon and that, depending of course how we define it (see below), it is a concept we may perhaps not need. The sense of the Holy (or, as I would prefer to call it, and I think it is the same thing, a sense of awe) is a sense of something greater than our own individual self and our own individual fate. Like any other sense or feeling it is not rational (I do not claim that it is irrational but that it originates in other than purely rational ways) but is composed of a number of components among which are emotional as well as aesthetic factors. Such a sense of the Holy (or of awe) like all else occurs within a framework of our existential a prioris which shape (but do not determine) the way we think, feel and appreciate. When Kant speaks of the sense of awe which he feels when contemplating "the stars above and the moral law below" he is suggesting a definition which derives from both rational and aesthetic considerations.

The concept of the Holy, then, can be seen as merely the product of a parochial belief in a particular religious faith; it can be seen as a feeling common to religiosity in its broadest sense which I would argue includes aesthetic feelings; or it can be seen as a transcendental feeling of shared humanity. Such a transcendental feeling of shared humanity may emerge from a realization of our shared interests and shared human condition: from the realization that we are all in the same boat and that we, together, have the obligation to steer it. The sense of awe (or the sense of the Holy) may be brought about by any or all of these. At its best, the concept or sense of the Holy (or the sense of awe) is a transcendental feeling of shared humanity and of a sense of beauty: it is a concept we not only need but one which emerges from aesthetics and from a realization of our shared interests and condition; at worst, this sense of the Holy is a parochial belief in a particular authority or faith which is beyond reason. Professor Jonas may—although I am not sure—mean by what he calls the sense of the Holy a transcendental feeling composed of aesthetics and a sense of our shared humanity: he may mean our feeling of something greater than us or our merely material condition. Such a sense of the Holy is, of course, quite a different thing than such a sense in a narrower parochial sense: a sense which does not transcend but is limited to a particular religious belief form. Bemoaning the loss of the one is quite a different thing from bemoaning the loss of the other.

By bemoaning the loss of the sense of the Holy, Professor Jonas may be bemoaning the fact that we often seem to have traded in a sense of awe (awe for something outside and transcending us, whatever that something may be) for an entirely egocentric and individualistic world-view. And most of us would agree that trading in this sense of the Holy or this sense of awe has ultimately not served us well. In any case, the sense of the Holy necessarily has an emotive and aesthetic quality which is beyond rational explication: some will get this sense of the Holy or of awe in attending mass, others in listening to Mozart. These different ways of experiencing this sense of the Holy or of awe do not discredit it for the particular person: indeed, for the individual, such a sense may serve to elevate them above the mundane and help them deal with life and the problems life brings. But the sense of the Holy I perceive or the sense of awe I experience when listening to the Exultate Jubilatum or to Beethoven's Ninth does not necessarily connect with the sense of the Holy another perceives in Church, Temple, or Mosque. Those of us who experience this sense of the Holy listening to Mozart and those who experience it at religious services both experience awe and a sense of the Holy. For both of us it is a feeling but it is a feeling we cannot hope to share across different aesthetic, religious, and cultural viewpoints and experiences: we can, however, realize that as humans we have the capacity for such feelings, that only compassionate rationality can help us understand and evaluate them and that we must respect and celebrate this feeling and its various ways of expressing itself in others as well as in ourselves. As with all feelings, this sense of the Holy (or this sense of awe) can be a force which stimulates our attempt to understand and find common ground with others or this sense of the Holy can be allowed to dominate us. After all, the sense of the Holy (or the sense of awe) relates to a given situation. In a sense, it is a symbol of such a situation. Symbols are the epiphenomena of a reality for which they stand and as such have great value in our daily lives and discourse. When, however, the symbol becomes more important than the reality for which it stand (when the religious symbol is more important than the religion itself or the flag is valued more than the country for which it stands) a dangerous transmutation of sentiment to sentimentality occurs. Likewise, a sense of awe (or of the Holy) when not controlled by reason can have dangerous consequences.

What Professor Jonas calls our sense of the Holy and what I have called our sense of awe does not, as I have mentioned, need to be conceived in a religious sense. When Kant speaks of the sense of awe he feels when "gazing at the starry sky outside me or the moral law inside me" or when I speak of a sense of awe in listening to the Exultate Jubilatum, walking in an alpine meadow looking at the grandeur before me or trying to conceive of how we as humans could live together for a common goal, religion, in the sense it is commonly used, may or may not play a part. In a sense the difference is the difference between religiosity and spirituality: and these two concepts are by no means necessarily associated with one another. Amour de soi même (which I have translated as regard for oneself) is entirely compatible with a sense of awe; indeed, I am not sure that if we lacked this necessary sense of ourselves and of our connectedness with others that a real sense of awe could emerge. Amour-propre (or self-love) on the other hand, is a pathological self-love: a sense of self-regard which has become self-love by being atomistic and asocial. Since self-love sees little which does not serve its own immediate interests as important, the sense of awe is stifled or in its most pathological and narcissistic sense only evoked by thoughts of one-self. When we insist that we can know nothing about each other except that we all want to pursue our own interests and ends in our own way, we have created a world in which amour-propre has become accepted and acknowledged not only as morally acceptable but even as morally foundational. Rousseau has, rightly I think, felt that as society ultimately creates morality, society also creates the soil in which amour de soi même is readily transmuted to amour-propre. A mutually reinforcing situation is created: in denying our human connectedness (beyond the fact that we all seek to live freely) and in denying our mutual human responsibility (beyond that of respecting each other's freedom), the proper atmosphere for nurturing self-love is created; as self-love begins to become the general condition of many members of an association, the idea of asocial, atomistic moral strangers gains a wider foothold. It is not surprising that in a state in which crass individualism is not only a highly held but a central value self-love is prevalent and the sense of awe, however produced, disappears.

Perhaps I am a throwback to the enlightenment but I still believe that reason can and will enable persons of good will (or persons who understand that their own personal fate is dependent upon peace—not the same thing) to forge an at least partly contentful and partly satisfying ethic. Realizing our human interconnections and utilizing the framework of what I have called the existential a prioris and searching with compassionate rationality for common ways of solving our problems would, I believe, serve to substitute for the religious sense of the Holy which Professor Jonas (rightly, I think) says is lost. But in realizing this vast interconnection and in sensing our common heritage and interests, a different sense of awe may develop.

While I agree that knowledge itself has moral force (and I am not at all sure that this has not always been the case) and while I am afraid of rampant technology and rampant science, I find it difficult to be as pessimistic as Professor Jonas is. Rather than evaluating scientific and perhaps social advances with extreme pessimism, I think that we need to evaluate them with a great deal of caution. While the negative or possibly negative consequences of technical developments need to be very carefully considered and weighed, they do not necessarily outweigh positive ones. All progress, all innovation, and all change carries within it the seed of risk. The fact that there is risk should not in and of itself have veto power: all risk is not alike just as all positive consequences are not alike. To risk destruction is quite a different thing than to risk some lesser and controllable or reversible form of misadventure. Our decision to go forward with change would, I think, depend on context and need, on a calculus of risk and benefit. We cannot stop new knowledge and advance until every possible objection of risk has been clarified: in the nature of things we can never reach an absolute answer but can only make a situation more determinate in its connections, relations, and consequences. Waiting for certainty condemns us to wait eternally and while that is possible doing so condemns us to stagnation or retrogression. What we can do is to proceed cautiously, tentatively, and thoughtfully: in other words, we can and must institute checks and safeguards throughout development and application of new knowledge, new science, new technology, and new sociology. But we can neither expect certainty nor wait for complete clarification of all possible consequences before proceeding. If we do, all progress stops and, inevitably, decay sets in.

One of Professor Jonas' points—a point which at first blush seems almost diametrically opposed to the rest of his thesis—is that having hope, being optimistic and working towards a better (or at least towards a no worse) future is a moral obligation. Although he himself is hardly an optimist, Jonas (and I think rightly) argues that without this hope or optimism, and without the consequent work that such a view obliges us to, no chance at all for human survival or ultimate improvement might be possible. If one accepts Professor Jonas' imperative "act so that the capacity for responsible action is also preserved in the future" as categorical, than having (or acting with) hope is a maxim which necessarily follows.

Fear of starting down a slippery slope where one thing may lead to another until what starts out as acceptable or even as desirable becomes disastrous often motivates our reluctance to innovate, experiment, or bring about change. The argument of the slippery slope, however, also depends on the particulars of the situation and context. Just because something is a slippery slope does not in and of itself mean that we cannot proceed: it means that caution is indicated. In real life, when slopes are slippery we proceed with caution and put down sand; when they threaten to be too slippery (at what admittedly is an arbitrary point) we erect barriers and only then stop proceeding. The presence of a slippery slope counsels caution: we proceed carefully, take appropriate precautions and are aware of danger.

Of course, the problem of modifying and controlling knowledge and technical advance or the problem of putting down sand or erecting barriers brings up the question of who is to control. Uncontrolled seeking after knowledge seems dangerous: attempting to create a weapon which could destroy the earth or seeking to produce an extremely virulent and universally fatal microorganism completely resistant to all known antimicrobials are both pieces of knowledge most of us would oppose having. But dangerous as it may be, most knowledge, most scientific or technical advance is not as drastic as that. We must be quite clear as to what we are about: when we speak of "control," we ultimately speak of some form of censorship. And censorship implies a body with the power to censor. That, throughout history, has not exactly been without danger and has, in fact, often been done in the name of a specific sense of the Holy.

Just as the moral rules we follow can be external (heteronomous) or internal (homonymous) in origin, censorship—for that is what we are talking about when we talk about control—can be internal or external. We, as adults, learn to set our own framework, lead our own lives, make our own rules, and take our own responsibility for our actions. In a viable democracy with a sturdy sense of a general will and which aims both to live communally and to respect individual aspirations the rules we live by will be set by such a process. If just rules are to be set by meaningful democratic political process, political democracy must be underwritten by economic, educational, and personal democracy. Such rules are necessarily rules which, in a sense, limit some of our personal freedom so as to enable all of us ultimately to lead fuller, freer, and more fulfilling lives. In that they interfere with completely free expression and action, such rules limit our choices. But such limiting is not arbitrary and is done by a democratically decided process and through and by the consent of the members of the community. It is a far different thing than the burning of books or the censoring of free speech by an arbitrary state. When our freedoms are hedged in a true democracy, they are hedged by due process and through the will of a well-informed, well-educated, and participatory electorate: they are an expression of a well formulated general will. Only such a process and such a general will can ultimately safeguard the future itself.

How, then, do we begin to formulate our ethics? As with all else, the first step would seem to be a definition and a recognition of the particular conditions of action as well as an understanding of the available raw materials. Once that is firmly understood, available tools must be examined and, if need be, constructed.

The way one defines ethics—whether as something "discovered" or something "crafted," whether purely rational or, and to what extent, partly empirical—in many respects determines the way we look at the resulting ethical precepts and principles. Those who cling to the idea of a discovered and purely rational ethic will tend to see precepts and principles as immutable; those who think otherwise will see precepts and principles as tentative guideposts, prima facie but not absolutely and unchangingly binding. Kant tended to the first view: to Kant morality was discoverable, rational, and immutable. It was anything but a social construct. Although tacitly understood by what Kant calls the common man, it was purely a product of logical reasoning:

> Philosophy which mixes pure principles with empirical ones does not deserve the name, for what distinguishes philosophy from common rational knowledge is its treatment in separate sciences of what is confusedly comprehended in such knowledge. Much less does it deserve the name of moral philosophy, since by this confusion it spoils the purity of moral themselves and works contrary to its own end.[14]

It is unclear at what level empirical information is accepted: certainly not only does Kant inevitably perceive the problems he perceives through the windows of experience but likewise he certainly derives his examples from that world. What Kant was after, was a search for the one highest principle of morality to which all others must conform:

> The present foundations, are nothing more than the search for and establishment of the supreme principle of morality. This constitutes a task altogether complete in its intention and one which should be kept separate from all other moral inquiry.[15]

This "supreme principle" Kant believes to have discovered in his various formulations of the Categorical Imperative on which universalization, respect for persons, and ultimately various maxims depend. If such maxims conform to the categorical imperative they are, according to Kant, unable to conflict with each other. That, in real life they in fact readily do, does not invitiate Kant's moral view; it does suggest that useful as his conclusions are, they can be used only insofar as they are found adaptable to real-life situations and problems. There is no doubt that the universalization of rules (that what I consider morally permissible for myself under a set of given circumstances cannot, under the same set of circumstances, be considered as morally impermissible for another) is logically compelling, indeed that it is part of our basic logical framework. But as such it becomes a tool helping further inquiry and not an immutable stumbling block beyond which, somehow, further inquiry ends. Here is not the place to carry such an argument, interesting as it may be, further. What I want to demonstrate throughout this work is that despite the diversity of sources from which moral rules are seen to be derived, the basic rules in the real world ultimately do not greatly differ. I would argue that this, in good measure, is because our framework of reasoning inevitably derives from the same bio-psycho-social reality which all sentient beings share and which, in that sense, is universal.

Ethics, as understood here and as I began to discuss in a previous chapter, is considered to be crafted by humans and is meant to help enrich and support the lives of all. As stated before, it can be seen as the application of compassionate rationality to our choice of options and actions insofar as they affect others. It is understood as an activity like any other human activity and one which, to be viable, must be tested in experience. If it is not, a purely formal and sterile ethic which does not connect with everyday experience and which is, therefore, not useful in enriching and supporting the lives of all can result: and such an ethic, being unrealistic, is likely to be (and is likely to deserve to be) ignored. What, then, is ethics in the sense in which I have and shall continue to use it? Perhaps one of the best explanations can be found in Dewey's Ethics:

> Ethics is the science that deals with conduct, insofar as this is considered as right or wrong, good or bad. . . . Another way of stating the same thing is to say that Ethics aims to give a systematic account of our judgments about conduct, insofar as these estimate it from the standpoint of right or wrong, good or bad.

> Moral life is called out or stimulated by certain necessities of individual and social existence. As Protagoras put it, in mythical form, the gods gave men a sense of justice and a sense of reverence, in order to enable them to unite for mutual preservation. And in turn the moral life aims to modify or transform both natural and social environments, to build a "kingdom of man" which shall also be an ideal social order—a "kingdom of God." These relations to nature and society are studied by the biological and social sciences. Sociology, economics, poli-

tics, law and jurisprudence deal particularly with this aspect of conduct. Ethics must employ their methods and results for this aspect of its problem, as it employs psychology for the examination of conduct on its inner side.

But ethics is not merely the sum of these various sciences. . . . It has to study the inner process as determined by the outer conditions or as changing these outer conditions, and the outward behavior or institution as determined by the inner purpose or as affecting the inner life. To study choice and purpose is psychology; to study choice as affected by the rights of others and to judge it as right or wrong by this standard is ethics.[16]

Rawls, although in many ways he seems to have a more "fixed" and Kantian notion of ethics, sees, not unlike Dewey, moral philosophy (or at least justice—he does not really extensively deal with morality in other ways) as emerging from intelligent and informed dialogue.

Moral philosophy is Socratic: we may change our considered judgment once their regulative principles are brought to light. And we may wish to do this even though these principles are a perfect fit. A knowledge of these principles may suggest further reflections that lead us to revise our moral judgments.[17]

To Dewey as to Rawls, ethics is constructed rather than discovered by humans but to Dewey it is more emphatically something crafted in a particular social setting. To Rawls such a dialogue is more an internal dialogue, a dialogue I would have with myself, rather than a necessarily social dialogue. Crafting an ethic (at least crafting our vision of justice) depends upon what Rawls calls "reflective equilibrium." Reflective equilibrium is a consideration of all the various convictions, principles and past particular judgments (all of which may have initial credibility) which can be brought to bear on a given problem, question or situation.

how well the view as a whole articulates our more firm considered convictions of political justice at all levels of generality, after due examination, once all adjustments and revisions that seem compelling have been made.[18]

To Rawls, as distinct from Dewey, this is a far more individualistic than it is a social task. Observers are outside that which they are observing rather than becoming a part of it. The veil of ignorance, useful as it is at times as a heuristic device, is only one of many examples of this type of individualist conception. Prudent individual choosers are placed behind a veil of ignorance in which they know nothing about themselves or about their society except that they understand their own needs and understand the opportunities society may offer. In this condition they are to make choices which then would become choices for all. The assumption is that all prudent, rational choosers acting for themselves alone and not in concert with each other would, under such circumstances, make substantially the same choice.

But for both Rawls and Dewey, ethics is here to serve man, not man to serve an immutable and somehow revealed and absolute ethic: precepts, principles, and rules are not so much something to which, almost in blind obedience, one must, once one has "discovered" them, conform as they are critically important but not immutable guideposts on the road to further inquiry. Shaping an ethic which can guide our lives and help chart our destiny is something we, as humans engaged in the common experience of living together, must participate in shaping, testing, and adapting. As a human activity which affects all of us, this activity is social: that is, if an ethic all can find helpful is to emerge, all who have the capacity to do so must be involved in shaping it and must contribute. Here, again, we have the idea of democracy, not in its political but in its moral aspect. Dewey, once again, states this rather succinctly:

> Externally viewed, democracy is a piece of machinery to be maintained or thrown away, like any other piece of machinery, on the basis of its economy and efficiency of working. Morally, it is the effective embodiment of the moral idea of the good which consists in the development of all the social capacities of every individual member of society.[19]

Since the existential a prioris I have enumerated form the framework for all we think and rationally undertake to do, they are involved in determining moral action. The way such a framework is seen or used will, to a large extent, depend upon the way a given society has structured itself. In a society in which libertarian principles and a minimalist ethic predominate, the wealthy and powerful have every opportunity to consolidate their power at the expense of the weaker. The weak and poor, despite their theoretically equal access to the physical and social necessities of life, will, under ordinary circumstances and without resort to force, be unable to consolidate their power. The poor and the weak, deprived of sufficient access to material and social necessities, may suffer but since their suffering is not seen as the direct result of another's action no one can be held responsible to ameliorate it. In such a society lack of power, lack of real opportunity for education (or health care) and a sense of hopelessness combine to produce a spiral in which the weak continue to be disadvantaged while the powerful continue to be free to exploit the situation.

When society structures itself on a minimalist (or close to minimalist) model and rules itself by an alleged political democracy which is not undergirded by economic, social and moral democracy de facto control by the powerful and wealthy is assured. In such circumstances the disadvantaged will perceive that conditions as they exist have rendered them virtually impotent. At first such a situation will lead to disaffection and indifference: to a feeling that what one does or how one votes matters little. As time goes on and especially as the poor are inevitably confronted with the life style and opportunities of those who are well-off, frustration is bound to lead to violence and upheaval. If it is to work politically, a truly democratic process in which all participate and in which mutual respect reigns must be based on true democracy in a much wider social sense. Democracy must be personal as well as educational and social and it should properly touch and modify every aspect of our daily lives. And, of course, economic or what Dewey calls industrial democracy must, if political democracy is to have substance, undergird it.

Democracy as a moral and not merely as a political ideal, consists in mutual respect for each other's diversity as well as in a search for commonalties which allow us to build bridges across our diversity. It is not a tyranny of the majority nor the freedom of every member to go his or her own way. Basic to democratic process is an agreement upon the process which is followed to make choices and an abiding belief that humans, when certain conditions are met, are capable of regulating their own and their community's lives. And part of such a contract is that individuals within a democratic society shall be willing to obey the rules made by a process they themselves had a role in shaping. If that is construed as coercion, it is a form of coercion all who had a fair opportunity to participate in the process of crafting the rules and of agreeing to the process by which rules and sanctions are decided, agreed to. I may not agree with being taxed for the benefit of a given communal enterprise: but as a member of a society in which I was given full opportunity to participate not only in crafting particular laws but also able to participate in developing the process by which valid laws were made, I am compelled to obey or be compelled to accept the consequences.

A belief in democratic process and the capacity of ordinary men and women to regulate their own and their community's lives is not a utopian ideal as long as the preconditions necessary for such a process are met. Having democracy as part of the moral life—indeed as one of its necessary foundations—implies that we are willing and able to grapple with problems which concern all of us by engaging in intelligent dialogue with others who may be of a different background or opinion. This is true whether democracy is seen as playing a dominant role in personal, educational, industrial, economic, political, or other social relationships.

Effective dialogue and through dialogue democracy can be seen as an intellectual homeostatic process in which the various forces (points of view, opinions, interests, beliefs, and world views) interact so as to deal with the problem at hand and to pursue a common goal. Homeostasis, in this point of view, operates no differently in the social than it would in the physiological or ecological setting. To reiterate: homeostasis is conceived as a dynamic equilibrium between various forces each of which seeks to maintain balance and each of which can continue only within the context of the whole. There has to be a healthy balancing of these various interests: healthy, because all are aware that their own particular interest can only survive and flourish in a setting in which the general good has been served. When one interest "swamps" instead of accommodates to another it is a pyrrhic victory: the basis for expressing that interest is destroyed in its victory.

In such a homeostatic process, democratic coexistence and dialogue on the one hand become a means towards promoting stability while seeking peaceful progress; on the other hand, democratic coexistence and dialogue become one of the ends towards which peaceful progress strives. This dynamic and yet stable process creates communal solidarity and underwrites survival and evolution. To be effective (that is, to accomplish a peaceful solution and deal effectively with the diverse problems persons, cultures and, ultimately, the world community face or faces), such dialogue must be carried on among persons of good will who are well-motivated and well-equipped to carry on such a dialogue: that is it must occur among persons willing to follow the processes and obey the laws they themselves have shaped and are in the process of shaping. Such a dialogue, held by humans with other humans who all share the same framework of existential a prioris and who share both an innate sense of compassion and a healthy drive for self-preservation, cannot hope to "solve" all problems it confronts or to build a universally satisfactory and complete ethic. However, it can hope to accomplish: (1) a general agreement on some broad ethical precepts, principles, and rules beyond merely mutual non-harm; (2) an ongoing search for ever broader areas of agreement and for a fleshing out of a more contentful common ethic; and (3) a delineation of those ethical precepts, principles, and rules which at least at present seem to lack a common solution and which would, therefore, be left to individual (be it personal or corporate individual) choice. In the process of such a dialogue persons will inevitably come to understand each other better: the process itself helps to engender trust and enables further dialogue. Thus, in a sense, such a dialogue is self-energizing and self-perpetuating.

To illustrate: broad principles or precepts which may easily find agreement, for example, may be (1) an understanding that all of us are united by a common framework of needs, interests, and capacities; (2) the necessity of keeping the peace, maintaining mutual respect, and utilizing an agreed upon process for resolving problems; and (3) the desirability of assuring full access to the basic biological and social necessities we all have and all know we have. As time goes on and further dialogue develops, such broad understandings can be deepened and fleshed out. A more contentful ethics will gradually emerge and gradually be adapted to changing conditions of life. At the same time, some specific issues—commonly those associated with particular customs or belief systems—will be seen as not amenable to such agreement. Mutual respect, tolerance, the necessity to keep the peace, and utilize agreed upon process as well as maintenance of a sense of humor will lead us to leave such issues, at least for the time being, unresolved and up to individual conscience and determination. As the process of working within the framework of these existential a prioris continues and as democratic coexistence and dialogue and, therewith, mutual trust becomes habitual, areas which at first seemed refractory may become amenable to resolution.

Thus far I have tried to show that what I call the existential a priori of ethics are the inevitable and necessary conditions in which all our activities must take place. At the same time, I have taken care to show that these activities, while they inevitably occur within such a framework, cannot be reduced to it. I have introduced the idea that compassionate rationality through these conditions, and through acknowledging that these conditions are our common lot, can sufficiently unite us so that we can profitably engage in democratically constituted dialogue and begin to formulate a more contentful ethic than libertarians would suggest. In doing this I have suggested that the various components of such a framework are homeostatically related and have stressed the importance of democratic dialogue which, I believe, constitutes an intellectual variation of homeostatic process. Moreover, our willingness and ability to engage in such a democratic dialogue—rather than our merely shrugging our shoulder and pretending that, beyond knowing that we all want to be left to pursue our own path, we have no common framework of mutual understanding—are the conditions necessary to ultimately achieving common solutions. I have suggested that unless democracy is seen more broadly than merely as political—unless political democracy is underpinned by other forms of personal and social democratic life—democracy as a political system and as a political ideal becomes unworkable and, indeed, self-defeating.

Willingness to engage in dialogue, however, is hardly enough. To engage in meaningful dialogue denotes the meeting of some preconditions. Dialogue requires that our biological framework is not in jeopardy: persons whose very existence is threatened, persons whose access to their biological or social needs is blocked or persons who are suffering, who are acting illogically or who have their freedom constrained by forces beyond their control cannot engage in the kind of meaningful mutual dialogue likely to bear fruit. The framework of existential a prioris in and through which we engage in dialogue must be intact for all of us before meaningful democracy can exist.

Those who are most skeptical about democratic process often point to the United States. The United States—the self-advertised "leading democracy" and often (especially by itself) held up as an example for all—is hardly an example of untarnished success. Poverty, homelessness, lack of education, and downright despair are rampant and actual, as well as functional, illiteracy is at an appalling level (a level far higher than in any other industrialized nation and far higher even than in many nations we consider "backwards"). The United States—even if it will not admit it—is hardly in a position to serve as "a light onto the nations." For this state of affairs, unfortunately, democracy often gets the blame: after all, the United States allegedly has a well-functioning political democracy: polls are honest, the choice of the voters is uncontested, and more and more all qualified voters regardless of race, creed, or sex are entitled to vote and hold office. What more could one ask?

Although much is spoken and written about democracy in the United States (and although the skeptics or opponents of democracy point at the United States to buttress their arguments) one can draw far different conclusions from current conditions in the United States. I would argue that, as things stand today, and while technically speaking political democracy functions, true democracy does not and under present conditions cannot flourish nor even exist. America, as it is today, may have the mechanics of political democracy but it lacks the necessary underpinnings to make political democracy truly functional.

To function well, political democracy must have several preconditions met. Individual liberty and the freedom to make political choices at the very least presupposes that satisfying the framework of conditions and interests which all individuals share is not neglected. Our interest in living freely can meaningfully exist only when the preconditions prior to it are met. To have an interest at all, we need to be alive, need to have our biological and social needs at least minimally secured, cannot be severely suffering, and must be able to think logically; to lead a meaningful life necessitates that we are given reasonable opportunity to live freely so as to develop our own interests and talents. If, behind a veil of Rawlsian ignorance we were given the opportunity to choose all but one from among having our biological and social needs met, not having to suffer unduly, having the capacity for basic logical thinking, and having personal freedom most prudent choosers would probably regretfully do without freedom. The freedom to starve to death when one wishes to live, the freedom to freeze when one would rather be warm, or the freedom to remain ignorant when one would wish to be educated is not freedom but the sort of cynicism which removes the preconditions necessary for real freedom to exist. To the hungry the freedom to assemble is considerably less meaningful than is a loaf of bread; to the functionally illiterate or to those unable to obtain health care when ill, freedom to make political choices runs a poor second; to those who suffer, their suffering subdues all other interests; and those unequipped with basic logical thinking cannot properly choose at all. Our ability to make our lives meaningful, beyond the luck of being or not being endowed with certain innate abilities, depends either upon power (in its various forms), adequate communal support, or sheer luck.

Political democracy, then, presupposes that adequate material resources as well as adequate and equitable social opportunities are available to all members of the community. When our value for freedom is entirely out of proportion to our value for other components of our bio-psycho-social framework, freedom itself suffers and ultimately can exist only for those in power. Freedom without access to basic material resources and social opportunities cannot lead to a properly functioning democratic society. In such circumstances political democracy lacks the necessary support of other social forms of democracy.

When societies give preponderant value to one of the components of our bio-psycho-social framework, the others necessarily will be shortchanged. If one sees the components of such a framework as having a homeostatic relationship in which balance among them serves to advance all interests, a strong preponderance of one interest or value at the expense of others distorts such a balance. Variations in valuing will, of course, occur: some societies will define the components and acknowledge what is and what is not adequate for each differently. But they cannot so overvalue one and undervalue another that some vital bio-psycho-social interests or conditions go begging or remain entirely unfulfilled. The connection between and among our interests is intimate and mutually supportive. If ultimately the goal of survival, evolution, and growth for every person within a society as well as for the society as a whole is to be met, the necessary basis for every individual within it must be assured.

In crafting an ethic, we must be mindful of who we are crafting an ethic for: are we crafting an ethic for a "particular moral enclave," are we crafting an ethic to which all (or at least most) humans whatever their background can agree or are we crafting an ethic which permits various cultures and societies to co-exist? As interests and cultures diverge, specific ethical content will diminish. Engelhardt is undoubtedly right when he claims that no universal ethical view about things like abortion or euthanasia can be established and that when it comes to such specific issues mutual tolerance and respect are as far as we can hope to go. Indeed, an attempt to resolve all such issues and to create a uniform view about them would lead to a homogenized world, a world in which homeostatic tension was kept to a minimum and in which bland uniformity would reign. Not only would such a world be uninteresting, such a world would be apt to lack the drive for change and growth. But the fact that we cannot hope—nor should desire—to solve all or even most such problems, does not preclude the fact that we as individuals, as well as we as specific moral enclaves, we as cultures or societies and ultimately we as inhabitants of this globe can begin to forge an ethic in which some very basic things are mutually agreed upon.

I will leave some specific illustrations to the last chapter. Suffice it here to say that, driven by our innate sense of compassion and enabled by our common sense of logic, our common interests can serve as a basis for a dialogue carried on amongst us. Normal humans, whose sensitivity has not been blunted to indifference by societal forces, are concerned about the suffering of others. They not only recognize common needs and common interests but see their own thriving as necessarily occurring within a community of others which enables it. Likewise, humans are aware that some are far better off than others and that some fail to have even their most basic needs met. Moreover, they are aware that such inequities, while sometimes a result of what has been called the natural lottery, are intimately connected with the way societies have structured themselves and that obligations to other members of our community exist even when critical inequities are the result of the natural lottery. Without this understanding solidarity will not be firm and without solidarity society will be in jeopardy. They know that the powerful and wealthy (be they the powerful and wealthy within a nation or the powerful and wealthy among nations) have played their role in the exploitation of those (be they individuals or nations) who are powerless and poor. Such recognition may be hampered by a pathological individual or national self-love fostered by social forces which gain personal short-range advantage. But unless blinded by such self-love (be it the self-love of individuals who are unwilling to give up some of their opulent life style so that others can have minimal needs met or the self-love or chauvinism of nations unwilling to reduce their own bloated standard of living so as to help other nations who are in want) persons will at least agree that severe problems of critical inequity exist within and among nations. And they will—aware of our common human condition—recognize such a state of affairs as unfair and unjust and, therefore, as something at least undesirable and to be remedied.

Recognizing critical inequity as undesirable and assuming ethical responsibility for remedying such a state of affairs are, however, two quite different things. The fact that something is undesirable and the fact that some state of affairs arouses our compassion does not by itself translate into an obligation. Two further considerations, however, will lead one from a recognition that such inequity is undesirable and unfair to an admission of ethical responsibility.

The first is the realization that while we may not be responsible in the sense of culpability for having caused such a state of affairs we, who are well-off, continue inevitably to profit from the way society has structured itself. White American males, for example—whether they want to or not—profit daily from the disadvantaging of minorities and women. Not taking responsibility for remedying gross social inequity, therefore, makes us responsible in the sense of being culpable for the continuation of the very inequity from which we profit. The second reason for assuming responsibility is the very fact that gross inequity weakens and eventually destroys solidarity and, therefore, ultimately destroys the community which is the necessary condition for our individual existence. Community, as I have pointed out earlier, has prior worth: prior because it is the necessary condition for all else. Once having assumed responsibility for dealing with gross inequities, defining what are tolerable and intolerable inequities and deciding on ways of expeditiously righting the wrongs we recognize can be accomplished only through the democratic process and dialogue.

A dialogue of this sort, a dialogue which can bring us to agree on some basic precepts of mutual behavior and mutual assistance, presupposes democracy. It is a dialogue in which all concerned must participate on an equal footing. So that political democracy can function, educational, economic and, I would suggest, moral democracy must first be developed. Moral democracy, however, presupposes several things: while it presupposes respect for the moral view of others, it also implies that agreements made in free dialogue and with appropriate process are binding and enforceable. When a society decides that supporting the poor or helping those who have been disadvantaged to gain their rightful place in the sun is proper, individuals within the society who have had ample opportunity to be involved in the process must be willing to participate and to do their fair share.

These various forms of democracy—educational, economic, moral, and ultimately, political—are mutually interdependent. I have argued that political democracy unless undergirded by other forms of democracy cannot, in more than a merely technical sense, function properly. The relationship among the various forms of democracy is not linear: each is inevitably linked with and dependent upon the other. Without economic democracy so that the basic needs of all are met, educational democracy is meaningless: hungry and homeless students do not do well in school. And yet economic democracy without educational democracy is likewise empty: persons given ample access to biological needs but lacking education will accomplish little. Moral democracy, in turn, requires economic as well as educational democracy to be functional and, in turn, economic and educational democracy are linked with moral democracy. Political democracy finally enables and in turn is enabled by these other forms.

What is some of the basic content that an ethic, within the framework of the a prioris and driven by a sense of compassionate rationality, can provide? First of all, we can—and I think that logically we must—acknowledge that we have basic shared interests; secondly, we can agree to use logical process to enable dialogue; and thirdly, we can agree that when areas of apparently insoluble conflict appear, mutual respect and tolerance are warranted. Such agreement is fundamental and it is not impossible or even unlikely that we can readily achieve it. Beyond this, we can agree that as humans with shared interest and with compassionate rationality, we inevitably have an additional interest: we are not uninterested in the welfare of those who share this globe with us and, as creatures endowed with compassionate rationality, at least to some extent obligated to acknowledge and act upon this realization. Such a requirement is not far removed from Kant's "kingdom" or "realm of ends": as moral beings we are logically compelled to include the goals and ends of others amongst our own. Using democratic process we can begin to shape an ethic which enables our interdependent coexistence. If we agree to using democratic process politically and to grapple with our ethical problems, we are, when we can, logically compelled to create conditions which provide a fertile soil for political democracy.

Political and economic systems are not quite the same thing. Democracy is a political (and, I would argue, a moral) system and can be contrasted to other political systems; capitalism or socialism, on the other hand, are economic (and, I would argue, likewise moral) systems. While some political systems by virtue of having a more compatible worldview may be more readily linked with some economic systems, economic and political systems are far from identical. To equate, for example (as is almost invariably done in the United States today), democracy with capitalism or with a free market is equating not even apples and oranges but motorcars and houses. Capitalist systems have flourished in dictatorships and monarchies and socialist systems have occurred in democracies as well as in monarchies. The linkage between capitalism and democracy—a linkage made consistently by the American government and the media—is made for the sake of propaganda not for the sake of clarity. Indeed, philosophical and moral democracy and capitalism lack a common worldview: democracy necessarily sees the community as central to its existence and the education and welfare of the individual as intimately linked to its own prosperity; capitalism, on the other hand, sees the individual as central to its worldview and sees the education and ultimately the welfare of the individual as that person's own concern and responsibility.

The notion of democracy requires respect not only for individual dignity but, likewise, has community as its goal. Democratic cultures necessarily must value the existence of community because without it individual dignity and democracy are not possible. Likewise, such cultures—if they are to have a truly functioning political democracy—necessarily must see to it that political democracy is underwritten and embedded in educational, economic, and moral democracy. When such cultures pay lip service to democracy but do little to ameliorate poverty, provide full education or foster the mutual respect moral democracy demands, they ultimately make political democracy into a sham. Having a well-functioning political democracy is certainly not in the short-term interest (even though I would argue that it is essential to the long-term interest) of the powerful or well to do: having a readily manipulable electorate is. The economic system called socialism—not its Soviet caricature called Bolshevism—likewise has community as its goal. It is predicated on individual dignity as well as on a sense of communal interdependence and, therefore, fits very well into the notion of democracy. Indeed, some of the most enduringly democratic nations on earth have a socialist economy liberally admixed with the market. A socialist infrastructure which assures all members of the community ample access to basic biological as well as social needs, not only can coexist but in a larger sense can enable both political democracy and a well functioning capitalist market. It enables political democracy because it provides a climate in which economic, educational, and moral democracy can thrive; it supports a well-functioning market for providing goods beyond basic necessities by allowing the emergence of a large number of consumers who indeed are well enough off so that they are able to consume.

Throughout this book I have maintained that ethics is not something humans discover or that it is absolute. In shaping our lives we cannot expect to wait for certainty, regardless of whether such certainty is scientific, social, or moral. Nor can we expect to have any proposition absolutely proven before acting. Propositions—be they scientific, economic, social, or moral ones—are proven in praxis and adapted by and within the context of our daily lives. I have maintained that ethics is crafted by humans within and for the human condition and that, like everything else, ethics is altered by social forces. A shared framework of interests and capacities—what I have termed the existential a prioris—used with compassionate rationality and rational compassion, can even by democratic process never produce an entirely contentful ethic. But it can begin to shape some content and can begin to make all of our lives safer, richer, and more fulfilling.

What might the content of an ethic crafted in such a manner look like? I have stated before that such an ethic cannot in fact and so as to preserve the complexity and diversity which stimulates progress, be complete; but such an ethic can and ought to enable us to understand and, therefore, communicate and live with our individual and corporate neighbors for our common good. Our inborn sense of compassion—a sense shared by all normal members of the human family and a sense which, albeit perhaps to a lesser degree, many higher nonhuman animals share—will lead us to pay attention to our neighbor's interests and to include such interests in shaping our own course of action; our shared sense of compassion will motivate us to care about the interests of our neighbors; our understanding of the existential a prioris will enable us to start understanding what these interests are; and since only by mutually supporting such interests can true communal solidarity (without which a community cannot remain stable and survive) be achieved and maintained, our sense of self-preservation (distinct from our merely inward focused sense of self-love) will counsel us to regard such interests as part of our own. Communities as well as individuals who are (as all must be) interested in their own existence, their own development, and their own thriving will—out of a sense of compassion and with compassionate rationality—craft an ethic which promises more than merely noninterference with each other.

Within such a framework and with such tools, individuals and communities will, at the very least, feel compelled to address some fundamental ethical problems. If we view freedom as necessarily social, if we view freedom not as an absolute but as enunciated and vouchsafed within community, ethical rules and ways of procedure will go well beyond those merely meant to establish our personal and corporate freedoms. Such rules would try to assure that all have at least the minimal basic requirements for the satisfaction of their common interests met before allowing others to go far beyond.

Specifically, communities and individuals who truly value freedom (not only their own personal freedom but the idea of meaningful freedom available to all in a fair and equitable manner) would feel compelled to see to it that other individuals and persons in other social structures at the very least did not remain hungry, cold, or ignorant and that they would not go without basic health care as long as adequate resources to remedy such a situation existed. There is no doubt that in many nations today providing for the minimal needs of all would require a redistribution of individual as well as national wealth: for example, the 1 percent of the population in the United States which owns over 90 percent of all property would have to "tighten their belts" so that programs to achieve true opportunity (and, therefore, true freedom) for all could be achieved; and in a similar manner wealthier nations would have to play their part in ameliorating the state of affairs of their impoverished neighbors. The ethical understandings we have and the ethical rules we craft ride piggyback on our understanding of what it is we owe to personal and corporate others and of what we ultimately (since our personal as well as national existence depends upon the existence and, therefore, upon the viability of our community) we owe to ourselves. When all is said and done, the problems of abortion, euthanasia, or the eating of meat may, for the time being at least, have to be left to individual choice: a choice that is made within the framework of a particular culture and its evolving beliefs. Such issues would become the subjects of an ongoing dialogue which not only respects individual freedom and cherishes diversity but also tries to continue to deal with common ethical problems which confront us. Dealing with and even just talking about such issues requires the satisfaction of prior needs and the existence of a framework of understanding and mutual respect which will allow us to draw closer together and will ultimately determine how these other issues will or will not be dealt with. I leave the illustration of some of these specifics to the next chapter.

5 Summing Up: Problems and Approaches

In past chapters, I first reviewed and then went beyond and expanded some of my prior work in which I suggest that the capacity to suffer is at least one of the markers which gives an entity prima facie, albeit not absolute, moral standing. In short, I have suggested that entities which have the capacity to suffer have primary moral worth and other entities, depending on their being valued by those of primary worth, have secondary worth. Additionally, the notion of prior moral worth was developed: the notion that being, nature, and community themselves have fundamental worth because they are the necessary conditions for any possible valuing.

To deal with the concept of obligation, it is necessary to be clear about the nature of moral standing: what entities, in a moral sense, matter and why they do. To have an obligation towards anyone, implies, among other things, that that someone or something has moral standing and that our actions have the capacity to affect such entities. Beyond this, I went on to develop various ways of conceptualizing community and the relationship (and hence the obligations) which individuals have towards each other and the relationship (and hence the obligations) which communities and their members have towards each other. I suggested that specific associations (whether societies or communities) could be conceptualized as corporate individuals. The relationship of such corporate individuals with (and hence the obligations of such corporate individuals to) other associations and eventually the relationship and obligations within the world community could be analogized to the relationship (and hence to the obligations) which the members of a community and the community have to each other.

What has been seen as the dialectic tension between an individual's (be it a single individual's or a corporate entity's) desire for freedom (for making its own decisions and for following its own life plans or cultural development undisturbed) and the interest of the larger community in which individuals or corporate entities are embedded, can, I have argued, be more fruitfully seen as a homeostatic relationship. In a homeostatic relationship a dynamic balance among various forces or interests subserves the common goal of development, growth and survival: a common goal because, unless such a goal is met, neither individual nor communal interests can be realized.

Individuals require community to live their lives freely and communities are dependent upon the development of individual capacities if they are to thrive. In essence individuals (be they single or corporate individuals) and communities must share the same transcendent goals of survival, progress, and development. In such a view the adversarial tension between a single or a corporate individual's striving for freedom and a community's striving for wider communal interests and solidarity (a community's necessary interest in the interests and suffering of its members) is dissolved or at least ameliorated and essentially resolved in an ongoing manner. This resolution is of interest to the individual (be it a single person or a corporate individual) as well as to the larger community in which such single persons or corporate individuals find themselves since one is critically dependent upon the development of the other. Such resolution requires a common basic moral agreement. So that a commonly agreed upon basic set of moral obligations and ways of behaving can be crafted, effective communication and dialogue among single or corporate individuals must take place.

It is evident that to engage in meaningful dialogue so as to forge a commonly agreed upon basic moral framework requires that peace be kept: without peace and without peaceful process no dialogue is possible and, on the other hand, without dialogue and with at least some common agreements among all concerned, peace can only be kept by force. The libertarian position, likewise, is founded on the critical importance of keeping the peace; but to libertarians only a minimalist ethic is possible and a common "contentful" ethic is beyond our reach. Moreover, from a libertarian point of view, a minimalist ethic suffices to keep the peace. According to libertarians, the possibility that effective dialogue can occur and that what Engelhardt calls a contentful common ethic we can subscribe to can be crafted, shatters on the supposed fact that persons from different cultures and belief systems lack common interests, are "moral strangers" and thus have no common basis for dialogue. Their only common interest is the interest to live freely and hence no more than a minimalist ethic which promises that individuals (whether corporate or single individuals) will refrain from interfering with each other's liberty and will scrupulously honor freely entered contracts can be expected. Except in specific "moral enclaves" any attempt to craft a more contentful ethic must fail. In such a view, the sole legitimate role of the state (be it a national state or, at least by inference, a supernational association) is assuring the liberty of its members and enforcing the adherence to freely entered contracts. Since a more contentful ethic cannot be crafted, beneficent action by individuals is supererogatory and beneficent action by the state (which, of course, would require taxation of some for the benefit of others) is not legitimate.

Engelhardt has argued that in a multicultural world both religion and rationality have been discredited. Therefore, neither religion nor rationality in today's world can help craft a generally agreed upon contentful ethic. A framework of common interests is lacking among what is conceived as moral strangers. Although libertarians (and specifically Engelhardt) argue that the hope of the enlightenment (peace and progress through the use of reason) has been discredited, even the starkest libertarians who would deny that any but the most minimal ethic can be created argue, as I have pointed out, on the basis of reason. Even those who agree with Engelhardt that we live in a world of strangers, that we must keep the peace so as to get on with our individual interests and plans and that we, therefore, must adopt a minimalist ethic limited to mutual non-harm (and the strict adherence to freely entered agreements) are left arguing on the basis of reason. They do so because in fact, and short of violence, we have no other meaningful way of reaching agreement.

I agree that a fully contentful ethic which unites all peoples everywhere (or even one which people in one society today would readily all agree to) cannot be crafted. And, I have argued, that to do so would not even be desirable since it would entrap us in dead uniformity. Since the homeostatic development of societies, cultures (and, I would argue, the development and understanding of ethics) requires the spur of diversity, such uniformity would be deadly. It would threaten to damage the future and, therefore, the prior worth of community. I agree that a fully contentful ethic, an ethic in which general agreement on a multiplicity of moral problems would be attainable, could be developed only among moral friends or within what Engelhardt calls moral enclaves. And even within such moral enclaves, unless such moral enclaves are what I have called "monastic communities," total agreement can never be achieved. A fully contentful ethic is not what I am after.

An ethic which is tolerant of other points of view is frequently said to be "relativistic": there is no actual way of differentiating on moral grounds among the various ways of behaving or among disparate views of morality. Although I have consistently argued for a common ethical framework within which sufficient room for various ethical beliefs can be accommodated, I do not imply that a kind of relativism in which "anything goes" is defensible. Anthropology, in describing the way in which societies behave is descriptive; ethics, in its very nature, is normative. While the normative enterprise most assuredly cannot be entirely divorced from the descriptive (discussing what "ought to be" necessarily must refer to "what is"), its task is quite different. In all that has gone before, I have argued for an ethic developed in an ongoing fashion by social human activity within a framework of common human experience and capacities.

An ethic which accepts common human capacities and experience as the necessary framework for its development cannot be relativistic. It may tolerate and hold coequal many different ways in which ethics are played out but it will fundamentally insist that different habits and customs can be measured by their ability to provide satisfactory lives to as many members of a community as is possible. It may, and to a large extent does, leave what is "satisfactory" to be quite different in various cultures and societies: what it is after is not so much a given standard of what constitutes "satisfactory" but rather some very basic standards of what is (according to fundamental human experiences and capacities) "unsatisfactory." Humans may worship or enjoy art in quite different ways: but all want to exist, none want to go hungry, none want to suffer, and all want to satisfy their often very different social needs and to pursue their own interests and talents. The relativist argument that all societies (whether they ceremonially mutilate female children, keep slaves, or gas Jews) are really equal, that one can pass no external judgment on their internal behavior, falls down when one considers such societies not from the point of view of those in power but from the point of view of those who are not: humans do not generally wish to be mutilated (albeit that social pressures can go far towards making them feel the necessity of having this done), do not wish to be enslaved, or to be gassed. Persons who would argue for a complete relativism and who claim that external judgments of particular societal ways of behaving are inappropriate fail to take account of the common human experiential framework and are generally unable to conceive themselves as slaves, inmates of concentration camps, black persons in the Ghettos of America, or the hungry in capitalist societies. They instinctively view themselves as members of the dominant and not as the dominated. Capitalist societies in which many go hungry or lack the opportunity for the full development of their talents so that a few can lead lives of opulence cannot, by the standard of those who are deprived, be considered to be as desirable as would societies in which goods and opportunities are more equally distributed. One need, of course, answer the question: why view from the vantage point of the unfortunate rather than from the point of view of those who have been more fortunate? Such a question suggests a very individualistic world view in which our individual fate can be seen as quite separate from that of our community. Several ways of answering such a query seem evident: (1) those who are "unfortunate" (the slave, the Ghetto dweller, or the person in the concentration camp) have been brought into their situation not by some natural disaster but by the deliberate action of their society which, rightly or wrongly, believes that it or powerful persons within it will benefit by acting in this way; (2) those who have been disadvantaged are just as much members of the human community as are those who are taking advantage of them: they have simply been disenfranchised; (3) communities which act in this way will lack solidarity: slaves, the hungry, the poor, or those locked into concentration camps to be exterminated cannot be expected to show solidarity with such a society and will, in fact, ultimately work to destroy it. It is in the interest of societies and ultimately it is of vital interest to the powerful within a society who depend in their very existence upon their societies stability, to create a society in which the point of view of those less powerful is given full and generous consideration.

A relativist argument, deprives one of all measures of "progress." If nothing is "better" than anything else one cannot judge what is or might be better than what already exists. What I have suggested is that a common framework of what I have called the existential a prioris of ethics together with our inborn sense of compassion and fellow-feeling can allow us to craft a common ethical framework. Since there are vast cultural and personal differences (many of which, so as to create a dynamic and developing world, should be preserved rather than being homogenized), a vast latitude of expression will be expected to be not only tolerated but embraced. Such a point of view is relativism within a framework of respect for basic human experiences, needs, and capacities as well as for the inevitable personal and cultural differences and peculiarities which exist and which function to underwrite progress and growth.

The fact that the crafting of a fully contentful ethic is beyond our reach, however, should not hinder us in trying to establish an ethical framework beyond the minimalist which a large consensus of persons from different cultures and belief systems would reasonably endorse. The components of such a framework and the ethics which spring from it are not seen as static but are envisioned as a developing system aimed at a common goal and produced through homeostatic interaction. In order to craft such a basic ethic, a framework of shared common interests and values is indeed necessary. I have argued that a framework allowing us to craft a basic ethic exists, is tacitly realized by all of us and that while these common shared interests and values assuredly do not make us moral friends they do allow for an acquaintanceship which can carry us far beyond the libertarian minimalist ethic.

The framework of which we have been speaking is not a set of principles or rules: it is a framework in which principles and rules can be crafted by persons who by virtue of being endowed with a basic sense of compassion care enough to do so. Ethics cannot be reduced to a static system of principles and rules: it must be crafted by fallible men for actual use in particular circumstances and particular societies within a common and commonly accepted framework. What such a framework does, is to establish the necessary condition within which discussion and ultimately the development of mutually agreed upon ways of proceeding can occur. In the human condition as we know it, such a framework is inescapably the necessary condition for creating ethical rules. I have called the components of this framework the six (there may be more) existential a prioris of ethics (and perhaps of religion) and have suggested that their existence allows us to be sufficiently morally acquainted to begin the task of resolving some of the problems faced not only within a particular society but among various societies which ultimately go to make up the world community. When these conditions are woven together to form a framework, the particulars of their weaving may differ depending upon culture and circumstance: but to function well they must relate homeostatically to each other in that one cannot overwhelm another without courting the destruction of all. These shared conditions are: (1) the necessity for existence of being; (2) our inevitable biological necessities without which being is not possible; (3) social needs which, while they differ from species to species and culture to culture remain social needs; (4) the desire to minimize suffering; (5) a common basic logic; and (6) our single and corporate individual desire to follow our own interests and talents and to live freely. I have argued that these conditions are, on the one hand, lexical in that the latter depend on the former and on the other hand mutually reinforcing.

Granting the existence of these existential a prioris does not imply that a meaningful and binding ethic will emerge. The framework which these existential a prioris constitute says nothing about the type or the justification of the agreements which may emerge. In past chapters, I have discussed the question of justification which in part at least depends upon our view of ethics: what it is and how it comes about. If we consider ethics as consisting of immutable basic truths which are discovered or at least discoverable, we will require a quite different set of justifications than we will if we see ethics as social and the crafting of ethics as a social task. In the view which I have argued for, ethics is a social construct underwritten by but not reducible to psycho-social-biological forces. It is enabled by a basic biological trait: what Rousseau has called a "primitive sense of pity" or compassion. As a biological trait, this trait is no more "ethical" or "unethical" than are other biological capacities. But as a biological trait it serves to make us sensitive to the well-being or suffering of others: it causes us to care about the effect our actions may have on others. Therefore, this sense of compassion serves as the driving force for our ethical thinking and acting and prevents ethics from becoming merely a sterile and purely intellectual game of chess. It impels us to care about our common framework and causes us to recognize and use the existential a prioris I have listed. This sense of compassion, I have argued (see chapter 4), is enabled by another innate trait: curiosity and, therefore, imagination. Without curiosity, we would not stop to investigate; without imagination we could not begin to answer the question curiosity prompts us to ask; and without compassion we would not care.

Crafting an ethic, then, has been seen as a communal task, stimulated by an inbuilt sense of compassion, directed by reason, and ultimately accomplished by a democratic process within the framework of what I have called the existential a prioris of ethics. An agreed upon process in which all have a voice and the agreement that all ultimately will abide by the decision made—even when they as individuals may disagree with the specific decision—is essential to the peaceful development of any ethic and of any community. This holds no less for a small association than it does for a state or, for that matter, than it ultimately does for the proper functioning of the world community. In all of these associations individuals (be they single individuals or corporate entities) ultimately must decide what their mutual obligations are and live up to them.

The way of going about developing a viable ethic which I have suggested here has been accused of being utopian. Utopianism (from the word Utopia meaning, as has been pointed out to me by Dr. Joachim Widder, "nowhere") is generally used in an essentialist sense: the sense which sees individuals or situations as self-sufficient and no longer in need or even with the possibility of development. In the essentialist sense, utopia is meant to denote visionary but not really possible reform; in a nonessentialist sense—if one can use Utopia in that sense, and perhaps one can—Utopia could denote a society working smoothly not towards a non-achievable perfection but towards steady improvement and betterment. If Utopianism is charged to what I propose in an essentialist sense, the charge defeats itself: by essentialist definition Utopia represents a perfect or the striving for a perfect (and, therefore, no longer perfectible) system or society; what I propose is a dynamic homeostatic system leading to a society which, while striving for improvement, is dynamic and quite reconciled to its own imperfectibility. In its usual essentialist sense, the charge logically fails: a system conceived as perpetually and dynamically developing cannot, in the essentialist sense, be a perfect or perfected one.

The point that process is all important in, if not eliminating, at least minimizing conflict is one made by Stuart Hampshire in *Innocence and Experience.*[1] Professor Hampshire, however, sees relationships as far more adversarial and sees a critical difference between the virtues of private and the virtues of communal relationships. According to Professor Hampshire, personal relationships properly are informed by what he calls "a fastidious sense of honor" whereas communal relationships must be guided by "largeness of design." Applying a fastidious sense of honor (in a sense an individual ethic perhaps based on Kantian precepts) to issues of public policy where one deals with issues largely involving unidentified lives and necessitating compromise cannot resolve such issues; largeness of design, on the other hand, will not do when it comes to interpersonal relationships. Resolution of conflict, according to Professor Hampshire, is achieved by what he calls "rationally controlled hostility." What keeps rationally controlled hostility from flaring into open warfare is the presence of agreed upon fair process. Rationally controlled hostility may, I think, well be another way of looking at the relationship as competitive and dialectic. In the present work I have suggested that homeostatic process rather than outright competition, a dialectic or rationally controlled hostility is a more fruitful way of conceptualizing the relationship among various interests within a community. Rationally controlled hostility is an armed truth in which reason prevents resort to force; homeostasis does not deny that different interests exist but it sees these interests as inevitably united and resolved by the common need for striving above all for the common goal of communal existence. When resolution by agreed upon "fair process" occurs it does so since forces are balanced: it is an agreement reached by a competitive and basically hostile process. Peace is maintained while the balance of forces, competition, and hostility persist; but what would happen if our reason told us that our strength sufficed to vanquish opposing interests? In rationally controlled hostility the individual interests do not as much balance each other as struggle with each other; resolution, at any time, is, as I have claimed, an armed truth. In a homeostatic system a plethora of interests balance one another and work together to produce an ongoing resolution of an ongoing problem: all parties realize that they necessarily have a common transcendent interest outside or without which their individual interests cannot flourish. Resolution is reached by a process in which all participate and in which rational compassion (and not rationally controlled hostility) plays a major role.

When it comes to crafting an ethic of some content—that is in establishing a set of generally agreed upon obligations and legitimate expectations as well as setting some commonly agreed upon goals and then going on to grapple with some specific problems—I have suggested that the process we must rely upon is a democratic process: democratic in a far more than merely a narrow political sense of democracy. Following and extending Dewey, I have argued that political democracy to be effective is possible only when democracy as a moral ideal is accepted and when, therefore, personal, social, educational, and economic (Dewey calls it "industrial") democracy exists in a de facto and not merely in a libertarian de jure sense.

Libertarianism and democracy are not well-matched. Community, and a sense of community, is vital to a democracy which is a democracy in its fundamental moral sense. Democracy in which those who have had a full chance to participate in an agreed process but who disagree with the decisions made can simply "opt out" cannot be a functioning and viable situation. While individuals as well as individual liberty, in the view I present here, must be cherished, individual liberty is seen as integrated into the idea of democracy itself. There is no such integration in libertarianism: except when they individually and freely choose not to be, individuals are basically isolated, single, and asocial. A true democracy necessarily has shared interests beyond the interest of each to live his or her own life undisturbed.

A democratic community cannot survive unless it fosters and encourages individual interests and enables the flourishing of individual talent. Therefore, a truly democratic community will see to it that all its members have ample and equal access to those goods and services necessary to allow their talents to flourish. It will, furthermore, define having fair "access" not merely as (the libertarian definition) not being actively hindered but as being actively facilitated: a truly democratic community interested in preserving and safeguarding its democracy, will deny the libertarian fiction that access is present when persons are too poor to avail themselves of health care or higher education because only their poverty but nothing else stops them. A society in which stark differences of opportunity de facto (even if not de jure) exist cannot maintain itself as a truly democratic society or, for that matter, as a well-functioning society at all. Albeit that history shows many examples of societies in which gross inequities were allowed to exist, history also shows two things: (1) such societies could persist only through the exercise of delusion and force; and (2) eventually such societies perished in violence and gave way to chaos.

Although a proper "fit" between economic and political systems is desirable if a society is to survive, economic systems must not be conflated with political systems. A variety of economic systems can more or less readily coexist with a variety of political systems. Economic as well as political systems are founded upon a particular worldview or philosophy. Since economic systems necessarily are embedded in the political and philosophical systems of a given society some sort of fit or accommodation between them is necessary. Both libertarianism and capitalism emphasize individual freedom of action and choice. Therefore, the economic system called capitalism is well-matched to the philosophy of starkly individualistic libertarian principles. Communal care for individual needs and community itself as well as concern for legitimate individual interests and individual dignity is a hallmark of any true democracy in the sense I have used democracy here; it is likewise a hallmark of socialism (here used in its democratic and not in its degenerated and perverted Soviet sense): these two, moderate socialism and democracy, therefore, seem well-matched.

Economic systems (be they entrepreneurialism in a free market economy or communism) are subsequent and not prior to the society in which they exist. Although this seems evident, not all will agree. Locke, for example, sees private property as prior to social association[2] and Engelhardt suggests entrepreneurialism not only as the (proper) foundation for medical but for general morality.[3] John Locke does so because of an insistence on a "natural law" or "natural rights" type of world view: a view which sees certain rules as being those of "nature or of nature's God"; to Engelhardt individuals as ontologically prior to community likewise are or must be endowed with innate liberty and, therefore, rights to property. It seems hard to accept a point of view which sees either property or entrepreneurialism as preexisting social association: to be meaningful my "property" has to be my property in a framework of others and entrepreneurialism requires a social system to be meaningful. Property rights—as all other rights—are not something which is "natural" and "discoverable." Rights—at least in my view—in a theoretical as well as practical sense are social constructs: things given to the members of an association and secured to them by the association. To speak of "rights" outside some sort of association seems like an empty gesture. The rights we as individuals have—the rights vouchsafed to us by our community—are rendered meaningful and kept secure only by virtue of the organization. Such rights are not absolute, eternal, or unchanging: they are an evolving construct whose particular nature will depend upon the society which promulgates and secures them. While to Locke, rights are natural, given by nature or by nature's God, Jefferson (who has often been said to be a natural rights advocate) has subtly but significantly changed this point of view: rights are not natural, not "somewhere out there" to be discovered. Rather certain rights, in any decent society, are inalienable:

> We hold these truths to be self-evident, that all men are created equal, that they are endowed by their creator with certain inalienable rights, that among these are Life, Liberty and the Pursuit of Happiness. That to secure these rights Governments are instituted among men, deriving their just power from the consent of the governed.[4]

Several changes from Locke should be noted. (1) Rights are self-evident rather than being strictly natural: although all men are "endowed" with these rights by "their creator" we know that Jefferson, the deist, was using this phrase in a metaphoric sense: the creator, I think, can, perhaps, be seen as a metaphor for community and communal rational process. These rights are self-evident because they are things all of us want for ourselves; they are thus evident to every thinking human being. They emerge from a common framework, from what I have termed the existential a prioris. (2) The "right" to property does not appear in this work of Jefferson's: the right to the pursuit of happiness does. Only a crassly materialist point of view—a view widespread in individualistic capitalist nations—would reduce happiness to merely its necessary material conditions. (3) The function of government is to "secure" such self-evident rights. (4) Governments derive their "just power from the consent of the governed": that is, a proper government is a proper participatory government in which all affected have their say. I would add that if all affected are to have their say, all affected must have the necessary conditions to make such say meaningful: the necessary conditions for the functioning of true political democracy (personal, social, educational, and economic democracy) must be met.

The fear that if we do not see rights as absolute but leave their enunciation and safeguarding to social process basic ("self-evident") rights may be ignored has much historical validity. But it has historical validity only when tyrannical government did not derive its just power from the consent of the governed or when such political consent was not underwritten by an informed electorate: in other words, when what was touted as political democracy was not underwritten by the necessary personal, social, educational, or economic preconditions. If we are to have a functioning community and if we believe that political democracy is the best alternative for shaping our community, then the necessity of assuring these self-evident rights to all becomes obvious. Assuring these rights is not done only because of our respect for persons; assuring these rights, motivated by compassionate reason, is done so that our community and with it our individual selves may survive and prosper. Our rights will be safest when they are not seen as written somewhere in the stars but when they are forged by man and considered necessary for community itself as well as for every member of it.

These self-evident rights are not operative unless certain preconditions are met. Persons who do not have the necessary condition for having rights amply met cannot be said to have meaningful rights: persons who are starving, cold, ill, homeless, or ill-educated can do little with such rights. Their right to life (when they starve to death) is ignored; their liberty is meaningless (what good is freedom of speech when one is hungry, what avails freedom of assembly when we are poorly educated?); and their right to a "pursuit of happiness" is a cynical fiction. A world view which encompasses a real belief in individual rights as well as a belief in democratic process to secure such rights, must recognize that individual rights and democratic process is possible only in a well-functioning community. Solidarity in such a community is necessary to its survival and, therefore, is necessary to the thriving of all individuals within it.

In like fashion and for the same reasons, societies as corporate individuals must strive to produce a world community held together in a similar manner. When we see each other as moral strangers (whether the "we" refers to individual persons or corporate individuals) striving for such a society and ultimately for such a world is impossible. Recognizing that we are not moral strangers, recognizing that we have at least a framework of what I have called the existential a prioris of ethics in common, will allow us to work together cooperatively within a dynamic society and, ultimately, within an evolving and dynamic world community. To achieve such a state of affairs individual interests (be they personal or corporate) must be conceived as ultimately achievable for all only in the confines of a well-functioning democratic community: therefore, personal or corporate individuals must be willing to contribute equitably and as necessary to the common good, a good which ultimately serves the contributor as it does everyone else.

Libertarians, seeing persons (except when they voluntarily associate in certain enclaves) largely as asocial beings with little connection to their community, insist that societal rules beyond those needed to assure maximal freedom to all would have to be agreed upon by all of those affected: those who did not agree with such rules could not be forced to adhere to them. Contributing equitably for purposes other than to support sufficient state power to assure personal liberty (including the strict adherence to freely entered contracts) is not something which can be enforced. Levying a tax on those who can afford to pay so as to create a system of public assistance and works would be possible: but such a tax would have to be voluntary and those who opposed it would be vouchsafed the right not to participate. This is not only ridiculous (who of us would really voluntarily pay a large income tax?) but inimical to democratic process. In a democracy all members as a condition of membership accept a process for creating the rules that all will live by. They are agreed—whether they individually agree or disagree with the specific outcome of such a process—to either abide by it or to take the consequences.

Of course, no society adheres completely to libertarian principles. To do so would, demonstrably, be self-destructive. In such a society, rampant competition—not only inevitable but morally desirable in the libertarian view—would determine wealth and power. Competition among the wealthy and powerful for more wealth and more power would, inevitably, shrink the number of the wealthy and powerful. Many would sink from their position of wealth and power and eventually join the poor and the weak. The weak and the poor soon recognize that their freedom is empty and that it is the freedom to starve, to freeze, and to comply. History has shown that such a process is not one apt to endure: inevitably revolution—and bloody revolution—with its consequent period of terror follows. All societies, even those most closely associated with a libertarian world view, will, in order to pacify the disadvantaged, have an at least minimal social program.

It seems that a libertarian system in which internal peace is a goal of the minimalist ethic must seek to prevent revolution. History has shown us that when conditions become intolerable to the disadvantaged, revolution becomes inevitable: only the time of its occurrence is then in doubt. To make a libertarian system predicated on internal peace workable, revolution would have to be prevented. To prevent such a revolution and to keep internal peace—even for a little while—a powerful "sovereign" (or some other form of repressive government—pace Hobbes!) who would have sufficient power to keep the hordes of poor and weak "in their place" and to prevent them from forcefully appropriating power and wealth is essential. Such a government would be instituted in the name of vouchsaving individual liberty by preventing persons from interfering with one another's freedom. A society at least at first dedicated to individual freedom but having little regard for communal beneficence and, therefore, social programs, is quite apt to spawn tyranny: the tyranny of those who are powerful and wealthy. The wealthy and powerful would continue to be in a position to exploit the poor and the weak and would have to rely upon force to prevent the revolt of those who feel themselves disadvantaged. They would do this in the name of assuring the liberty of all: after all, the poor and the weak are free to compete; the fact that they are poor and weak (and that their ability to compete is, therefore, not real) is either bad moral luck or is, in fact, their own fault. The tyranny which would necessarily result would be apt to be supported as long as it allowed the powerful and wealthy to continue to pursue their particular interests. The powerful and the wealthy have repeatedly either been the tyrannical government (Bourbon France, Czarist Russia and, ultimately, the Soviet State) or have supported a tyrannical government as long as it, in turn, supported them (Nazi Germany).

All societies levy and collect taxes and create systems of public works and public assistance. They do so either because they subscribe to democracy in its widest sense (and, therefore, recognize that for one to prosper all must have certain basic needs satisfied) or because they recognize that to do so provides a hedge against mass disaffection and eventual unrest. Some societies, however, have been deeply penetrated by the world view and philosophy of libertarianism so that they create public works and provide public assistance grudgingly and, as it were, under protest. From what has been said before, it is not surprising that such societies generally will have capitalism as their economic system. In such societies competition—while perhaps somewhat controlled and not entirely rampant—is seen as one of the most important social driving forces. It determines wealth and power: and wealth and power, not beauty, truth, justice, or humanity are the primary values in such societies. Depending upon the limits placed on competition such societies will tend to concentrate wealth and power in fewer and fewer hands: the fact, for example, that in the United States more and more wealth is concentrated in fewer and fewer hands is well-known. A shrinking middle class with more falling into poverty results.[5] Here too the weak and the poor will recognize the emptiness of their "freedom." Persons living in an American poverty area or ghetto are "free" in an only very peculiar sense of the word: they are free to starve, to go homeless, to go ignorant but not free to truly avail themselves of the real opportunities society may offer or to participate meaningfully in democratic process. When such persons are disorganized, frustration and hopelessness will eventuate in violence, crime, and cruelty; when they ultimately become organized, and that is inevitable, frustration can regrettably easily turn into a bloody even if justifiable revolt. Such a revolt is regrettable because it is unnecessary: the social conditions which forced the issue could, but for individualistic greed, easily have been changed. Furthermore, such a revolt will, before it produces any good, generally (see the French and Russian revolutions) be followed by chaos and terror. In the United States today such a revolution is, I think, not yet unavoidable; at least not quite yet.

It remains to examine a few examples of today's problems. In doing this I do not delude myself that solutions in the sense of permanent or ultimate solutions to these vexing problems can be found: finding solutions (moving from lesser to greater determinacy, if you will) is something which requires the working together of many persons with many skills and backgrounds; and ultimately it requires the democratic participation of the entire community. What I want to do in what is to follow is to give a few examples of how the crafting of an ethic and the practical structuring of rules and understandings we can all live with are possible among persons who are neither moral friends nor moral strangers. The claim, made in different ways by both Professor Jonas and Professor Engelhardt, that in a pluralist world and outside specific enclaves, religion has failed to enable us to craft an ethic or provide a structure which all or most would agree to and that religion is bound to fail in providing such a structure in the future, is, as I have said, one that I can readily subscribe to. It is unlikely that a "true religion" which all will readily subscribe to can or will be found; indeed many of us, myself included, do not believe that such a faith exists or that it can, in fact, exist.

However, I find the libertarian claim that reason also has and must continue to fail impossible to subscribe to. The enlightenment has failed to produce a widely accepted, specific, and transculturally applicable ethic but the concepts and world view of the enlightenment have enabled progress towards a general ethical framework. It has allowed us to grope towards a united world in which a recognition of what unites us as humans and a commonly agreed upon process of how we might profitably deal with our problems is being forged. However, in my view the libertarians are right when they claim that we cannot forge an ethic which, in each particular, we all will subscribe to. But that is not necessary: what is needed is a general broad area of agreement about basic issues, sufficient mutual respect to tolerate particular points of view about many other specific issues and a willingness to continue the process so that a dynamic and evolving system of talking about our differences and fashioning ethical points of view to deal with new contingencies can occur. A recognition of our common framework, a fair democratic process, curiosity, imagination, and rational compassion can go far in achieving this goal.

The sayers of doom will reflect that the enlightenment has done little good: the world has become no better and has perhaps even become worse. And certainly the events of this bloody and unhappy century might lead one to agree to this proposition. Lenin was certainly right when he said that one who wished to live a quiet life would do well not to be born in this century. But such a statement, suggesting that one lived a quieter, a less threatened life or a "better" life in past centuries, presupposes an interesting view of what "one" is: one certainly was not a slave in pre-civil war America nor an ordinary black person in pre-1960 America; certainly one was not an ordinary laborer in either Europe or America; certainly one was not a Chinese Coolie or a member of the lowest caste in India; and most likely one was not a woman in any part of the world. The world in the past was a quieter, a more secure and happier place to live for some, a much harsher, much more insecure and far unhappier place for many. Those who lived well, then as is now the case in the capitalist world, did so "on the backs" of those whose lives were materially and intellectually impoverished by the very circumstances of their society. Whatever progress there has been, has been hard fought against those for whom the world was secure, safe, and happy and often fought against overwhelming odds. This ongoing and complex struggle—to reduce it simply to a class struggle, albeit that is certainly a part of it, is to deny that far more complicated issues than merely class are at stake—is not one which has not had many setbacks, and many disappointments.

Let us take a brief look at the good old days and contrast them to the state of affairs today. Colonial days in America—if you did not happen to be a native or black American—were generally days of hard but rewarding work: the tasks were many and the hands few. After the revolution, despite all verbiage about "men" as "created equal," conditions for slaves went from bad to worse. Where tasks were too onerous for whites, slaves whose lives were materially deprived and intellectually stunted, were used. As the need for more labor grew, immigrants were imported and at the very least were very badly used. The tracks of the transcontinental railroad bear witness to an abuse of humanity few would like to recall. To believe that most persons came to America seeking liberty is a pious fiction: many poor laborers, especially Italian, Irish, and Oriental, were seduced into coming by agents seeking to acquire a cheap and ready source of labor. Some of these persons died, some "made it" into main stream America and many were left over to form a uniquely American form of proletariat.

Uncontrolled and unmodified capitalism requires an exploitable class. Native Americans and black Americans provide a good example. Native Americans were difficult to exploit directly: they were in their own milieu and culture. They were, by and large, neither willing to work for the white man on their own territory on the white man's terms, nor—given the fact that they were not uprooted in a cultural sense—could they be easily enslaved. Instead they were eliminated: their culture and basis for living destroyed and they themselves often exterminated. Our ability to remedy the situation today, though as much as is humanly possible needs to be done, is minimal.

The fate of black Americans was rather different. Africans were uprooted from their culture, torn from their families, severed from their language and linguistic roots, and separated from their religion and social setting. They were given a new and to them meaningless name. Their depersonalization was as vicious as was that of the inmates of Auschwitz. Often—since among their new groups many came from distinctly separate cultures within the larger African culture—they did not even have the tenuous connection with their previous culture as did victims of Nazi concentration camps. In America slavery at first was economically very profitable: not only because inexpensive labor was available but also because the slave represented a new, a renewable and a potentially growing commodity. Slavery was abandoned largely because it was no longer economically as profitable as simply creating an exploitable underclass of (at first largely but not only) blacks: body slavery had merely changed to wage slavery. As time went on, this underclass proliferated while, as I mentioned in chapter 4, the need for manual labor decreased. Other exploitable immigrant classes (hispanics, for example) as well as a group of traditionally poor whites were added during these years. The conditions in the United States today are the fruits of past exploitation. With that in mind the plea to "give us your poor, your huddled masses yearning to be free" or the appeal to a "land of opportunity" has a hollow, and I would argue, a most cynical ring!

Just as whites exploited blacks in America because they had the power to do so, those in power all over the world exploited those who were essentially powerless. In like manner and driven by the same forces the more powerful western nations exploited the weaker nations they had colonized. Much of the problems of what we call "developing" nations are the direct result of such exploitation. Just as the exploitation of blacks, women, and other minorities especially in the United State continues, the exploitation of the former colonies continues. Moreover, the cheap labor available in the developing world, which used to be an asset to the rest of the world, has, in some respects, become a liability; the natural resources so badly needed in the past have often been depleted or exhausted. While the exploiter continues to gain advantage from past and, to some extent, from ongoing exploitation, the threat posed by the exploited to the exploiter grows.

In Europe, the French revolution brought the possibility but not the reality of a life with dignity to all. It remained for the socialist labor movement to carry on an ongoing and remarkably successful struggle in Europe; in America, the attempt of a similar labor movement to manifest itself was brutally crushed in, among others, the Pullman strike and the Haymarket riot. But in both Europe and America at the turn of the century, it was quite usual for a laborer not to own a flat or even a room but to hire a bed for an eight hour period each day. De jure segregation in the South and de facto segregation in much of the North forced blacks into a situation from which they still suffer today. And while laws and a veneer of political correctness prevent some of the grosser abuses today, opportunities can hardly be said to be equal. Nevertheless and despite the evident and, in my view, inexcusable inequities which pervade and, I believe, destroy American society today, one cannot, if one takes a long view, deny that some things, at least, have improved. If nothing else, that should give one hope and should serve as a spur for further improvement. The problem, far from solved, is at least in some measure moved "forward": a forward defined by inreasing opportunity and lessening deprivation for some even if not by any means for many enough.

Just as those who cling to the mythology of the "good old days" have created largely a fiction of the state of affairs then, doomesayers and pessimists will claim that, despite all efforts to the contrary, things today are really no better than they were before. From this they will often conclude that any attempt to improve things is bound to fail and in turn draw from this the conclusion that there is no point in trying to do so. Those who cling to the fiction of the good old days are just as myopic as are those who claim that the so-called good old days were very "bad old days" and that they have not improved. In much of the western world (the United States sadly enough is a flagrant exception) most of the poor are not starving, or homeless, or without medical care. While homelessness in the United States is widespread and provisions for the homeless are less than inadequate, it is unthinkable for a worker in the rest of the western world not at least to have a room or an apartment. And while homelessness in the United States is a severe (and shameful) problem, even in the United States employed persons seldom go without some, even if not adequate, housing.

Despite some de jure and lesser de facto changes one would not choose to be black, hispanic, female, or foreign born in the United States today and one would still not wish to be of a lower caste in India. Nevertheless, opportunities for blacks, hispanics, women, or the foreign born and life for members of the lower casts is not as dismal as it used to be. In the United States, for example, substantial improvements—at least de jure improvements—have occurred: in the 1950s there were virtually no black students in white colleges and virtually no women in professional schools. In the 1950s and even early 1960s segregation in the South was not only accepted but legally enforced; today, while de facto equality is far from established, at least the idea of de jure equal treatment (grudgingly it is true and often evaded) has been established. Racial, religious, ethnic, and gender slurs and stereotypes have been replaced by an all too thin veneer of what has been called "political correctness." Even though in the 1980s and 1990s things are arguably worse than they were in the 1970s—at least there appears to be more racial, religious, ethnic, and even gender resentment as well as more hostility and less tolerance towards those who are different than we happen to be (racism is not an exclusive white province, heaven knows!)—things are without a shadow of a doubt better than they were fifty or eighty years ago. Neither mythologizing the good old days nor denying the fact that substantial progress has been made is helpful: neither point of view can help engineer the changes we need to bring about. While the school of thought which yearns for the good old days would have us turn back the clock, the school of thought which denies progress would, since they are bound to fail anyhow, have us abandon all efforts. Both can serve as a wonderful excuse for washing one's hands and worrying only about oneself.

Throughout this book I have maintained that ethics is not something humans discover or that ethics is or can ever be absolute. For that reason alone it is not perfectible, cannot be made "perfect" but can only be improved and made more satisfying. In shaping our lives we cannot expect to wait for certainty or expect perfection, regardless of whether such perfection or certainty is scientific, social, or moral. Nor can we expect to have any proposition absolutely proven before acting. Propositions—be they scientific, economic, social, or moral ones—are proven in praxis and adapted by and within the context of our daily lives. I have maintained that ethics are crafted by humans within and for the human condition and that, like everything else, ethics are altered by social forces. A shared framework of interests and capacities—what I have termed the existential a prioris—used with rational compassion and by democratic process can never produce nor hope to produce an entirely contentful ethic. But by the use of such a framework we can begin to shape some content and can begin to make all of our lives safer, richer, and more fulfilling.

Libertarians as well as, peculiarly enough, the more radical forms of communism seem to use rationality without compassion. The one uses a form of reasoning in which asocial individuals in a loose and basically asocial association are free to deny all beneficent obligations; the other uses a form of reasoning which in holding a strange view of a social community as the center of its consideration ends up by neglecting individuality and individual aspirations. Both end up with the same end result: a community in which members feel little solidarity, in which trust for each other and for the community of which they are a part disappears and a community which is well on its way to destroying itself. In the kind of ethic I am suggesting, rationality must be tempered by compassion just as compassion must be controlled by reason. Looking at things from a purely rational view produces an ethic devoid of humanity just as only allowing our compassion to control us leads to an ethic of sentimentality. Both turn out to be unhelpful when it comes to having to deal with real individual as well as with public problems. Dealing with the long established problem of poverty and disadvantage in the United States today cannot be done by using either a "libertarian" approach (an approach which, albeit modified, got us into the mess we are in in the first place) or by using a radical socialist approach. Reason without compassion would allow us to shrug our shoulders and either deny the problem or deny our responsibility for and to it or reason without compassion might guide us to form a society in which individuals serve merely as cogs in a community which supplied basic needs but denied human aspirations.

Examples of using rationality without compassion in personal as well as in more public spheres are many. When physicians set "cure" as their goal and forget to adequately control a patient's pain, they are following a line of reason devoid of humanity just as libertarians and the type of capitalism libertarian philosophy supports will follow a line of reason which leads society to neglect the needs of the poor. And both defeat themselves: patients whose pain is not adequately controlled will be less likely to be truly "cured" and societies which neglect the needs of their members ultimately must fall and destroy themselves. Rationality (depending upon one's basic view of community and interpersonal obligation) can, on the other hand, lead one to reason that only through community can individual needs be met (something I would subscribe to) and, therefore, go on to entirely neglect the role and importance individuality and personal capacities or interests play in creating a viable and progressive community.

Using compassion without reason is at least equally dangerous and inevitably leads to a kind of sentimentality which neither can be helpful to the solution of individual nor to the dealing with communal problems. Physicians who allow compassion and pity to control them, will refrain from doing disagreeable and often painful things which are crucially necessary to their patients ultimate well-being; societies which neglect reason in favor of pure compassion will deal with the problem of poverty by "throwing money" at it without attempting an aimed, rational, and reasonable approach to dealing with such problems.

In what is to follow, I want to examine some specific problems and show how a working out of solutions is possible. To do this I shall assume and not reargue (for the entire book has been an argument of these points) the following: (1) as human animals (together, perhaps with higher nonhuman animals) we share a framework of bio-psycho-social "givens" which I have called the existential a prioris; (2) a necessary part of this framework is a common sense of basic logic which—in view of our common givens, stimulated by compassion and driven by "compassionate rationality"—allows and indeed prompts us to reason together; (3) since we share an interest in maintaining the peace we share an interest in allowing fair process to deal with our problems; (4) to be fair, a process must give ample voice to all concerned; (5) part of such fair process is a mutual agreement that all, even those who do not agree with the outcome, will abide by the results; (6) such a fair process, since it recognizes that meeting individual interests is possible only in a community which evolves and ultimately vouchsafes it, is an ongoing, dynamic homeostatic process in which individual ends are shaped within the context of communal needs.

Furthermore, I have and shall continue to emphasize that such problems are social: what Jonathan Moreno calls the "myth of the asocial individual"[6] applies with equal force to persons as it does to corporate individuals. Just as no individual can truly conceive of him/herself as asocial (as uninvolved in a community of others), no society in today's world can look upon itself as "asocial" in the sense of not necessarily being enmeshed in and with all other societies. Our individual relationship with others and the relationship between individuals and their community are mirrored by the relationships which pertain between and among different communities and cultures. The day for personal or corporate isolationism (if, indeed it ever had a viable "day"!) is long past.

It is not my intention to give ready solutions to difficult questions but to try to look at a sample of problems in our society and in our world, from a different point of view. There are, I believe, three problems which are inevitably interconnected and which constitute at least an important part of many other problems today: overpopulation, poverty, and lack of education. Additionally the United States (unique among most nations and most certainly among most industrialized nations) lacks basic health care coverage for all. One cannot deal with one of these problems out of context with the others: building a just health care system, for example, is, as we have seen, difficult if not impossible in the context of a basically unjust society. These are problems which have a long and unhappy history, a history which has inevitably created a traditionally exploited class of persons who, in fact, are the very ones in whom poverty is greatest, education poorest, population growth the fastest, and basic health care the most lacking.

In the United States the problems of poverty, lack of education and lack of health care for a large segment of the population (problems which in many of the industrialized nations have been reduced to a minimum) are among the most vexing: while this is true of the population at large, it is especially true of a segment of the population which for want of a better term can be called the "underclass" or the "hard-core poor"; persons in whom poverty is not an intercurrent event but in whom poverty and lack of employment has been present not merely for a relatively short time but has often been present for generations. While overpopulation in the United States is thought not to be a general overall problem, it is a problem among the hard-core poor: and, therefore, since the hard-core poor are members of the community just as are the middle class or the wealthy, it is a general and overall problem and one which has added much to perpetuating the problem of poverty itself. The poverty areas in the United States which in their hopelessness and squalor approach some of the worst conditions in third world nations are fed by this unbalanced population growth.

Overpopulation throughout the world is a distinct and severe problem: indeed it may be the fundamental problem of the twenty-first century. The world health organization, among others, has stated that we cannot today feed the entire world unless we become vegetarians; further, if populations continue to grow at the present rate, nourishing the earth's population will prove to be an impossible task even if we do. Persons who are starving and with their backs to the wall, will necessarily have their drive for self-preservation dominate if not entirely extinguish their compassion. This alone is a disaster: a world in which compassion for one another has been extinguished or is minimal is a world in which peace cannot be maintained. Individual compassion can be extinguished or suppressed in two ways: it can be suppressed or extinguished by an upbringing in an individualistic and opulent environment in which the sense of self-regard is converted to self-love; or it can be suppressed or extinguished when an immediate threat to survival becomes dominant. In either case, habits of compassion are lost in individuals and (often deliberately) not fostered in the young.

We are confronted with a clear choice: prevent overpopulation or face the consequences of famine, hunger, pestilence, and war. Technological progress has allowed survival of children and adults who, heretofore, would have died. Some diseases have been eliminated, others (such as schistosomiasis or malaria) probably could be. But one cannot clog the drain of a bathtub and keep the inflow of water at full speed without overflowing the tub and flooding the house. Unless we choose not to treat or to prevent disease (not really a palatable thought!), controlling birth rates seems to be the only viable alternative.

In my view religious objections to birth control—however good their motivation to care for the resulting offspring may, at least in theory, be—are an anachronistic, irresponsible, and ultimately disastrous idea to promulgate. Arguing against birth control cannot be based on a rational argument. Religious arguments against birth control are arguments from an a-rational belief supported by emotion but not supportable by reason: they are not irrational (that is they do not claim things which can be clearly disproven: that two plus two is sixteen, for example) but they are a-rational in that they accept as their ground of argument an a-rational (even if not an irrational) premise. Such a premise may be that using birth control is counter to the will of God (a-rational since one cannot prove what the will of God is; irrational because it claims that the will of a God said to be unknowable can be known) or it may be that preventing the birth of children deprives such purely potential beings (or even pre-beings) of the chance of entering the kingdom of heaven. It is not an argument based on compassion (unless it is compassion for nonexistent beings who are deprived of heaven) nor one supported by reason.

If we subscribe to the ethical framework I suggested, if we use compassionate rationality to order our thoughts and chart our course and if we at all believe that being has moral force, the attempt to interfere with birth control is ethically indefensible. Standing outside a poverty area teaming with children some of which are sold and almost all of whom are homeless and starving is not just stupid: without being based on an a-rational or irrational premise, it is irresponsible, cruel, heartless and, in that it condemns more children who need not have been created to these very conditions, is ultimately evil. An ethic created by humans using compassionate rationality and recognizing a necessary framework of human capacities and experience could not judge other. A point of view which speaks against birth control under such circumstances can only be based upon an a-rational, irrational, or indefensible vision.

In past chapters I have suggested that the natural trait of compassion (what Rousseau calls the primitive sense of pity) is critical for our understanding of ethics: it serves as a stimulator not only of ethical acting but of concerning ourselves about ethical problems to begin with. As any other natural trait, the sense of compassion is morally neutral. But since the sense of compassion plays such a crucial role in motivating our ethical behavior and forming our inclinations, fostering this sense of compassion, in individuals as well as communities, may become a moral obligation; doing those things which stifle it would then be ethically inadmissible. (See Kant's view on this matter in chapter 2.) As individuals we have done all we can to shield ourselves from seeing the appalling conditions in American poverty areas; have evaded facing the fact that a large segment of the American population (including large numbers of children) go hungry, homeless, and without medical care. In perpetuating the fiction that America is the land of opportunity, we have shielded ourselves from the fact that for many who live in the United States the very concept of hope does not exist and speaking of opportunity is cynical. Because many of us live all too well, we have allowed ourselves to forget those whose lives are impoverished and blighted; and, what is worse, when such facts are mentioned the victims themselves all too often are the ones who are blamed. So that some can enjoy opulence, others must live in squalor: those who are immensely wealthy (and regrettably even those of us who are merely well-off) enjoy this state of affairs at the expense of others who can barely exist. The United States, which considers itself to be the land of opportunity, and which has promised so very much to all has delivered so very little to many.

The statement that little has been delivered to many suggests that passive persons within a community should have the good things in life somehow "delivered" to them: that is, passively provided by the society in which they live. I do not mean to suggest such passivity. But I do suggest that in providing meaningful opportunity societies must do more than merely provide passive access. When it comes to biological or social needs defining access as merely having no one actively stop you is cynical: to suggest that the starving do have free access to the supermarket but merely lack money or that poor persons who wish to further their education have "equal access" to college when they have no funds, defines access in a trivial way. Equal access, to be truly equal, must actively seek not only to allow persons to avail themselves of opportunities but must actively seek to create conditions in which speaking of equality is not a mere sham.

There are some recent works which suggest (and, indeed claim) that some of our population (notably members of the underclass and notably blacks) are endowed with a somewhat lower IQ than are members of the middle and upper class, notably whites.[7] These books suggest that there are (significant) IQ differences among all ethnic groups and that these differences are not a function of social conditions but of heredity. They conclude from this that spending large sums on social programs so as to bring about social changes are ill conceived. Essentially their argument is a justification for those who are well-off and entrenched in power to maintain the status quo: a status quo perhaps modified by condescending and mostly private largess. From this view emerges a notion of a "cognitive elite" which controls, and apparently justifiably or at least inevitably controls, the affairs of the nation. This cognitive elite, most importantly, comes about by genetic and not by social selection. It is not that the brightest who have had equal opportunity in society to shine make up this "elite": rather, those in society who make up this so-called cognitive elite do so by virtue of genetic endowment and not by virtue of social conditions. They are in a position of power, one would infer from this argument, because they are best equipped to be there not because having been born into affluent families they have been given the best opportunity to place themselves in a position to maintain their power. A self-fulfilling prophecy in which those who are in power because they, allegedly, are superior are given every opportunity to remain in power is created.

In the *Bell Curve* the authors make dire predictions (and, I am afraid the way things are going not inaccurate predictions) of what will happen and what, by inference, is already happening. At fault is the "welfare state" and not the abhorrent social conditions which have spawned the problem. It is the very idea of the welfare state as such and not the way the welfare state has half-heartedly been conceived and implemented in America today which is at fault. The authors fail to look at other models of the welfare state: for example, the moderate welfare state in its various forms as it exists in many parts of Europe (say in the Scandinavian nations or in Austria) today. To the authors a welfare state seems necessarily to be crassly paternalistic, and must eventually lead to what they call the "custodial state": a state conceived of as a "high tech and more lavish version of the Indian reservation for some substantial minority of the nation's population while the rest of America tries to go about its business. In its less benign forms, the solution will become more and more totalitarian" (p. 526). Aside from wondering what the "more benign forms" might be, one is left with the "less benign forms" which, I suppose, can range through the whole gamut of repression. The authors acknowledge that their description is "not really projecting but reporting." In other words, even this apologia for a right wing agenda, admits that we are well on our way to a totalitarian state: an opinion I (but for quite different reasons and with, I think, considerably more revulsion) share. They see the causes of this state of affairs as (1) and even though they acknowledge brilliant exceptions, the general genetic inferiority of the underclass; (2) our failure to deal with this state of affairs realistically; and (3) the whole notion of a welfare system as well as the (to them) ill-conceived and wasteful attempt to correct what they see as a genetic flaw by social means. To the authors the genetic "facts" of inferiority are a "given;" the real villain is the whole notion of the welfare state and its social programs. In their final chapter the authors suggest what Professor Gould in his *New Yorker* article has rightly called a "grotesquely inadequate" (p. 148) solution, a solution which, not surprisingly enough, seeks to cure the disease with yet another stiff dose of individualism.

Here is not the place to speak to their thesis nor to their "solution" except to say that many if not most experts consider their data, their thesis, and their conclusions to be flawed.[8] Among other things, not only do many experts doubt the validity of IQ testing and especially of IQ testing which is not specific for particular socioeconomic and ethnic groups (ghetto language and experience are quite different from white American language and experience and the language and experience of the white underclass is different yet) but only American blacks were used with no attempt to do relevant testing in black groups from other nations.[9] And this despite the fact that there are almost no "true blacks" (in a genetic sense) and, for that matter, not, in a genetic sense, that many "true whites" who have been in the United States for more than a couple of generations left in America today. One cannot help but wonder what would have happened if similar tests had existed in the middle ages (or in Russia up to the early part of this century) and if such tests had been applied to serfs who, from all reports, were "less intelligent" than was the nobility or the emerging middle class: the cognitive elite of their day. It was a notion of a social democratic welfare state (a notion which emphasized the education as well as the economic improvement of the masses) which in much of Europe enabled the current state of affairs: not an ideal state of affairs, a state of affairs in which class structure (albeit in many ways less crassly expressed) certainly continues to exist, but a state of affairs in which class structure is far less noticeable and in which the hard-core poor, while not entirely eliminated, are relatively rare. At least most people are assured an at least minimally adequate "cushion" of basic benefits as well as access to free health care and higher education. The notion of a communist state, on the other hand, while ameliorating some of the conditions (most persons had enough to eat and few persons were homeless or without basic medical care) and for the very reason that socialism was conceived in a nondemocratic fashion, resulted in exactly such a totalitarian state. Both agendas— the agenda of the extreme right and the agenda of the extreme left— inevitably will lead to the same thing: unsatisfied, stunted people, a "cognitive" (or power) elite and eventually a shattered society.

Their solutions of more individualism are either naive, ill-conceived or downright cynical. As do most right-wingers, their emphasis on individual opportunity misses the point that the opportunity to shape our lives and alter our destiny in fact (and not merely in theory) presupposes the satisfaction of our biological necessities as well as implying a supportive social nexus. Such solutions do little more than support and perpetuate an oppressive status quo and they do so by a dangerous appeal to an at best questionable scientific insight.

I strongly doubt that had the cards been stacked differently so that IQ testing had shown whites to have a slightly lower IQ than blacks, an argument that whites are less deserving of education and other opportunities than are those of other races would be made.

That, of course, is the case because whites today—at least in the western world—are in power: they, in other words, "stack the cards." Those who are inclined to give a genetic explanation of poverty (and with it an argument that trying to raise the level of the poor on par with that of others is a hopeless venture) will, of course, argue that the very reason that whites enjoy this power is to be found in their genetic superiority. But such an argument not only grossly ignores other forces but conveniently overlooks the fact that the same or similar races have developed quite differently by growing up and living in different cultures. Serbs growing up and living in what was once Yugoslavia have developed quite differently than Serbs who grew up and now live in neighboring Austria or in the United States and black children raised in European white families appear to have had a quite different fate than do American black children given the benefits of socially unreinforced Head Start. It is peculiar indeed, that an argument which emphasizes genetic racial or ethnic aspects of development and downplays the role of cultural, social, and economic forces should (of all things!) be made by Americans in America today: America initially was largely built by persons from a traditional underclass some of whose members within a generation or two played a major role in the social, economic, and intellectual life of the nation and of the world. It is a queer (and I believe disingenuous if not indeed downright cynical) argument which blames the undoubted fact that until recently relatively fewer black Americans have made significant intellectual contributions to American life "genetic inferiority" rather than on a black person's critically different history, social structure, and true opportunity: black persons were hardly inclined when they were cruelly transported and kept in slavery to regard America as the land of opportunity and they have little reason to regard it in such a way today. What is surprising is not that there are relatively fewer blacks who have made such contribution but that despite all obstacles there have been so many: the history of black intellectual achievements in the United States, which already started during the times of slavery, is hardly one which supports a thesis of a people who are (if there were to be such a thing) "genetically inferior."

It is readily apparent (and not denied) that blacks (just as do whites, orientals, and any other group) have a spectrum of IQ which stretches from the lowest to the highest: nor can it be denied that all ethnic groups within the framework of their cultural possibilities have demonstrated intelligent behaviour of the highest sort. Given cultural, social, and technical possibilities, and by whatever criterion one chooses to use, all ethnic groups have made major contribution to human life. Cultural frameworks are critical here: until Chagal, there were few if any Jewish painters of note. Judaism traditionally eschewed this art form on biblical grounds and only liberation from Orthodoxy and the ability to live as members of the community within other cultures brought about a change. Moreover, and like-wise for cultural reasons, women until recently have made only spotty, even if significant, major contributions: yet few would argue that such a lack of contributions is a function of intelligence rather than that it is a function of culture and, therefore, of prejudice and possibility.

Studies, which purported to show that children in "Head Start" did improve but in their later childhood and teen years "dropped back," were used to support the thesis that programs such as Head Start are essentially wasteful and ill-advised. No attention was paid to the fact that children who participate in such a program of neces-sity come from a deprived social setting and that they almost inevitably continue their social life within its embrace (or, some would argue, clutches).[10] Continuing to live in such a setting, despite programs such as Head Start, is very likely destructive if not indeed devastating to a person's further development.[11] But that hardly argues against programs such as Head Start. On the contrary: what it does do is to argue for expanding programs such as Head Start so that the basic social problems of poverty and blighted environment in the home are ameliorated. Individual success occurs in the con-text of the community and its social structure. One wonders what would have happened to the children of medieval (or more recently Russian) serfs had they been taken out of their homes for a few hours per day to be sent to the equivalent of Head Start and for the rest of the time kept in their old milieu!

A story might be appropriate here: I have a friend (once a stu-dent of mine) who grew up in one of the very worst ghettos on the South side of Chicago. His father was shot when my friend was seven years old while carrying a birthday cake to his wife (he appar-ently got into the line of fire during a "shoot-out"). My friend grew up like most ghetto kids, I suppose: theft and drug deals were (as they even more are today) the order of the day. He was lucky: when he was about ten he was identified by a social worker as a particu-larly bright and promising person. With the help of the social worker, his mother was able to obtain sometimes two or two and a half jobs at a time so that she could afford to send him to a private school and leave the ghetto environment. Following this, he went to and graduated from one of the best universities in the area and then came to us. After two and a half years, he received an offer from Harvard to take a year off from medical college and obtain a Master of Public Health. Upon returning, degree in hand and because I was about to leave for a lecture tour in Scandinavia, I suggested that he might travel with me, study the health care system there, write a report and, provided a solid report were written, receive university credit. We did just that. For me it was one of the finest learning experiences. A few days after getting there, and while walking down the street in Oslo, he turned to me and said: "you know this is the first time in my life that I do not feel like a black man in a white man's world." His was moral luck combined with an extremely high native ability and tenacity. I doubt that, given my intelligence and tenacity, I could have done the same thing. What must it be like day in and day out to feel as a stranger (and a despised stranger) in one's own nation? Can compassion not at least give us a hint and can compassionate rationality and good will really not find a solution?

Suggestions of genetic inferiority are, of course, not only used (and, perhaps or even no doubt, meant) to support a basically conservative if not indeed a reactionary agenda, an agenda which, woefully short on the compassion part of compassionate rationality and furthermore based on shoddy reasoning, would keep those who are "down" down; they are, likewise and with equal importance, used to justify not doing anything to alter what no one can deny are indeed abominable conditions. In the long run, of course, an agenda such as this (an agenda short on compassionate rationality) is destructive of community and of its basic concepts. Few would really believe that blacks today feel (or ought to feel) very much solidarity with the greater community in the United States today. Indeed, the basic ethical question is not whether the average IQ of a given group—for whatever reason—is or is not a few points higher or lower than is that of another: I strongly doubt that, given valid measurements it is or would be; but that is a question those interested in such measurements and the validity of such measurements can concern themselves with. The basic question is why a rather trivial statistical difference not applicable to any particular individual in the group should be a relevant ethical criterion for inevitably continuing the disadvantaging of a given entire group. Denying the group the advantages necessary so that individuals can escape from the confines of their social situation not only deprives talented individuals within the group the possibility of living satisfactory lives and of developing their talents; denying the group such advantages eventually will deprive the community of a pool of critically needed talent while shattering its solidarity. When one holds that the underclass is the underclass because of its genetic endowment and not because of its social setting and then and therefore decides not to try to improve the social setting one creates a circular and self-fulfilling prophecy.

There is a difference between arguing that individual genetic endowment provides the framework of intellectual possibility which is then (necessarily as well as significantly) fleshed out by cultural, social, and other environmental conditions and arguing that this framework is a racial or ethnic characteristic. One cannot doubt that severely retarded persons will not be able to achieve intellectual preeminence, although the amount of achievement such persons can make when opportunities are provided is formidable. But that is hardly the same as arguing that certain racial groups are intellectually inferior on a genetic basis and then concluding that and therefore any effort to provide help to escape destructive social forces is ill-conceived. In my view both the initial premise of intellectual inferiority and the conclusion are flawed: the first flawed technically and scientifically and the second ethically, humanly, morally and, not least of all, pragmatically.

The basic point gets us back to a consideration of community, of its meaning and of its role. No one privy to the facts or equipped with eyes, ears and modest compassion can argue that there is not in the United States today a class of traditionally poor who often, but not always, are black persons. The basic discussion does not deny the presence of such a class: indeed it recognizes its existence; the discussion centers about the genesis, the explanation and (at least for most of us) the eradication of what largely has become traditional poverty: poverty which is not poverty because a previously reasonably well-off individual has fallen on hard times but poverty which is a poverty which has been present for generations and which is endemic in the community in which such individuals live. If we view our society as consisting of competing forces whose interests are opposed we end up with a "them" and "us" mentality in which community is at best a temporary tool for getting on with our tasks. If, on the other hand, we view society as a community of persons who so as to meet their individual goals and develop their individual talents necessarily make the life and vitality of the community itself one of their major goals, a different sort of possibility emerges.

I want to make what I think is an important distinction between "being poor" and "being in poverty." When I first came to this country we certainly were poor: the Nazi state had stripped us of all but our lives, some small amount of personal property without material value and five dollars for the three of us. My father, who was a physician, had to repeat all of his qualifying examination (starting with anatomy, physiology, and biochemistry and then going through the whole gamut of clinical specialties as all medical students have to—and in a foreign language) while my mother obtained extremely underpaid work. The apartment we lived in was inadequate, there often was little food and certainly never any extras (I remember that I often, but not always, received a nickel every two weeks for a bottle of soda which a friend of mine—who received a similar sum every two weeks—and I would then share). But we were not "in poverty": we were simply "poor." Ours was a tradition of learning and success through learning: there was always a New York Times (even if there was little food) on the table, there were always books on the shelves, there was always good music and good intelligent conversation. Furthermore, and perhaps most important of all, we could readily see others who had shared the same fate and who had gone on to succeed.

Being in poverty is quite a different thing. It means not only not having enough or little variety to eat, it does not only mean living in a poor apartment and having virtually no extras. It often means having no place to live (except perhaps a crime and rat infested neighborhood), having no tradition of learning, no tradition of success through learning, no role models to look to, often not only no family structure but little familiarity with others who do. Above all and because of this, it not only means having no hope but it denotes a lack of understanding of what the concept "hope" is all about. That, in many cases, is what has happened to the underclass in the United States today.

The explanation for traditional poverty has many facets. In Marxist terms—and I believe that while the Marxist explanation is hardly the entire explanation no explanation that ignores it altogether can hope to succeed—an exploitable class is necessary so that those in power (which of course means those with wealth) can continue to enjoy their power. And while the way this manifests itself differs with history and culture, one can (and could in the past) see this sort of thing in all parts of the world. How such an exploitable class came to be in any particular cultural setting depends on that culture's world view and on the material as well as the nonmaterial forces in history.[12] One thing can, I think, be safely stated: the presence of a traditionally exploited class (no matter how powerful the exploiter will be) creates and reinforces a "them" and "us" mentality which will eventually and inevitably weaken the society in which it is found. It is, interestingly enough, a phenomenon not unique to capitalist nations: it is a totalitarian phenomenon which with some cultural variations could equally easily be seen in the former Bolshevik states.

What is being said about society can, with some modifications, of course, be likewise applied to the world community. Again from a Marxist perspective—a perspective which, I believe, is hardly the entire explanation but is a perspective which cannot be ignored— exploitable societies are necessary so that more "advanced" (i.e., materially affluent) societies can continue to enjoy their position in the world. Likewise, one thing can be safely stated: the presence of traditionally exploited nations (no matter how powerful exploiting nations may be) creates and reinforces a "them" and "us" mentality which will eventually and inevitably weaken and finally destroy any idea of a global community.

In today's societies as well as in today's world our individual (personal or corporate) existence, prosperity, and survival are possible only if we begin to deal with the fact that we have common long-term goals. Our individual short-term goals may be achievable when they run counter to the goal of communal solidarity and survival: but they are achievable only at the price of sacrificing our longer term goals. This is as true of individual persons as it is true of individual cultures. In ages past, we could afford (though doing so was neither ethically justifiable nor pragmatically wise) to ignore the long-term consequences of pursuing our immediate goals: the consequences for those who did the disadvantaging were comfortably far away. With the advent of modern technology, pursuing our short-term at the expense of our long-term goals has had ever more immediate consequences: in a sense our long- have tended to move closer to our short-term goals.

Different societies have recognized and dealt with such problems within their borders in different ways. The world community, on the other hand, is just beginning to deal with such problems on a global scale. The question will be asked: why does anyone (or why does any particular society) have an ethical obligation to accommodate their personal short-term goals to long-term ones? Why should I (or why should a given society) not live in a way which maximizes short-term profit and which makes my (or a given society's) life the most pleasant and comfortable, even if this is done at the expense of those less well-off and even if doing so will, some years hence, damage my own or the world community? Ethically speaking, why should I care? I have suggested that the answer to this question can be found in a combination of arguments: it can be found in a Kantian argument which suggests that the moral life necessitates paying more than lip service to a realm of ends; it can be found in a Utilitarian argument which seeks the greatest good for the greatest number; and, above all, it can be found in a pragmatic argument which sees us as at the very least morally acquainted, which sees us applying compassionate reason within a framework of existential a prioris, and which recognizes the "prior worth" that community as a dynamic, homeostatic system in which individual and communal interests necessarily merge has. Such justifications at least in part must ground themselves on a realization of our inevitably common purpose and goals without which neither individual persons nor corporate entities can survive.

The justification of the status quo can, among other things, be found in the notion of moral strangers; the justification for altering and working together on altering such a status quo can be found in the whole idea of "moral acquaintances" willing to recognize and work within their common framework of existential a prioris and willing to use compassionate rationality to work out common moral problems. Curiosity will drive us to examine the fate of others different than our own and the reasons for it; imagination will allow us to come to terms with the fact that we ourselves might very easily have been among the disadvantaged instead of among the more lucky; compassion will drive us to seek to remedy such situations; and rationality will help guide our compassion so that our remedies may have a real chance to succeed. Compassion without rationality could well result in our merely "throwing money at the problem": a thing which is not only useless but which can, as I shall again mention, aggravate the already severe problem. Rationality without compassion, on the other hand, could lead us to seek shelter in a libertarian type of argument in which our obligation to remedy would lack moral force. Compassionate rationality—balancing compassion by reason and helping stimulate reason through compassion—would help us work towards truly remedying the situation.

In real terms such a view would necessitate some form of affirmative action: of taking steps to see that the consequences of such disadvantaging and especially of traditional disadvantaging are, as far as that is possible, undone. I see this sort of affirmative action (both affirmative action for traditionally disadvantaged groups in this nation and the affirmative action which I feel would be appropriate on a global scale) as rooted in the historical events which have led to and perpetuated such disadvantaging as well as grounded in the obligation to take one's part in righting an ongoing wrong from which one, whether one wants to or not, profits. Beyond this: unless the disadvantaging of persons within our borders and of nations on a global scale is undone (a thing which will take many decades but which, nevertheless, must be started with "all deliberate speed") the community (both the national community and the global community) will fall apart and destroy itself. As deplorable as violence and its consequences are, revolution and war will become inevitable.

Although examples of historical disadvantaging of one group by another are many, one can use the experience of black America as one of the most flagrant examples of such historical disadvantaging. It should be evident that such disadvantaging within the American nation bears a more than superficial resemblance to the disadvantaging of the nonindustrialized world on a global scale.[13]

When it comes to explaining the existence of black ghettos today, a glance at American history should suffice. As I stated before, American blacks in general are persons whose ancestors were literally torn from their roots. If they survived transport on slave vessels, such persons were forced into slavery and separated from their family, community, religion, culture, and language. Their traditions, their religion, their family structure, and the very habits of their daily lives were rudely interrupted. Bereft of all roots, these slaves were entirely at the mercy not only of hostile forces but of hostile forces they could not understand. Whites profiting from the slave trade (and these included a large number of commercial enterprises some of which were owned or operated by the Catholic church) had little incentive to oppose the very thing from which they profited. It was in the interest of the white establishment to promulgate and reinforce the notion of black inferiority, indeed the notion that these poor persons belonged to a different species.[14] When slavery was abolished, it was abolished largely because keeping slaves was no longer as profitable as it had been. As property, slaves had to be housed, fed, given some sort of health care, and some sort of care in their old age; as free persons who could be hired at minimal wages, they did not have to be housed, fed, and minimally cared for. They were free to "enjoy" the fruits of freedom in the context of a hostile society which continued with every attempt to prevent their material, intellectual, and political success. When fathers were sold away from their wives and children (a regular occurrence) families were disrupted and a largely matriarchal society was created. During slavery many states made it a crime to teach blacks to read and write; intelligence and education did not (as it did in the Jewish experience) confer a survival advantage.

With the abolition of slavery many blacks moved north only to find that their largely physical skills were marketable only at starvation wages and that the attempt to gain intellectual skills were generally foiled by inferior schools and a lack of true access to higher education. They, therefore and together with some whites, soon were a substantial part of the American underclass, the hard-core poor. Keeping Blacks in that position was and to some significant extent even today is an advantage for whites: the position of the white upper and middle class in America today is to a large extent a product of the prior exploitation of blacks. Well-off whites profited directly and poor whites had not only a better shot at getting a menial job but also were and continue to be provided with a socially handy way of feeling superior to someone while achieving little themselves. For the nation, however, such an advantage did not last long. As society developed, available menial jobs tended to disappear: ditch-diggers, porters, and other unskilled laborers were less and less in demand while the exploitable underclass persisted and grew. Add to this a welfare system which, among other things, has tended to break up families by forcing fathers to move away from their families so that their children could get benefits otherwise denied to them: a policy, interestingly enough, often established by the very people most verbal about the value of what they call "family values!" A matriarchal society in which often no family structure is evident was perpetuated. I do not mean to imply that the traditional father-mother-children are the only way in which "family" can be conceived or to suggest that very many ghetto mothers do not do their very best to create an acceptable environment for their children. There is no doubt that many single parent or nontraditional family groupings can do very well indeed raising children whose future will not be blighted and will, in fact, be every bit as good as is the fate of children raised in more traditional families. I do suggest that in a society in which people are in poverty and in which no or little tradition of success exists even the traditional as well as the nontraditional family may find it virtually impossible to remain intact and to raise children with a decent chance to succeed.

At this time, the United States has a largely ghettoized underclass with little real opportunity to escape the ghetto: a segment of the population effectively excluded from what has euphemistically been called the "American dream" and a society with much to be angry and hostile about. Even those blacks who have managed to escape the ghetto are treated far differently than are whites. Such a state of affairs, although it may still help advantage whites and may still help members of the white underclass "feel good" because of their supposed "superiority," today disadvantages and ultimately threatens to shatter the community in which it is allowed to exist.

The disadvantaging of any particular member of a society by other members (or the disadvantaging of any particular society by another) results in the inevitable advantaging of another segment (or society). This is the case even when those who are advantaged are themselves opposed to such a state of affairs. Societal as well as global resources and opportunities are not unlimited: what is given to one cannot be given to another. When one segment of society (or when one society) profits from the disadvantaging of another segment (or society), the advantaged segment (or society) is loathe to forfeit its advantage and is apt to develop a host of explanations and justifications meant to show either that such disadvantaging does not take place, that it is beyond the control of those who profit from it or that, all things considered, it is justified.

In the *Bell Curve* the authors claim that only by a return to individualism can America's problems be properly handled. A person, they say, should not be judged as a member of a group but as an individual. Few of us would, I think, disagree with that statement. The authors of this book readily admit that members of any group may fall anywhere along the Gaussian curve and that, consequently, they deserve to be treated as what they are rather than what their group is.

> group differences in cognitive ability, so desperately denied for so long, can best be handled—can only be handled—by a return to individualism. A person should not be judged as a member of a group but as an individual.[15]

But given the unwarranted and, I think, erroneous assumptions made here in the book and given the so-called "solutions," the stark individualism the authors suggest can only lead to perpetuating rather than eliminating this sad situation. My thesis right along has been that true and meaningful individualism (the capacity to develop one's talents and pursue one's life plans) is possible and is viable only in the context of an enduring community. Such a community—a community which makes ethical social decisions with compassionate rationality within a framework of what I have called the existential a prioris—will of course respect individual capacity and choice. To make this meaningful, however, individual possibilities must be explored by means of an equal opportunity not only to express a knowing individual choice but above all as opportunity to develop individual talent. Communities will see individual possibilities not merely or predominately as genetically conditioned—indeed, whether they are or not will be largely immaterial—but will see individual possibility as truly existing not only where it exists without being actively hindered but where, indeed, it is actively facilitated. In a community such as the United States and despite the fact that social conditions at the very least hinder "access," speaking of "equal access" to opportunity is at the very least disingenuous if not downright cynical.

Affirmative action—which seeks to redress a past and present wrong by giving an advantage to the disadvantaged—has been said to advantage one person or group at the cost of disadvantaging another person or group. And when it is a "zero-sum game" there can be no doubt that this is partially but only very partially true. What, it is asked, is fair about disadvantaging a middle-class native born white male who has had no role in creating conditions today in order to advantage a member of a disadvantaged group? Do two wrongs really make a right? The argument which makes whites responsible in the sense of being culpable for the past wrongs of slavery or of the reconstruction period must be rejected as surely as must those who would make Germans living today (and born after the Nazi period) responsible in the sense of being culpable for having a role in Nazi atrocities. The concept of collective guilt makes little sense and would, in fact, perpetuate the very situation it bemoans: basically it is a racist concept which holds that all "x's" by virtue of being "x's" are guilty. The problem here is the broad way in which the term "responsibility" is used: the word responsibility can denote both culpability (responsibility for having done something) and obligation (responsibility to do something). There are other reasons than having been culpable for past wrongs which would make one responsible for playing one's part in redressing a wrong. These fall, I think, into at least two groups: (1) those of us who are white males (even when we have had no role in causing such disadvantage and even if we detest the very existence of such disadvantage) inevitably are benefited by our membership in the advantaged group; and (2) the very fact that a wrong is being committed by or in an allegedly democratic community to which we belong, of which we are an integral part and in which we have some say, makes ameliorating and, if possible, righting that wrong our obligation.

There can be no question that white native born males enjoy an advantage over others who are not members of their particular group. That does not mean that native born white males in this country invariably are better off than are their non-American born, non-white, non-male counterparts. But it does mean that as a group and as individuals within that group distinct explicit and tacit advantages accrue: whites and males continue to receive a higher salary for the same type of job as do nonwhites or non-males;[16] white males have a higher incidence of coronary artery surgery than do non-whites or females (the presumption, one I do not necessarily share, being that having coronary artery surgery for the indications done in the United States today is an advantage);[17] females tend to be adjudicated as "incompetent" by the courts when under similar circumstances males would be ruled "competent";[18] under similar circumstances, bank loans for black families are more difficult to obtain than are bank loans for whites;[19] blacks are treated quite differently by police as well as courts; and there are many more examples. The United States is a racist (and to a lesser extent a religiously prejudiced and class-ridden) society: a society in which the idea of race, and to a lesser extent of religion and class, has penetrated deeply and in which, under a thicker or thinner veneer of political correctness, it forms the background to virtually all that is thought, written, or done. While there can be no serious question that important explicit legal and explicit social changes have taken place, there can also be little doubt that culturally racism (and with it religious bias and class consciousness) is alive, well and not limited to any particular race, religion or class. The anti-black feelings and policies of whites in turn have resulted in anti-white feelings among blacks. We have become a nation in which a sense of distrust and dislike (whites for those not like them, Christians for non-Christians, blacks towards whites in general, and Jews in particular, etc.) has divided and threatens to destroy us. Changing this situation—not merely by decrying it but by willing to participate in the solution rather than being part of the problem or a pure spectator (which since we cannot escape personal involvement in a nexus in which we are enmeshed, is, in fact, not possible)—can, therefore, also be argued for on prudential grounds.

There are other than purely prudential grounds which must motivate us to become a part of the solution: grounds which make us responsible both in the sense of responsibility based on being "culpable," and in the sense of being responsible by virtue of the general responsibility of participating in one's neighbor's weal and woe as well as in the sense of ameliorating injustice. As I have mentioned, those of us who are white males (even when we have had no role in causing and even if we detest the very existence of such disadvantage) inevitably are benefited by our membership in the advantaged group. We are not only directly advantaged (we generally earn more money, get more deferential treatment in everyday life as well as in our contacts with the authorities, etc.) but we are and perhaps more importantly also advantaged because coming from a white and especially from a white middle-class background we have inherited a family structure, a familiarity with positive experiences, a different way of using language, and a constellation of values which place us into a position in which our success at an equivalent expenditure of energy is far easier than would be success were we to belong to a minority group. Things like a particular family structure, a familiarity with positive experiences, a different way of using language, and a particular constellation of values are advantageous not necessarily because, by some external or eternal yardstick, they are inherently better or worse: such things are advantageous because in our particular culture the behaviour which results from these conditions tends to help persons pursue their particular interests, develop their talents and fashion their particular lives in a more fulfilling way.

Equipped with these advantages a white native born male of average intelligence and with average luck (especially if he comes from a middle-class background) will find it much easier to be successful in pursuing his interests and developing his talents than will a highly intelligent black person in the ghetto. A black person of average intelligence and with average luck will find himself clearly unable to pursue his interests and developing his talents as would his white counterpart. The social situation as it exists today inevitably advantages the white middle-class native born male over other members of the society and, in the United States, especially over black members; as a result, the disadvantaging of minorities continues. Advantaged persons will often cry out that "affirmative action" when it gives certain "points" to members of minority groups treats them unfairly and will claim that "fairness" consists of judging everyone purely on their "merits": that persons ought to be judged purely on their own personal achievements seen out of context with their social setting; explicit achievements when it comes, for example, to grade point average when seeking a particular position or when applying for admission to graduate or professional schools. But such explicit achievement was inevitably at least in part enabled or discouraged by the social nexus. A white middle-class native born male grew up understanding the concept hope: this allowed him to strive to fulfill his desires; he grew up in a family where he as well as they were familiar with the process and with the success of others in similar situations: this provided understanding and support; he grew up having gone to better schools, using a different language and vocabulary and behaving in ways judged more appropriate for testing and interviews, and so forth. Good golfers playing with golfers who are less proficient do not consider that placing a handicap is unfair to them; indeed, the rules of particular social settings (particular games or golf courses) regularly stipulate handicap. They know that to have a fair game requires an equal de facto chance for all who participate: if handicaps would not be used, those with the best chance would inevitably win. It is strange not to apply such a process to the vastly more important game of life.

Impoverished nations are frequently in a similar situation as impoverished minority groups. Theirs is a history of exploitation by the industrialized nations, exploitation which enabled those nations to flourish and which continues to advantage them. The exploitation of exploited groups has run into difficult times because such groups have not been trained for the jobs needed today while the more menial jobs of yesterday have disappeared. Likewise, the vast natural and human resources in impoverished nations have largely been exhausted either by being used up or by not being prepared for the demands of a new age. The industrialized nations responsible for this exploitation enjoy the lifestyle they do today because of yesterday's exploitation. They, like the native born white middle-class male in the United States, continue (whether they choose to be or not) to be advantaged by ongoing disadvantage. Here too a system of affirmative action which attempts to remedy an ongoing wrong is needed.

The formation of legal structures which arbitrated disputes and removed at least many of the more severe punishments from private or narrowly social sanction to publicly decreed punishment thanks its existence largely to the necessity for "keeping the king's peace." The peace of the realm inevitably would be disturbed by private vengeance or when persons "took the law into their own hands." It is of benefit to all that the "peace of the realm" be maintained. Those things threatening that peace, therefore, were and continue to be arbitrated by arms of the legal structure: neither private vengeance nor vigilantism can be allowed in a stable society. The decision of what should and what should not fall under the rubric of "need to be controlled" or "need to be taken out of private hands" is a social decision which, in a democratic society, will hopefully be made by and through all concerned. In other words: how individuals act cannot always be a private matter and legitimately some of the ways in which individuals may act fall under public control. I would argue that affirmative action on a national and global scale is equally needed if "the king's peace" is to be maintained.

The relationship among nations is similar to that among individuals. Like individuals in former times, societies and the people which compose them are dependent upon the peace of the realm (in this case the world realm) so as to live their own private or corporate lives. Individuals are expected (and at times mandated) to relate to each other and to their community in certain but not in other ways. The aim here is the peace of all so that all may thrive, prosper and, within that framework, pursue their own interests and develop their own talents.

Just as individuals and their community must interact in certain ways if peace is to be maintained, individual societies or nations must relate to each other and to the larger world community in certain ways. The aim here is likewise the maintenance of peace, a peace essential if the particular communities which compose the world community are to thrive, prosper and, within that framework, pursue their own interests and develop their own culture in ways they choose. When individuals act either to impinge on other individuals or when they act in ways which seriously disturb the community and its peaceful survival, sanctions (which when they are decided upon by legitimately established process are held to be legitimate sanctions) will be applied. In a world in which distances have shrunk and technical possibilities have magnified, a similar way of proceeding is needed. Some of the things which may happen in Sri Lanka or outer Mongolia inevitably and ultimately will affect those living in Oslo or New York. Asocial individual beings are no more possible than asocial nations: that is, nations whose behavior is not intimately and necessarily interwoven with that of all of its neighbors. What is an external (a problem which concerns the particular or the world community) and what an internal problem (a problem which purely concerns individual persons or individual societies) is not by any means easy to determine. In the long run, this differential depends upon social decisions which, one would hope, are made in a fair and democratic fashion by all concerned. Here also compassion tempered by reason as well as reason tempered by compassion may help guide the way into improving an untenable status quo.

National sovereignty, just as individual sovereignty, must be seen to operate within a framework of meaningful international laws and norms. Starvation in India, repression and denial of basic freedoms in China, concentration camps in Nazi Germany, Apartheid in South Africa, or ghettoization and police brutality in the United States will inevitably affect all other states and nations. When I brutally beat my children, the community cannot sit still: it will interfere and put a stop to my acting in this way; when I heap trash on my lawn and create unsanitary conditions, the community likewise will stop me. Ultimately my actions threaten the peace of all. When nations grossly mistreat their citizens or when there is starvation, persons will seek to flee to "safer" areas. In turn, this puts undue pressure on the living space and economy of host nations and threatens the peace. The problems in Europe and in the United States with legal and illegal immigration, the problem of what to do with asylum seekers and, indirectly, the rise of right wing groups in Europe as well as in the United States, groups which among other things seek to arouse hostility against "foreigners" can be directly or indirectly traced to the social, economic, and political problems in some other land. As Professor Habermas, in an article in a German newspaper, so aptly pointed out, persons do not leave their country or their culture lightly; when they flee they do so because economic and/or political situations have become intolerable. To claim that conditions or policies which directly or indirectly threaten the peace of all are a "purely internal concern" of another nation is as untrue as is the claim that dumping garbage on my lawn or mistreating my child is of no concern to the community at large. Having compassion for the illegal immigrant and for the asylum seeker without tempering that compassion with reason could easily lead to simply allowing all who would to enter a host nation: such a move might, in short order, destroy the host nation itself. Reason, motivated by true compassion for those who are suffering, would prompt one to do more than to apply merely the sop of immediate admission or eventual destruction: it would actively work towards ameliorating conditions elsewhere while and at the same time doing as much as possible for those in acute need. Compassion tempered with reason would prompt us to prevent the problem while doing all we can to alleviate the misery of those afflicted. In the long run, preventing disease is far less costly (in both human and monetary terms) than curing a disease after it has started: but that does not argue against curing disease.

Compassionate rationality can help us to chart a course between the Scylla of sentimentality and the Charybdis of insensitive reason without the leaven of compassion. It will help us to recognize and feel for the problem as well as for those enmeshed in it while at the same time working at solutions aimed not only at ameliorating the immediate fate of those who have been disadvantaged but at the same time and by doing this preserving a viable community for all. It can do this in dealing with the exploited and traditionally disadvantaged within a nation as well as in working at correcting the problem of exploited nations within the world community.

The western world in its treatment of refugees or asylum seekers has consistently attempted to differentiate between economic and political refugees. Somehow, those who feared persecution for political reasons are seen as "deserving" while those who flee starvation or want are considered to be undeserving of asylum. In the first half of this century, refugees and asylum seekers came largely from more or less developed nations: the Soviet Union, Nazi Germany, Fascist Italy, Franco Spain, and others. Resistance to accepting these refugees—especially but not only Jewish refugees from Nazi Germany—deeply implicated western nations in the results of the holocaust: many who died would not have died had more generous policies existed. Moreover and even after the full extent of Nazi atrocities were known, no real attempt to rescue people were made: in fact, pilots were expressly forbidden to bomb Auschwitz or the access roads to it despite the fact that Buna (a sub-camp of Auschwitz in which rubber-like products were produced) was regularly bombed. Western nations in general and the United States in particular were implicated in the holocaust in at least three ways: (1) not only were there no efforts to rescue Jews, every effort to thwart even those who could legally enter was made.[20] (2) Attempts to bomb extermination or concentration camps were forbidden or discouraged. (3) Ways of dealing with survivors of concentration camps were half-hearted and largely ineffective: the west did all it could not to accept survivors while attempting to foil all attempts to reach Israel—the only haven left.

In the second half of this century, most asylum seekers and refugees have come from underdeveloped nations. Many such nations had brutal and repressive dictatorships; in others, persons went hungry or found it impossible to support their families. Here too, industrialized nations bear a large share of the blame: these nations have been the traditionally exploited. Just as the opulence of the wealthy rides piggyback on the disadvantaging of others within a capitalist society, the development of the industrialized nations until very recently rode piggyback on the exploitation of what are now called "underdeveloped" nations. Today traditionally disadvantaged groups in some of the underdeveloped nations as well as in the United States (and to a lesser extent in other parts of the western world) and traditionally disadvantaged nations throughout the world constitute not only a national and world disgrace but also a national and world threat. Doing justice has become a method of self-preservation.

I have argued throughout the book that the idea as well as the reality of individual freedom as well as the genuine possibility of political democracy presupposes that basic needs have been met: to speak of freedom to assemble to the homeless or of freedom of speech to parents unable to feed their children is disingenuous, hypocritical, or downright cynical. Beyond this, establishing and maintaining a functioning and viable (as opposed to a nonfunctioning and, in the long haul, nonviable sham) political democracy requires the meeting of at least minimal basic economic, social, and educational requirements for all members of a participatory community. Maintaining a true democracy around the world (a democracy which in various cultures will, of course, take various forms but a system in which all have a meaningful and respectful way of interacting with one another to make decisions) has become more than merely an internal national concern.

Licensing health-professionals or attorneys, setting speed limits, or levying real estate taxes are clearly "internal" concerns of a given community; persecuting minorities or members of opposition parties or creating conditions of inequity which cause severe and widespread homelessness and hunger is quite another matter. What does and what does not count as an internal matter cannot be left entirely to the discretion of individual societies or countries; ultimately, it is a matter for an international body to decide by accepted and fair international procedure. In general, things which can seriously threaten peaceful relations among nations or things which displace large hordes of people who then inevitably burden other states and consequently threaten their peace, will fall under international control.

How can the sort of approach to ethics that I propose help in sorting out such a problem? Since we share a common framework of bio-psycho-social givens, we inevitably know as much about others: we know that these personal or corporate others have a drive for being, biological as well as social needs, wish to avoid suffering and wish to pursue their own interests and we know that by virtue of our common sense of logic we can engage in dialogue. As normal human beings, we are equipped with a sense of compassion as much as we are normally equipped with sight. This sense of compassion, enabled by curiosity and stimulated by imagination, will cause us to take more than a passing interest in our neighbor's weal and woe. Transformed by reason (and realizing that our own individual personal and individual corporate destinies depend upon our membership in a community) this sense of compassion can serve us in going about the business of establishing a way of fair procedure in which all participate and in crafting an ethic which will allow the larger community to prosper and grow. Such a view rests upon a metaphysical concept in which neither freedom nor the necessary social connectedness of all sentient beings is seen as the sole concept. Rather it is a concept which presupposes both necessities: freedom as individual aspiration enunciated, enabled, and vouchsafed in a community and connectedness as the connectedness among free individual persons and among free corporate entities homeostatically and, therefore, dynamically related in pursuit of a common goal.

There are different ways of conceptualizing and addressing the problems of poverty, inadequacy of education, and inadequate access to health care as they exist in the United States today. Among these are (1) denying the existence or gravity of these problems; (2) claiming that there is "nothing wc can do," by one of two methods: (a) that we as individuals are impotent to do little if anything meaningful to help (the claim of impotency) or (b) that we can do nothing since doing so would necessarily (since ultimately it would require taxing the wealthy for the benefit of the poor) restrict freedom and liberty; (3) blaming the victim in one of two ways: (a) attempting to show that the socially disadvantaged are not really socially disadvantaged as much as they are genetically underequipped: in a sense a nonmoral way of blaming the victim; and (b) claiming that, because of indolence, laziness, and lack of stamina, it is the failure of those disadvantaged to grab the opportunities that exist which is at fault; and (4) sentimentalizing and, as it were, "idealizing" poverty and consequently attempting to act not only compassionately but in truth sentimentally and, therefore, neither reasonably nor consistently. There are variations on as well as permutations and combinations of these themes: but it is these themes which in one way or another have underwritten most attempts to evade recognizing and effectively addressing this problem.

The first of these ways of conceptualizing and dealing (or excusing not dealing) with these problems should, one would think, be rather easy to deal with. Confronted by statistical facts and existential conditions about them, those who deny the existence of such conditions would be expected to give up this idea. Amazingly enough, this is not the case. When confronted with these facts persons may agree but then continue to forward the same claim (one would think an unreasonable but unfortunately and in fact a not rare event), persons may retreat to protestations of impotence or persons may resort to victim blaming. And a combination of all three is, perhaps, the most frequent. Often individuals to whom you point out indisputable statistics will counter by saying a variation of "I can't imagine how this can be, I never see any of it." To a limited extent this may be true: most middle- and upper-class persons live in virtual enclaves sheltered (except when they become the victims of criminals many of which are driven to this by their poverty) from the equally segregated areas of the poor. And yet, "not seeing" is, at least in part, likewise a function of not choosing to see. The homeless, the poor, the hungry and the desperate abound in the larger as well as in the smaller cities of the United States. "Not seeing them" is as often a protective mechanism, a deliberate closing of the eyes.

The first variation of the second of these ways of conceptualizing and dealing (or excusing not dealing) with such problems—the protestation of impotence—is in part true: there is little any individual can do by individual action to remedy the situation. In part this excuse rides piggyback on the very same notion of isolated individuals as does the second variation of this excuse. It may be true that as individuals acting alone and conceiving ourselves as isolated beings we can do little, albeit that does not mean that we cannot do anything at all. But we are not, in fact, asocial and isolated beings: we are, whether we like to admit it or not, inevitably members of the community, capable of inciting communal interest and capable of joining in communal action. We can speak to those we inevitably contact in our daily lives, can exchange information and viewpoints, and learn from and influence each other. Finally, we are members in a community, allegedly democratic, and allegedly dedicated to carrying out the will of the people. As members of this community we not only can participate in its debate and share in its decisions but likewise inevitably must play our role in formulating its general will. Such a general will, when it comes to the kind of issue we are concerned with here, depends upon the prevalent type of approach used in conceptualizing and dealing with the problem. And, finally, we as individuals can help at least some of those who approach us and solicit our aid. When we only live in uni-dimensional social enclaves, only choose to eat in fine restaurants and live in expensive hotels and when we chose only to communicate meaningfully with those in our immediate sphere of interest in a similar social class we inevitably will be blind to what affects those less lucky. And we will have purposely blinded ourselves. In not fostering (indeed in stifling) our sense of compassion, we will inevitably be culpable. The second variation of this is precisely the libertarian account of morality we have been countering throughout the book. It is an account which is, I feel, not only seriously flawed philosophically but is also an account which tries to dismiss the role which compassion plays in morality and in making moral choices. Its basic metaphysical assumption that we are moral strangers is one which unites the first and second variation.

I have dealt with what I have called the "nonmoral" variation of the third of these ways of conceptualizing and dealing (or excusing not dealing) with the problems (that which would have our "underclass"—their term, not mine—not socially but genetically disadvantaged) as well as with what I have called the "moral" variation (which attributes lack of "gumption" rather than lack of opportunity to the members of this class) before. Both of these are attempts at victim blaming and are not only untrue but basically irrelevant in a community concerned about its members well-being.

The fourth way of conceptualizing and dealing with this situation is radically different: persons who act this way recognize the existence of this problem, assume responsibility and truly attempt to help. Unfortunately, this often results in solutions which have more sentiment than rationality. Contrary to one of my criticisms of libertarianism (that reason is not allowed to interact with compassion), this approach fails to temper compassion with reason. The result is often an attempt to "throw money" at the problem in a futile attempt to affect rapidly visible results and often in an attempt not to help those who are in need of our help but to assuage our own (justifiable) feelings of guilt and to make us (not the poor) "feel better." When results are at best halting and partial they are likely to be abandoned or inconsistently applied. In the final analysis this approach has been no more helpful than have the others. Indeed, this approach to caring for the poor has often resulted in a jumble of so-called entitlements which have often aggravated the very problem they have set out to solve. Unless reason and compassion work together for a common goal, unless reason articulates compassion and compassion tempers reason, no morally satisfactory approach is likely to occur.

I have remarked before that the excuses made for the deplorable conditions as they exist in the United States today are symmetrical to those used by the apologists for the Nazi regime: (1) it didn't happen or we didn't know about it; (2) there isn't anything we can or could do; and (3) the fault lies largely with the victims themselves. The first three of the ways of conceptualizing problems in the United States today bear more than a faint resemblance to the excuses which were and are being made by the Nazi apologists. I claim that there is a similarity between the conditions in Nazi Germany and the problems we face today: this similarity is not only in the situation itself but in the way we tend to conceptualize and ultimately deal (or fail to deal) with them.

In the United States, attempts to address the problems of poverty, racism, lack of health care, and inadequate education, have consisted of a hodgepodge of approaches. At the same time the very forces which, at least in my view, played a critical part in creating this problem have not only been allowed to go unchecked but have often been held up as virtues. American schools by and large help fortify and condition students to readily accept the myth of crass individualism and the myth of purely personal achievement as well as indoctrinating them with a view of American history, opportunity and political process which while an enticing fiction is a total distortion of reality. Sentimental appeals to a view of history which would have the United States be a haven of the poor and suppressed (what I would call "the huddled masses yearning to be free" lie), instead of balancing the country's role as a haven with that of simultaneously an exploiter do little to help us face the problem. The way children are educated in the United States today tends to fortify the notion of the asocial, freestanding individual which is so popular a feature of American civilization today. Moreover, such a fiction does little to foster and much to crush a feeling of compassion for others. Schools, furthermore, rely much on memorization and fail to foster curiosity, encourage imagination and train reason. The use of compassionate rationality, therefore, is not something that comes easily to those trained in such a system.

I have stressed throughout this book and continue to stress that developing and using a true democratic process is the main hope the United States and the world has to develop a just and lasting system of peace and prosperity. The United States is indeed technically a democracy: by and large elections are not rigged and all citizens (at least theoretically) have the right to vote. But in fact, the United States today is no longer a well-functioning democracy.

The preconditions (similar preconditions stressed by John Dewey) of personal, educational, social, and economic democracy have not been met. Following John Dewey, I have reiterated and stressed that democracy is, first of all, a moral ideal: to be politically viable democracy needs to be underpinned by democratic personal, democratic educational, democratic social, and democratic economic relationships. To be viable democracy must penetrate every fiber of our national and personal lives.

The hodgepodge of attempts to solve the problems we face has suffered from both the extreme of callousness and the extreme of sentimentality. Callousness would largely ignore the traditionally unemployed, the poor and the ignorant; where government programs exist, they exist more to stave off rebellion than to give meaningful aid. And, on the whole in such a view, government programs should be discouraged; relief if available would be a matter for individual and optional charity. The "thousand points of light" (with each point being an individual helping another individual) so much favored by former President Bush is an example. Such an approach is an adaptation of the libertarian world view and places full responsibility for dealing with their problems upon the persons having them or upon largely capricious (and often ill-conceived and arbitrary) largess. On the other hand, sentimentality would see the poor not only as deserving of communal support and help but as having no responsibility to help in determining their own fate. The approach has ranged from vilifying to glorifying the victim; neither approach can work. To make matters worse: where occasional tentative and realistic efforts have been made, they were generally insufficient and, when they failed to yield rapid results, tended to be downplayed or abandoned. Head Start and job training programs, which did yield some promising results, are examples.

Attempts to deal with the international problems of immigration and asylum, likewise have suffered from one of the two extremes: on the one hand are the undoubtedly well-intentioned but ill-conceived attempts to at once open all borders and allow all who would to flood in; on the other hand, have been attempts to exclude all who would seek asylum (except, of course, those the nation has a need for!). The one extreme is compassion unmodified by reason: when challenged, there is no argument except an appeal to hope ("we'll manage somehow" or "something will turn up") and sentiment; the other extreme is reason (of a strange sort, it must be admitted) disconnected from all compassion: when challenged, those who advocate complete exclusion take refuge into a version of "squatters right" or a libertarian type of argument. Neither of these extremes in approaching internal or external problems suffices.

Dealing with the problems of "third world," "emerging" or "nonindustrialized" nations (whatever euphemism one chooses, it ultimately refers to a group of nations who have been generally badly exploited) likewise has suffered from these two extremes: on the one hand, sentimentality leads one to the myth that such are "good" by virtue of being poor formerly or currently exploited; on the other hand, a libertarian form of non-compassionate rationality will invoke a lack of beneficent obligations to excuse either further exploitation or, at best, non-help.

The approach I advocate is a concerted attack on the roots of the problems. I am neither a sociologist nor an economist and so what I advocate is necessarily tentative, fragmentary, and incomplete. What I sketch is a philosophy of approach and not the approach or its details itself. But that does not discredit it: solving problems in today's complicated world requires the democratic interaction of numerous skills, backgrounds, and peoples. Since I believe that ultimately only a democratic process can help to deal with our problems justly and effectively and since democratic political process must be underpinned by personal, educational, social, and economic democracy the task is mammoth. In dealing with the problems at hand, we should be informed by an ethic we (or at least most of us) can subscribe to and which was forged in awareness of our common framework of existential a prioris. Our enormous general problems, furthermore, need to be examined and dealt with by using compassionate rationality.

Earlier in this chapter I have stated (see above) the conditions under which our problems could be approached. The whole book has been an argument for this approach. To reiterate and then illustrate:

1. As human animals (together, perhaps with higher nonhuman animals) we share a framework of bio-psycho-social givens which I have called the existential a prioris: this allows us to recognize the interests of other individuals as well as of other communities. Critical to this is the inborn drive of all beings for existence or being. It is a natural drive and as such not a moral requirement. But in the framework it plays a central role. The question "why should I be" is, in the final analysis, an incoherent one.

2. A necessary part of this framework is a common sense of basic logic which—in view of our common givens, stimulated by compassion and driven by compassionate rationality—allows and indeed prompts us to reason together. Our inborn sense of compassion, enabled by curiosity and stimulated by imagination, causes us to feel distinctly uneasy when confronted by the reality of others who could be helped going without.

3. Since we share a desire to exist, to develop and to thrive and since we realize that we and our community are interdependent, we share an interest in maintaining the peace. Furthermore, since we—as individuals and as a community which is the necessary condition for individual existence—wish to exist and to chart and determine our own destiny, we share an interest in allowing fair process to deal with our problems.

4. To be fair, a process must give ample voice to all concerned: all individuals within a given community and all communities within a world association.

5. A necessary part of any such fair process is a mutual agreement that all, even those who do not agree with the outcome, will abide by the results.

6. Such a fair process, since it recognizes that meeting individual interests is possible only in a community which evolves and ultimately vouchsafes it, is an ongoing, dynamic homeostatic process in which individual ends are shaped within the context of communal needs.

The problem of poverty and racism rampant in the United States and the exploitation of less fortunate nations by the more affluent will inevitably lead us to advocate some form of affirmative action. Our problems can only be addressed if all of us are willing to contribute sufficiently so that the grievous wrongs of the past and the resulting continuing advantaging of some over other groups can be brought to an end. The task before us is massive: it is one which cannot be accomplished in a world of moral strangers. It necessitates a burden of taxation on those who are well-off so that the problems of those who have been traditionally disadvantaged can be addressed. We shall have to levy more, not fewer, taxes. Our aim as a nation properly should not be primarily the protection of the middle class or the further pampering of the wealthy but the amelioration of the problems of the traditionally poor: those who are without hope today. If we as a nation, as well as those of us who are well-off within that nation, are to survive, peace must be kept. Ultimately this can only be accomplished if the terrible problems of poverty, lack of education and, therefore, lack of opportunity are effectively dealt with. I do not suggest that money alone can solve these problems but I do urge all to realize that without such funds (and without massive funds) problems of this sort cannot even start to be ameliorated.

What I have in mind, however, requires far more than money. It requires a reconstruction of our world view and of society itself. As I see it, the problems of poverty, lack of education, and lack of true democracy are all different aspects and part and parcel of the same basic problem. Basic to the kind of reconstruction I have in mind is a different kind of education starting at a young age. In the United States our system of education, rather than stressing stark individualism as a positive trait, would instead have to emphasize our interconnectedness. It would seek to foster our compassion, nourish our curiosity, stimulate our imagination and train our reason. Without such a reconstruction, nothing else can be achieved. But that will not serve to release the hordes of traditional poor from their bondage or put bread on their table or hope into their hearts in sufficient time to prevent the disaster which looms ahead and which those who are well-off in the short-term conveniently and in the final analysis disastrously ignore. We must simultaneously work on ameliorating existing conditions of poverty and inequality and provide an educational milieu in which longer range goals can be achieved. Society spawns its institutions including its educational system and, therefore, these institutions reflect the society of which they are a part. The few who hold power in a society which has allowed and continues to allow the few to hold it, will inevitably attempt to thwart such efforts. Power, peacefully if at all possible regretfully non-peacably if not, must be wrested from their hands.

In a true democracy an educated, interested, and interactive electorate could overturn a frozen status quo: true democracy is, therefore, not in the interest of those who wield enormous power in our society and throughout the capitalist world. This power is largely wielded by international cartels. Decisions and policies made are apt to originate in board rooms in New York, Tokyo or Bonn. The so-called "tri-lateral commission" (founded in 1973 by David Rockefeller of the Chase Manhattan Bank and an organization which despite its immense power, we seldom hear about) is an organization which unites Capitalist interests from Japan, the United States, Western Europe and by now perhaps other areas. A quotation I cited in a previous work[21] from a report of that commission, bears repeating:

The vulnerability of democratic government in the United States comes not primarily from external threats, though such threats are real, nor from internal subversion from the left or the right, although both possibilities could exist, but rather from the internal dynamics of democracy itself in a highly educated, mobilized and participating society.[22]

The threat to democracy, in other words, is the democratic process itself. I have argued that meaningful and effective political democracy cannot exist without personal, educational, or economic democracy. When a society lacks these necessary conditions, political democracy cannot function and is demoted to a form of window dressing, a basically meaningless circus in which the ill-trained, ill-informed and often impoverished are confronted with an inconsequential choice while being given the impression that they truly govern themselves. Democracy (true democracy not merely an inauthentic form of political democracy) is, I believe, the only fair and just way in which we can go about to forge a common ethic and begin to grapple with our problems. In a society in which so many are ill-educated, uninterested, and hardly in meaningful relation with one another, democracy will be difficult to achieve. But it is not impossible.

My thesis has been that individual as well as national isolation is not only ethically untenable but likewise works to defeat homeostatic mechanisms working towards individual, national, and international survival and progress. When individuals or nations conceive of themselves as minimally connected, isolated and asocial entities, when they see their individual or corporate selves as moral strangers who share merely the desire to pursue their own interests and nothing else with one another, homeostatic balance is lost and our very being itself is put at risk. If we as a nation and as a peaceful and viable world community are to survive and prosper, we must accept the inevitable notion that we are morally acquainted. We must be willing to explore, celebrate, and strengthen each other's similarities as well as each other's differences in a homeostatic framework so that they can result in a nonhomogenous but dynamic society.

Hans Jonas—pessimist though he tended to be—stressed that hope (or optimism), since without it no possibility of averting disaster remained, was a moral obligation.[23] It may well be. There is, despite of the terrible conditions we confront, some hope of peaceful change. That hope resides in our recognizing that (1) we, as sentient beings, share a common framework of experience and capacities and that, at the very least, we are not moral strangers but are morally acquainted; (2) we are a potentially viable and functioning society (or world): that, in other words, while perfection cannot be attained and Utopia is beyond reach steady improvement is well within our reach; and (3) the alternative to such a world is bloody revolution or war; and, furthermore, that if we (1) as private or corporate individuals recognize the necessary relation which society and beyond it the world society has for our individual strivings; and (2) acknowledge that the same holds true for all others within our society and world, we shall at least have a start on things. Furthermore, we must recognize that neither reason nor sentiment alone will serve us in dealing with our problems and, therefore, must commit ourselves to recognizing, legitimizing, and finally dealing justly with the basic needs of others. Therefore, we will have to commit ourselves to some form of compassionate rationality in going about our work and to developing its details as we go. Finally, we will have to recognize that solidarity within our community and ultimately solidarity within the world is vital to our own survival, and, therefore, that we must strive to create our ethic (and solve our problems) so that the idea of free individuals capable of developing and expressing their tastes and talents is more than a mere word or, bluntly put, a sham.

The problems I have spoken about—those in the United States as well as those in the global community—are not isolated from one another. The problems faced within the nation are internally connected and, in turn, the problems faced by the global community and some of the other societies within it are interconnected with each other. The mal-distribution of material resources has in turn led to an attrition of social, educational, and economic resources which have turned political democracy into a charade. The mal-distribution of resources caused by and perpetuating a mal-distribution of power has caused a vicious cycle in which those in power ignore their long-term interest and conceive their narrow, short-term interest to lie in solidifying power. Proper distribution, in my view, does not imply that all must earn the same or have the same material goods: it implies that the basic biological, social, and educational needs of all must be met before some are allowed great luxuries. Mal-distribution exists when such conditions are not met. That is the state of affairs in the United States today and it, likewise, is the state of affairs when it comes to the distribution of goods among the nations of the world. Such mal-distribution, I have argued, is not a function of mere chance, bad luck or lack of initiative and effort; such mal-distribution, in its genesis as well as in its maintenance today, is an expression of a mal-distribution of power.

I have presented an argument to show that we are morally responsible for remedying this situation. It remains to briefly sketch a conceptual approach. The libertarian approach would deny responsibility and leave any possible remedy to private initiative. Thereby it would perpetuate and solidify the status quo. The approach I advocate—an approach suggested by reason and by compassion working synergistically—would be one in which imagination allows us to recognize the plight of the individual within the statistical numbers and to feel compassion with such a fate. Furthermore, such an approach would see all these problems as basically interrelated and not as separate and really separable problems. The basic problem of poverty is inseparable from that of education, lack of health care and, ultimately, lack of true political democracy. One feeds and spawns the other. Such an approach would, however, also be one which realizes that merely acting out of compassion and merely providing material resources will not solve or even greatly ameliorate the problem. The approach I advocate would focus on supplying basic material resources to all, teaching and advocating family planning but above all, on education and a viable environment and support structure for the young.

Such a plan can only be successful when we turn from conceptualizing these problems (be they the problems of our traditionally poor within the country or of impoverished nations throughout the world) as "their" and begin to recognize them as "our" (in the deepest sense for it could be us as well as "they" who are deprived) problems. The well-off (as individuals or as a class) are not asocial entities disconnected from those who are poor! We must recognize that in addressing our problems, the problem of creating a viable democracy by changing our attitude towards our obligations and towards our community constitutes both the means and the end. As long as we hold ourselves to be asocial individual or corporate beings who are not or only minimally connected with other individual or corporate beings no problem can be solved. Only by recognizing that we are basically similar and that we share a basic framework of interests and capacities with one another can we begin to craft a basic ethic and, therefore, grapple with our problems. We must recognize that we are not moral strangers: we are morally acquainted. Recognizing this will allow us to develop the solidarity needed to accomplish our task.

Notes

Introduction

1. E. Remarque, *Liebe Deinen Nächsten* (Kölnulr, Deutschland: Kiepenhener und Witsch, 1984).

2. D. S. Wyman, *Das Unerwünschte Volk*. Frankfurt a/M, Deutschland: Fischer Taschenbuch; 1989, from the English and now out of print *The Abandonment of the Jews: America and the Holocaust, 1941–1945* (New York, NY: Pantheon Books, 1984).

3. D. S. Wyman, *Paper Walls: America and the Refugee Crisis* (Amherst, MA: University of Massachusetts Press, 1968).

4. See n. 2 above.

5. J. D. Moreno, The social individual in clinical ethics, *J Clinical Ethics*, 1992, 3(1):53–55.

6. H. T. Engelhardt, *Bioethics and Secular Humanism: The Search for a Common Morality* (Philadelphia, PA: Trinity Press International, 1991), xiii–xv, 96–101.

7. Ibid.

8. E. Bloch, *Das Prinzip Hoffnung*, vol. 1 and 2 (Frankfurt a/M, Deutschland: Suhrkamp, 1990).

9. H. Jonas, *Das Prinzip Verantwortung* (Frankfurt a/M, Deutschland: Suhrkamp, 1984).

10. Ibid.

Chapter 1

1. In this chapter, I shall rely on two prior works: (1) E. H. Loewy, *Suffering and the Beneficent Community: Beyond Libertarianism* (Albany,

NY: SUNY Press, 1991). (2) E. H. Loewy, *Freedom and Community: the Ethics of Interdependence* (Albany, NY: SUNY Press, 1993). The arguments will only be briefly reiterated here and the interested reader is referred to these two works to flesh them out.

2. Ibid.

3. I. Kant, *Foundations of the Metaphysics of Morals* (trans. Lewis White Beck), (Indianapolis, IN: Bobbs Merril Educational Publishing Co., Inc., 1985), 53.

4. E. H. Loewy, *Freedom and Community: the Ethics of Interdependence* (Albany, NY: SUNY Press, 1993).

5. I. Kant, Duties towards animals and spritis, in *Lectures on Ethics* (trans. Louis Infield) (Gloucester, MA: Peter Smith, 1978), 239–241.

6. J. Bentham, *The Principles of Morals and Legislation* (New York, NY: Hafner, 1948).

7. E. H. Loewy, *Suffering and the Beneficent Community: Beyond Libertarianism* (Albany, NY: SUNY Press, 1991).

8. H. T. Engelhardt, *The Foundations of Bioethics* (New York, NY: Oxford University Press, 1986), 116–120.

9. These ideas can be found explicitly or tacitly throughout Rousseau's work but are especially spelled out in his *Social Contract*. J. J. Rousseau, *Du Contrat Social* (R. Grimsley, ed.) (Oxford, England: Oxford University Press, 1972), and his *Discourse on Inequality. Discourse sur l'Origine et les Fondements de l'Inégalité parmi les Hommes* (Paris, France: Gallimard, 1965).

10. C. Darwin, *The Descent of Man* (New York, NY: H. M. Caldwell, 1874).

11. See n. 4 above, 33, 100–107, 163–164.

12. This concept, found in A. Schopenhauer, *Preisschrift über die Grundlage der Moral*, in Arthur Schopenhauer, Sämtliche Werke, Band III (Frankfurt a/M, Deutschland: Suhrkamp, 1986), has been used by myself on several occasions, especially in E. H. Loewy, *Freedom and Community*.

13. The whole issue of the interrelationship among the concepts of compassion, self-preservation, self-regard, and self-love, as well as the issue of what we would today call moral development, as envisioned by Rousseau, can be seen in three of Rousseau's major works: the Social Contract, the Discourse on Inequality, and Émile. (Found in Rousseau, *Oeuvres Completes* Paris, France: Éditions du Seuil, 1971, vol. 1–3). For translations of these works and so as to flesh out my inadequate French, I have relied, for the Social Contract, on the excellent Grimsely translation (*Du Contrat Social*,

[R. Grimsley, ed.] Oxford, England: Oxford University Press, 1972) and on that of G. D. H. Cole found in one volume with his translation of the Discourse on Inequality (*The Social Contract and the Discourse* [trans. G. D. H. Cole] New York, NY: Everyman's Library, 1973).

14. J. Moreno, The social individual in clinical ethics, *J Clinical Ethics* (1992), 3(1):53–55.

15. I. Kant, Kritik der Urteilskraft (W. Weischedel, ed.) (Frankfurt a/M: Deutschland: Suhrkamp, 1974), as well as his essay on eternal peace, Kant I: Zum Ewigen Frieden: ein philosophischer Entwurf, in *Immanuel Kant, Werke XI* (Wilhelm Weischedel, ed.) (Frankfurt a/M, Deutschland: Suhrkamp Verlag, 1964), 195–244. Kant implicitly as well as explicitly stresses the necessity of a social nexus for all intellectual activity.

16.In her *Lectures on Kant's Political Philosophy* ([R. Beiner, ed.] Chicago, IL: University of Chicago Press, 1982) Professor Arendt eloquently shows that Kant's view was not that of the solitary thinker in his garret: Kant would deny that one could fruitfully do scholarly work that way. To Kant, thinking implied "orienting" one's thoughts by and with the thoughts of others. It is this necessity of exchanging ideas which made of Kant an early and eloquent defender of internationalism and of the right of all to visit each other's countries. Indeed, one would surmise that for Kant the notion of moral strangers would have been an odd one.

17. See n. 4 above.

18. T. Hobbes, *Leviathan* (New York, NY: Collier Books, 1962).

19. The references here are to the same works of Rousseau listed in n. 13.

20. E. H. Loewy, *Freedom and Community*.

21. This idea of a field was first developed by my wife, Roberta Springer Loewy and appears in her Ph.D. thesis, *Integrity and Personhood: Looking at Patients from a Bio/Psycho/Social Perspective* (Loyola University of Chicago, Department of Philosophy, 1996). She has pointed out that the concept of homeostasis can be applied not merely in a physical or psychological but likewise in a moral sense. For example (an example pointed out to me by my wife and used in her thesis): the concept of autonomy requires a notion of integrity. Integrity could, among other things, be understood in an evolving homeostatic sense. So that an individual's autonomy can persist "the field's equilibrium between equally dynamic and often disparate internal and external elements must be maintained. One of the presuppositions necessary for this view is that no entity . . . is either self-sufficient or entirely self-determined. While persons have a hand in the decisions they make and the fate they choose, it is only one part of an exceedingly complex process . . ."

22. See n. 4 above, 128–132, 149–153.

23. F. Tönnies, *Gemeinschaft und Gesellschaft* (Darmstad, Deutschland: Wissenschaftliche Buchgesellschaft, 1963).

24. Many works of fiction and nonfiction attest to these happenings. Persons who were devoted Communists and who had truly found a "home" in the party and in its system, when confronted with the way their personal ideals, which had caused them to join the party to begin with, clashed with the behavior of the Communist party, left and paid an extremely heavy price: sometimes with their lives, sometimes in equally important psychological ways. One might, from many, select the works of Arthur Koestler or of Ignazio Silone as examples.

25. The problem of justification was previously discussed in a prior work (Loewy, *Freedom and Community*, 58–70). In my present discussion, I have relied heavily on two of John Dewey's works: *The Quest for Certainty* in J. A. Boydston, *The Later Works of John Dewey*, vol. 4 (Carbondale, IL: Southern Illinois University Press, 1988), and *Logic, the Theory of Inquiry* in J. A. Boydston, *The Later Works of John Dewey*, vol. 12 (Carbondale, IL: Southern Illinois University Press, 1988).

26. S. Hampshire, *Innocence and Experience* (Cambridge, MA: Harvard University Press, 1989).

27. See n. 4 above, 67–68.

28. W. D. Ross, *The Right and the Good* (Oxford, England: Clarendon Press, 1938).

29. This critically important passage in Kant is quoted from Becks's translation of Kant's *Foundations of the Metaphysics of Morals* (Indianapolis, IN, The Library of Liberal Arts, 1985), 41–42. The origial version can be found among others in Kant's *Grundlegung zur Metaphysik der Sitten* in *Immanuel Kant Werkausgabe VII* (Wilhelm Weischedl, ed.), (Frankfurt a/M, Deutschland: Suhrkamp Verlag, 1989), 55.

Chapter 2

1. H. T. Engelhardt, *Bioethics and Secular Humanism: The Search for a Common Morality* (Philadelphia, PA: Trinity Press International, 1991), xiv.

2. Ibid.

3. Ibid.

4. Ibid., 3.

5. Ibid., 103.

6. Ibid., 104.

7. Ibid., 119.

8. Ibid.

9. Ibid., 135–136.

10. J. Dewey, The Historical Method in Ethics, ed. J. A. Boydston, in *The Later Works, 1925–1953*, vol. 17 (Carbondale, IL: Southern Illinois University Press, 1991), 357.

11. T. Hobbes, *Leviathan* (New York, NY: Collier Books, 1962), 103.

12. Ibid.

13. Ibid.

14. Ibid., 104.

15. Ibid., 113.

16. Ibid.

17. Ibid.

18. Ibid.

19. R. Nozick, *Anarchy, State and Utopia* (New York, NY: Basic Books).

20. J. Rawls, *Political Liberalism* (New York, NY: Columbia University Press, 1993), 264.

21. J. J. Rousseau, *Du Contrat Social* (Paris, France: Garnier-Flammarion, 1966).

22. J. J. Rousseau, Discours sur l'Origine et les Fondements de l'Inegalité parmis les Hommes (Paris, France: Gallimard, 1965).

23. G. D. Cole, Preface, trans. G. D. H. Cole in *J. J. Rousseau: The Social Contract and the Discourse* (New York, NY: Everyman's Library, 1993), 383–384.

24. J. J. Rousseau, *Discourse on the Origin of Inequality*, trans. G. D. H. Cole in *J. J. Rousseau: The Social Contract and the Discourses* (New York, NY: Everyman's Library, 1993), 47.

25. Ibid., 75–76.

26. Ibid., 75.

28. Ibid., 73.

29. J. J. Rousseau, *Emile,* trans. A. Bloom (New York, NY: Basic Books, 1979), 211–214.

30. D. Hilberg, *Die Vernichtung der Europäischen Juden* Band 3 (Frankfurt a/M, Deutschland: Fischer Taschenbuch, 1990), 1076–1099.

31. This passage is translated by myself from a quote provided by Hilberg, see n. 30 above, and first appearing in the newspaper *Aufbau* (New York 23 Aug 1946, 1–2).

32. The frightening thing is how very often this phenomenon could be observed. It is well documented in the works of Simon Wiesenthal (see Wiesenthal S: *Recht nicht Rache* Frankfurt a/M: Deutschland: Ulsstein; 1992) as well as in Klee E: *Was sic taten, was sie wurden* (Frankfurt a/M: Fischer Tuschenbuch, 1994). Although well documented in the Nazi setting, I would suspect that the same phenomenon can be observed among all humans: American veterans involved in Vietnam atrocities have, for rather obvious reasons, never been well studied and are (given the political and historical circumstances) probably not capable of being studied. The frightening thing, if I am right, is that such a capacity to commit the greatest atrocities while being later able to lead quite normal and socially acceptable lives may lie dormant in all of us.

33. W. L. Shirer, *The Rise and Fall of the Third Reich* (New York, NY: Simon & Schuster, 1960), 966.

34. A. Schopenhauer, *Preisschrift über die grundlagen der Moral,* in *Arthur Schopenhauer Kleinere Schriften* (Band III Arthur Schopenhauer Sämtliche Werke) (Wolfgang Frhr. von Löhneisen) (Frankfurt a/M, Deutschland: Suhrkamp 1989), 742.

35. E. H. Loewy, *Freedom and Community: The Ethics of Interdependence* (Albany, NY: State University of New York Press, 1993).

36. U. Kronauer, *Vom Nutzen und Nachteil des Mileids* (Frankfurt a/Main, Keip Verlag, 1990).

37. For an excellent review of these various attitudes towards compassion see: K. Hamburger, *Das Mitleid* (Stuttgart, Deutschland: Klett-Cotta, 1985) which is unfortunately not translated into English. The attitude of Mandeville, it might be noted, very much presages the attitudes of what has later (erroneously, I think) been termed social Darwinism.

38. I. Kant, *Die Metaphysik der Sitten,* ed. Wilhelm Weischedl (Frankfurt a/M, Deutschland: Suhrkamp Verlag, 1989).

39. I thank the development of this notion to Dr. Friedrich Heubel who also drew the passage in note 46 to my attention.

40. I. Kant, *The Doctrine of Virtues*, trans. Mary J. Gregor (Philadelphia, PA: University of Pennsylvania Press, 1964), 126. This quotation is from section 35 of this work in both its original German (*Tugendlehre*) and in the translation. I have taken the liberty to make a few slight changes in the beginning of this translation. The concepts of "Mitleid" and "Mitfreude" are difficult ones to translate: Roughly speaking, it denotes the sorrow or the joy one feels at contemplating the joy or sorrow of another.

41. D. Hume, *A Treatise of Human Nature*, ed. L. A. Selby-Bigge (Oxford, England: Oxford University Press, 1968), 415.

42. Ibid., 414.

43. J. J. Rousseau, *Discourse on the Origin of Inequality*, trans. G. D. H. Cole in *J. J. Rousseau: The Social Contract and the Discourse* (New York, NY: Everyman's Library, 1993), 61.

44. I. Kant, *The Metaphysics of Morals*, trans. M. Gregor (Cambridge, England: Cambridge University Press, 1991), 250. This translation is adapted from Mary Gregor's translation with some changes made by myself: for example, the German Mitleid is translated not as "sadness" (which would be Traurigkeit) but as "compassion" and the term Mitfreude is translated as "deriving pleasure from the pleasure of others," terms, that I think, are much closer to the actual meaning. Likewise, other minor changes have been made.

45. I. Kant, *Critique of Practical Reason*, trans. L. W. Beck (Indianapolis, IN: Library of Liberal Arts [Bobbs-Merrill Educ Publ], 1956), 74. I have slightly adapted this translation to reflect some changes: the term "Triebfeder" which L. W. Beck translates as "incentive" I have chosen to translate as "motivating force" a term closer to the German "Triebfeder" as well as to the Latin synonym (elater animi) also used by Kant.

46. Again, I thank this clarification of Kant's views on inclinations to Dr. Friedrich Heubel. The passage is taken from I. Kant, *Religion within the Limits of Reason Alone*, trans. Hoyt H. Hudson and Theodore M. Greene, in *The Philosophy of Kant: Immanuel Kant's Moral and Political Writings*, ed. Carl J. Friedrich (New York, NY: Random House, 1977), 394.

47. See reference citation for Kant, n. 45 above, 64.

48. R. Sullivan, *Immanuel Kant's Moral Theory* (Cambridge, England: Cambridge University Press, 1989), 206.

49. Ibid., 27.

50. I. Kant, *Foundations of the Metaphysics of Morals*, trans. L. W. Beck (New York, NY: The Library of Liberal Arts, 1986), 80.

51. This last section (which I had first omitted from the quotation) was again drawn to my attention by Dr. Friedrich Heubel who, rightly, felt that if the quotation initially given were allowed to stand alone it would give the appearance that Kant might hold the feeling itself for unlikely. The quotation is from the same paragraph as the preceding: I have changed one word in Beck's translation: in the last part, Beck translates what in German reads "mithin aus unserem eigentlich selbst entsprungen ist"; as "hence from our proper self"; I have taken the liberty of rendering this passage as "hence from our genuine self."

52. J. Dewey, *Ethics*, ed. Jo Ann Boydston, in *John Dewey: The Later Works*, vol. 7 (Carbondale, IL: Southern Illinois University Press, 1989), 232.

53. The section about care ethics is a composite of two prior papers: E. H. Loewy, Care ethics: a concept in search of a framework (Cambridge Quarterly 1995), 4(1):56–63 and E. H. Loewy, Of Caring, sentiment and anencephalics: A response to Sytsma, *Theoretical Medicine* (1996), in print, 1996.

54. C. Gilligan, In a Different Voice: Psychological Theory and Women's Development (Cambridge, MA: Harvard University Press, 1982).

55. N. Nodding, Caring: A Feminine Approach to Ethics and Moral Education (Berkeley, CA: University of California Press, 1984).

56. L. Nelson, Against caring, *J Clin Ethics* (1992), 3(1):8–15.

57. J. Dewey, *Human Nature and Conduct*, eds. P. Baysinger and J. A. Boydston in *John Dewey: The Middle Works*, vol. 14 (Carbondale, IL: Southern Illinois University Press, 1988), 135.

58. J. Dewey, *Logic Conditions of a Scientific Treatment of Morality*, eds. J. A. Boydston and D. Rucker in *John Dewey: the Middle Works*, vol. 3 (Carbondale, IL: Southern Illinois University Press, 1977), 3–39.

59. C. Darwin, *The descent of Man and Selection in Relation to Sex* (Princeton, NJ: Princeton University Press, 1981), 71–73.

60. Ibid., 71–72.

61. E. Klee, *Euthanasie im NS-Staat: Die "Vernichtung lebensunwerten Lebens"* (Frankfurt a/M, Deutschland: Fischer Tacshenbuch Verlag, 1991).

62. J. J. Rousseau, *The Social Contract or Principles of Political Right*, trans. G. D. H. Cole in *J. J. Rousseau: The Social Contract and the Discourse* (New York, NY: Everyman's Library, 1993), 000.

63. Ibid.

64. Ibid., 194.

65. R. Grimsley, ed., Introduction in J. J. Rousseau, *Du Contract Social* (Oxford, England: Oxford at the Clarendon Press, 1972), 26.

66. See n. 62 above, 140.

67. See n. 23 above, 374.

68. I. Kant, *Grundlegung zur Metaphysik der Sitten*, ed., Wilhelm Weischedl in *Immanuel Kant Werkausgabe VII* (Frankfurt a/M, Deutschland: Suhrkamp Verlag, 1989).

69. Ibid.

70. See n. 62 above, 195.

71. E. Cassirer, *Rousseau, Kant, Goethe* (Hamburg, Deutschland: Meiner Verlag, 1991).

72. See n. 23 above, 373.

73. J. Dewey, *Freedom and Culture*, eds. J. A. Boydston and B. Levine in *John Dewey: The Later Works*, vol. 13 (Carbondale, IL: Southern Illinois University Press, 1991), 149.

74. See n. 23 above, 382.

75. J. Dewey, *The Public and Its Problems*, eds. J. A. Boydston and B. A. Walsh in *John Dewey: The Later Works*, vol. 2 (Carbondale, IL: Southern Illinois University Press, 1991), 331.

76. Ibid., 327–328.

77. Ibid., 328.

78. Ibid., 259–260.

Chapter 3

1. T. Nagel, *The Possibility of Altruism*, Princeton, NJ: Princeton University Press, 1970), 14

2. Engelhardt in his *Foundations of Bioethics* refers to infants and young children as "persons in a social sense."

3. J. Dewey, *The Public and Its Problems*, eds. J. A. Boydston and B. A. Walsh in *John Dewey: The Later Works 1925–1953* (Carbondale, IL: Southern Illinois University Press, 1988), 327–328.

4. J. Dewey, Creative Democracy: The task before us, eds. J. A. Boydston and A. Sharpe in *John Dewey: The Later Works 1939–1941* (Carbondale, IL: Southern Illinois University Press, 1991), 226.

5. Ibid., 229.

6. Ibid., 228.

7. H. T. Engelhardt, *Bioethics and Secular Humanism: The Search for a Common Morality* (Philadelphia, PA: Trinity Press International, 1991), 119.

8. J. Dewey, *Freedom and Culture*, eds. J. A. Boydston and B. Levine in *John Dewey: The Later Works 1938–1939* (Carbondale, IL: Southern Illinois University Press, 1991), 155.

9. I. Kant, *Critique of Practical Reason*, trans. L. W. Beck (Indianapolis, IN: Bobbs-Merrill Educational Publications, 1956), 76.

10. E. H. Loewy, *Suffering and the Beneficent Community: Beyond Libertarianism* (Albany, NY: State University of New York Press, 1991).

11. E. H. Loewy, *Freedom and Community: The Ethics of Interdependence* (Albany, NY: State University of New York Press, 1993).

12. See n. 7 above, 11.

Chapter 4

1. L. A. Blum, *Friendship, Altruism and Morality* (London, England: Routledge and Kegan Paul, 1980), 9–10. A fair part of my argument here has been enriched by a reading of Blum as well as by a reading of Thomas Nagels's *The Possibility of Altruism* (Princeton, NJ: Princeton University Press, 1970).

2. Hanna Arendt in *Kant's Political Philosophy* shows that this concept is quite basic to an understanding of Kant. Wittgenstein in *On Uncertainty* likewise indicates that we cannot—without an inevitably social framework—know (and by implication, therefore, reason or understand) anything. It is evident that to Dewey (among others) in Creative Democracy: the task before us. In *John Dewey: The Later Works 1939–1941*, eds. J. A. Boydston and A. Sharpe (Carbondale, IL: Southern Illinois University Press, 1991) and in *The Public and Its Problems* in *John Dewey, the Later Works 1925–1953*, eds. J. A. Boydston, B. A. Walsh (Carbondale, IL: Southern Illinois University Press, 1988) reasoning implied not only persons reasoning together and trying out ideas with each other but indeed that democracy as a moral ideal as well as a practical political reality was ineffective without this.

3. M. Midgley, *Wickedness* (London, England: ARK Paperbacks, 1986), 60–61.

4. J. J. Rousseau, *A Discourse on the Origin of Inequality*, trans. G. D. H. Cole in *J. J. Rousseau: The Social Contract and the Discourses* (New York, NY: Everyman's Library, 1993), 73.

5. J. J. Rousseau, *Emile*, trans. A. Bloom (New York, NY: Basic Books, 1979), 211–214.

6. R. H. Rawney, *Religion and the Rise of Capitalism: A Historical Study* (New York, NY: American Library, 1954).

7. H. T. Engelhardt, Health Care Allocations: Response to the Unjust, the Unfortunate and the Undesirable, ed. E. E. Shelp in *Justice and Health Care* (Dordrecht, The Netherlands: D. Reidel, 1981).

8. E. H. Loewy, *Freedom and Community: The Ethics of Interdependence* (Albany, NY: State University of New York Press, 1993), 215–219, 222–224.

9. H. T. Engelhardt, *The Foundations of Bioethics* (New York, NY: Oxford University Press, 1986), 36, 75.

10. C. Turnbull, *Forest People* (New York, NY: Simon & Schuster, 1961).

11. See, among many others, V. Frankl, *Man's Search for Meaning* (New York, NY: Simon & Schuster, 1970). E. Wiesel, *Night* (New York, NY: Bantam Books, 1982). P. Levi, *Survival in Auschwitz* (New York, NY: Collier Books, 1987).

12. H. Jonas, *Das Prinzip Verantwortung* (Frankfurt a/M, Deutschland: Suhrkamp, 1984).

13. Ibid., 56.

14. I. Kant, *Foundations of the Metaphysics of Morals*, trans. L. W. Beck (Indianapolis, IN: Bobbs-Merrill Educational Publishers, 1978), 6.

15. Ibid., 8.

16. J. Dewey, *Ethics*, eds. J. A. Boydston and P. F. Kolojeski in *John Dewey: The Middle Works, 1899–1924*, vol. 5 (Carbondale, IL: Southern Illinois University Press, 1988), 7–8.

17. J. Rawls, *A Theory of Justice* (Cambridge, MA: Harvard University Press, 1971), 49.

18. J. Rawls, *Political Liberalism* (New York, NY: Columbia University Press, 1993), 28.

19. See n. 16 above, 424.

Chapter 5

1. S. Hampshire, *Innocence and Experience* (Cambridge, MA: Harvard University Press, 1989).

2. J. Locke, *Second Treatise of Government* 3, ed. C. E. Macpherson (Indianapolis, IN: Hackett Publishing, 1980).

3. H. T. Engelhardt, Morality for the medical-industrial omplex: A code of ethics for the mass marketing of health care (*New England Journal of Medicine*, 1988), 319(16):1086–1089.

4. T. Jefferson, The Declaration of Independence, eds. C. A. Beard and M. R. Beard in *The Beard's Basic History of the United States* (New York, NY: Doubleday, Doran and Co., 1944), 453.

5. The fact that the gap between rich and poor in the United States is widening (just as it is in the post-communist nations) has frequently been remarked upon. See, among others, M. B. Zuckerman, Dreams, myth and reality (*U.S. News and World Report* 25, July 1988), 68; and especially Congressional Budget Office: The Changing Distribution of Federal Taxes 1975–1985 (Washington, DC: U.S. Government Printing Office, 1987); as well as U.S. Department of Commerce: Statistical Abstracts of the United States, 1989–1995 (Washington, DC: U.S. Government Printing Office).

6. J. Moreno, The social individual in clinical ethics (*J Clinical Ethics* 1992), 3(1):53–55.

7. One of the most influential recent books in this regard has been Richard J. Herrenstein and Charles Murray's *The Bell Curve: Intelligence and Class Structure in American Life* (New York, NY: The Free Press, 1994). There have, however, been others. The rise of this sort of argument and the popularity among the general population that such books have achieved at the very time when there has been a political swing to the right is, in my view, ominous: unfortunately such arguments serve those who are well off and, therefore, have a stake in maintaining the status quo as well as those who have nothing but their white skin to point to "with pride" (and who fail to recognize that they too stand to lose in the long run) equally well.

8. Among the scholars who have for many years cast doubt upon the whole enterprise of IQ testing as it relates to what in effect is a resurgence of the eugenics movement, the works of Stephen J. Gould stand out. His *Measure of Man* (especially the chapter called "The Mismeasure of Man") as a basic source and his recent work published in the *New Yorker* magazine (The New Yorker 28, November 1994, pp. 139–149) should be read by anyone tempted to listen to the siren song of the bell shaped curve.

9. I myself, in the 1960s, took an IQ test which had been designed especially for blacks living in the ghetto areas. I do not know whether this test is considered to have any validity today but the fact that my own IQ on this test was slightly less than 60 (together with the fact that my IQ on the same sort of tests administered to whites is at least ten or twelve points higher!) still gives me pause when I see IQ tests used in this manner.

10. There are several books which begin to give some idea of what living and growing up in a ghetto is like. A. Kotzlowski, *There are No Children Here: The Story of Two Boys Growing Up in the Other America* (New York: Doubleday, 1991), for example, gives eloquent testimony to what happens to such blighted lives. A few children "make it out." But their "making it out" almost invariably is a product of very high grade intelligence and a great deal of luck. Another book, a careful study of the problem, and one which is highly recommended, is J. Kozol, *Savage Inequalities: Children in America's Schools* (New York, NY: Crown Publishers, 1991).

11. Ibid.

12. I will enter into the question of these nonmaterial forces in history: many of us feel that what I here call the "nonmaterial" (the religious, aesthetic, and intellectual forces) cannot, in fact, be separated from the material. I would argue that, at the very least, what I have called the nonmaterial forces are conditioned by the material circumstances in which they manifest themselves.

13. I have difficulty in finding a proper name for such disadvantaged nations: the term "third world" suggests the presence of a first and second; the term "developing nations" is basically condescending since it suggests that the western world's level is necessarily the frame of reference; and the term "emerging nations" likewise suggests that such nations are moving from a lesser to a better state. Therefore, I have chosen to use "industrialized" and "nonindustrialized" nations although this too suggests that industrialization is preferable to not being industrialized. What I mean to do is to refer to those nations or groups of nations who have been the victims of largely western (albeit also Japanese) exploitation and who, as a consequence, have a degree of poverty approximated only in the United States and unmatched in the rest of the world.

14. The fact that they did not themselves truly believe their own argument can be seen from the fact that, although having sexual relations with nonhumans is considered sodomy and baptizing nonhumans is considered blasphemy, whites frequently had sexual relations with and almost invariably baptized their slaves. A fictionalized but rather accurate version of the black experience during slavery can be found in Roots: accurate for the preslavery and slavery experience but, I think, astonishingly inaccurate when it comes to the post-slavery experience. Although the post-slavery

experience described by the author was what happened in his family, that experience was hardly shared by the majority of blacks who were free! The conditions in American ghettos today bear witness to this.

15. Richard J. Herrenstein and Charles Murray's *The Bell Curve: Intelligence and Class Structure in American Life* (New York, NY: The Free Press, 1994) 550.

16. Leeds, MA: Part-time status and hourly earnings of black and white men (*Economic Inquiry*, 1990), 28(3):544–553.

17. See M. B. Wenneker, Apstein AM: Racial inequalities in the use of procedures for patients with ischemic heart disease in Massachusetts *Journal American Medical Society*, 1989), 261:253–257; as well as J. N. Tobin, S. Wassertheil-Smoller, J. P. Wexler, et al., Sex bias in considering coronary bypass surgery (*Annals Internal Medicine*, 1987), 107:19–25.

18. S. H. Miles and A. August, Courts, gender and "the right to die" (*Law Medicine Health Care*, 1990), 18:85–95.

19. Although things appear to be getting better, there has been a continuous disparity between loans afforded to black and white clients, even when circumstances appear to be identical. Among others, see N. Deogun and J. R. Wilke, Nation's banks accused of bias mortgages: Suit says bank discriminates against blacks applying in Washington, DC (*Wall Street Journal*, Fri., Sept. 22, 1995), A7A(W), B12B(E), col. 1, 9 col.; H. Bass, Chevy Chase Federal reaches $11 million pact: Accord settles U.S. charges that S&L didn't offer mortgages to blacks (*Wall Street Journal*, Tue., August 23, 1994), A2(W), A2(E), col. 2, 10 col. in.

20. The documentation of these facts is large. Among others: D. S. Wyman, *Das Unerwünschte Volk* (Frankfurt a/M, Deutschland: Fischer Taschenbuch, 1989), (from the English and now out of print), *The Abandonment of the Jews: America and the Holocaust, 1941–1945* (New York, NY: Pantheon Books, 1984), and D. S. Wyman, *Paper Walls: America and the Refugee Crisis, 1938–1941* (Amherst, MA: University of Massachusetts Press, 1968) should be mentioned. I can personally remember the callousness of the West (the lies we were told by the American consul about a "full quota" at a time when the quota was often barely half-full; the initial denial of even a transit visum by France, Belgium, and Holland when we finally managed to secure a British visum: a denial which effectively [but luckily only temporarily] locked us in; the sad story about the turning away of a shipload of refugees by the United States despite the fact that they all possessed visas which would have been valid in a short time period, etc.) during the Nazi times and the equally if not even more callous treatment of Jewish survivors of the camps.

21. E. H. Loewy, *Freedom and Community: The Ethics of Interdependence* (Albany, NY: State University of New York Publishers, 199?), 243–244.

22. There is a small but persuasive body of evidence about the existence and function of this commission. Two sources are: M. Crozier, S. P. Huntington, and J. Watanuki, *The Crisis of Democracy: Trilateral Task Force on the Governability of Democracies* (New York, NY: New York University Press, 1975) and H. Sklar, *Trilateralism* (Boston, MA: South End Press, 1980). The quotation itself is taken from page three of Professor Sklar's work.

23. H. Jonas, *Das Prinzip Verantwortung* (Frankfurt a/M, Deutschland: Suhrkamp, 1984).

Index